WHY DEMOCRACY?

WHY DEMOCRACY?

BY
ALF ROSS

HARVARD UNIVERSITY PRESS
CAMBRIDGE, MASSACHUSETTS
1952

Distributed in Great Britain by

GEOFFREY CUMBERLEGE
OXFORD UNIVERSITY PRESS
LONDON

Printed in Denmark

FR. BAGGES KGL. HOFBOGTRYKKERI
COPENHAGEN

PREFACE

This book is intended for democrats. Actually we all claim to be democrats. Even the Communists now profess "democracy." But what does it actually mean to be a democrat? Can we be sure that democracy actually is so obvious a thing, and that its future development is marked out clearly, as so many of us would like to believe? I think it is worth while to ponder the matter over more carefully, and that is precisely what I have attempted to do in this book.

The writing of this book came about due to the impressions I had of the German occupation of Denmark. It so happened that it was the "Herrenvolk's" practical demonstration of the methods of dictatorship in Denmark that caused me to remember the meaning and value of democracy. The translation is placed before American readers in the belief that the ideas and aspirations which form the *American way of life* are in essence the same as those which inspire the West European democracies. Historically they have grown out from the same roots, and today form the spiritual and cultural background of the Atlantic community. The problems of adjusting democracy to a world in development are therefore the same on both sides of the Atlantic. Conditions, social as well as historical and political, are naturally different in several respects. I have therefore in this edition ommitted some parts which were written with regard to particular European aspect, and on the other hand, have developed others in respect of American democracy.

Denmark is one of the small democratic nations. Politically we only count for a little in the international arena. But it is perhaps easier in certain ways to put democracy into practice in a small than in a large society. In Denmark one does not find the same strained economic and social conflicts which often typify the larger society, and which can make the realisation of a living democracy difficult. It is my hope that my analysis of the relationship between democracy and socialism will contribute to making it understandable for the American public that the social democrats in our countries are more democratic than socialistic. This means that they believe in the possibility of combining democracy and social progress, but under no circumstances will fail the democratic ideals of freedom in favour of social experiments. In the European social democracy I see the strongest bulwark against the threat of communism.

The reader will see that in this book I am neither preaching a particular faith nor attempting to prove, with fancied scholarship, that a particular attitude is the only right one. I know very well that beyond all facts and all insight lie personal attitudes which do not allow of objective discussion. What I want to say is this: much tends to show that in the years to come we shall be moving toward a development which is going to lay down for a long time the forms in which social life shall be lived. Many single steps are in a small way a choice in the direction of either democracy or dictatorship. Perhaps the fruit is ripening now without our noticing it. For that development every one of us has his own share of responsibility. It is important, therefore, that we understand what the choice implies. To arouse consciousness of this, to throw light on this crucial matter as clearly as possible, and for the rest, to let everyone choose his own point of view—that is the aim of this book.

I am indebted to Mr. David Gatley-Philip, London, who undertook the translation. My grateful acknowledgements are due to the Trustees of the Rask-Ørsted Foundation, Copenhagen, for a grant of funds to defray the expense of translation.

ALF ROSS.

COPENHAGEN, 1952.

CONTENTS

I. INTRODUCTION 1

II. RETROSPECT
   1. THE PLACE OF DEMOCRACY IN THE HISTORY OF MANKIND. . 6
   2. DEMOCRATIC IDEAS IN THE MIDDLE AGES: CONTRACT THEORY, POPULAR SOVEREIGNTY, AND THE RIGHT OF RESISTANCE . . 9
   3. THE REFORMATION, THE MONARCHOMACHISTS, AND PURITANISM 16
   4. THE INDEPENDENCE OF THE UNITED STATES 23
   5. THE FRENCH REVOLUTION 33
   6. CONSTITUTIONAL MONARCHY 37
   7. MODERN DEMOCRACY 39

III. THE THEORISTS OF DEMOCRACY
   1. THE DOCTRINE OF THE ABSOLUTE RIGHTNESS OF DEMOCRACY (ROUSSEAU) 41
   2. BENTHAM'S UTILITARIAN "PROOF" OF THE ABSOLUTE RIGHTNESS OF DEMOCRACY 49
   3. THE ARISTOCRATIC-CONSERVATIVE CRITIQUE: THE FEAR OF MASS TYRANNY 53
   4. THE FASCIST-NAZI CRITIQUE OF DEMOCRACY 63
   5. THE COMMUNIST CRITIQUE OF DEMOCRACY 66

IV. WHAT IS DEMOCRACY?
   1. THE APPROACH TO THE PROBLEM 75
   2. THE CUSTOMARY IDEA OF POLITICAL DEMOCRACY 79
   3. DEMOCRACY DEFINED IN RELATION TO AN IDEAL 86

V. THE IDEAS OF DEMOCRACY
   1. INTRODUCTION 91
   2. DEMOCRACY AND THE RESORT TO FORCE 96
   3. THE CONCEPT OF LIBERTY 99
   4. DEMOCRACY AND POLITICAL LIBERTY: AUTONOMY (SELF-GOVERNMENT) 103
   5. DEMOCRACY AND POLITICAL LIBERTY: FREEDOM OF EXPRESSION AND OF ORGANIZATION 108
   6. DEMOCRACY AND PERSONAL FREEDOM: INTELLECTUAL FREEDOM 125
   7. DEMOCRACY AND PERSONAL FREEDOM: THE IDEA OF PUBLIC SECURITY 127
   8. DEMOCRACY AND EQUALITY 130

9. Democratic Mentality and its Effects Outside of Political Life. Other Forms of Institutional Democracy, and Democracy as an Attitude. Misuse of the Term "Democracy" 136

VI. The Case Against Democracy 145
   1. The Nonspecific Shortcomings 146
   2. The Negative Revaluation of the Ideas of Democracy . 150
   3. New Points of View 152

VII. The Social Conditions of Democracy
   1. Introduction 168
   2. Democracy and Capitalism 170
   3. Democracy and Socialism 178
   4. Democracy's Chances in a Time of Crisis 190

VIII. The Technique of democracy
   1. Direct or Representative Democracy 202
   2. Direct or Representative Democracy: Control Over the Legislative Power (Direct Popular Consultation) 210
   3. Direct or Representative Democracy: Control Over the Government 215
   4. Direct or Representative Democracy: Control Over Public Servants 217
   5. Direct or Representative Democracy: Unicameralism or Bicameralism? 221
   6. Democracy's Self-Defense. Limitations on Freedom . . 231

IX. More Than Your Freedom 244

WHY DEMOCRACY?

I.

INTRODUCTION

A generation ago, when James Bryce wrote his famous description of modern democracies, the fortunes of democracy had reached their zenith. He summed up the development during his lifetime in these words: "Seventy years ago, as those who now are old can well remember, the approaching rise of the masses to power was regarded by the educated classes of Europe as a menace to order and prosperity. Then the word 'democracy' awakened dislike or fear. Now it is a word of praise. The popular power is welcomed, extolled, worshipped. The few whom it repels or alarms rarely avow their sentiments. Men have almost ceased to study its phenomena because these now seem to have become part of the established order of things."[1]

These words were written, immediately after the first World War, the war that was fought "to make the world safe for democracy." It then seemed that the war had resulted in an overwhelming victory for the democratic principles. The empires that had been the foci of the autocratic principles had collapsed. The Kaiser went to chop wood at Doorn; the heir to the throne of the Habsburgs went to study at a Belgian university; the Romanovs were exterminated. With the exception of Russia, the new states that arose from the ruins of the defeated powers all declared for the democratic form of government. Indeed, the constitutions of these states (the German Weimar Constitution, 1919; the Czechoslovak Constitution, 1920; Estonia's, 1920; Poland's, 1921; Latvia's, 1922; Lithuania's, 1922) were often in many respects more consistently democratic than those of the older democratic countries. They rested on the republican form of government. They

[1] James Bryce, *Modern Democracies* (London, 1921), vol. IV, p. 4.

granted equal and universal suffrage, proportional representation, legal parliamentarism, and in some instances (the Baltic states) a unicameral legislature. Even in the Balkans democracy and parliamentary government gained ground.

At the same time democracy was extended and consolidated in a number of older democratic nations. Either privileged franchise in the case of the upper chamber, or universal suffrage, or both, were introduced in Denmark (1915), the Netherlands (1917), Sweden (1918), Italy (1919), and Belgium (1919). In particular, women were granted the vote in many countries, so that among the democratic nations only France, Belgium, Switzerland, and Italy still had only manhood suffrage. The principle of proportional representation also gained increasing ground; it was introduced in Denmark, France, Italy, Switzerland, Belgium, and the Netherlands.

This, then, was the position of democracy in 1920.

Twenty years later, however, the picture was quite different. Democracy had yielded ground, step by step, in many states and found itself everywhere on the defensive against aggressive dictatorships. During those years there were two related, but opposite, trends: on the one hand, the defeats of the League of Nations and its decay; on the other, the victories and growth of the dictatorial idea.

Russia had from the start cast a shadow across the victorious forward march of democracy. The tsarist autocracy had been replaced by the "dictatorship of the proletariat," actually the dictatorship of the Communist party, which, even though it was to have been merely a transitory phenomenon in principle, actually showed all the signs of consolidating itself as a permanent system of government. Indirectly, the Russian Revolution was one of the decisive factors in the trend of developments elsewhere. Fear of Communism remained the leitmotiv of the bourgeois democratic parties in Central Europe. It was because of this fear that these parties failed to give the working class parties the necessary support in the latter's fight against nascent fascism. At the same time the workers were themselves divided, for the Communist International (the Comintern) proclaimed that Social Democracy and the trade-unions it controlled—and not growing Fascism!—were the proletariat's enemy number one. The middle-class democrats in Italy sold themselves to Mussolini in 1922, and those of Germany to Hitler in 1933. In Spain, Poland, Lithuania, Turkey, Bulgaria, Greece, and Austria, too, democracy gave way to a more or less covert dictatorship in the twenties and thirties.

In the older democracies, on the other hand, democracy developed further in those years. It was only then that the effects of the equal and universal franchise became apparent. Owing to electoral reforms in connection with a steadily increasing political activity among such people as rural laborers and civil servants, who had until then been indifferent to politics, the Social Democratic Labor parties everywhere increased their numbers and in the Scandinavian countries, for instance, came close to controlling over half of the total vote. It was only natural, therefore, that the workers everywhere assumed political power—Branting in Sweden, 1920; MacDonald in Great Britain, 1924; Hornsrud in Norway, 1928; Stauning in Denmark, 1934; Blum in France, 1936.

Yet even in those countries, democracy was in danger. From the dictatorships came propaganda—fascist or communist—that spread like an infection all over the democratic community. Capitalist circles began to toy with the idea that the time might yet come when a Hitler would be needed to "put the worker in his place". In France, the financial world was more antidemocratic than anti-German. The republic had been repeatedly in danger since 1934, and the collapse of 1940 revealed how far advanced was the inner dissolution. The infection penetrated even the United States. Roosevelt's New Deal aroused violent hatred within big industry and finance. Corruption, espionage, blackmail, and pure gangster methods were resorted to in order to fight the workers and their unions. It is no exaggeration, said Harold Laski, that by 1940 the

Nazi ideas had forced their way deep into the American business world, notwithstanding all formal confessions of democracy.[1]

Democracy was under fire from the extremist parties both of the right and of the left. These extremist parties may have constituted no political danger in the relatively well-stabilized Western and Nordic democracies, but they contributed to the creation of a mentality that might well undermine popular rule from within. Even within the bourgeois parties, private armies were resorted to. The methods of fascism began to bear fruit little by little. Especially among youth did the spirit of dictatorship exercise its attraction as something new, heroic, appealing to passions. It was almost forgotten that democracy had itself once been a battle cry. Freedom was won, the struggle was over; democracy was something banal and commonplace, no longer capable of inspiring. Its gospel had become dogma, its organizational work mere routine, and the movement a church. The life that once had filled the political struggle stiffened more and more into forms and conventions. These developments prove once more that freedom is not something one can own by prescriptive right, but a boon which every day must be fought for anew.

In these circumstances it became fashionable even for the supporters of democracy to talk with weariness and skepticism of popular government. A healthy person does not appreciate his health until he has experienced sickness, nor does the well-fed man value his daily bread until he has had to go without. In the same way, a free people must experience the loss of freedom under dictatorship before it begins to remember the value of freedom. War and occupation provided the object lesson that forced the people of many European countries to reflect. They came to know what it means when a people has given its self-determination away and unconditionally surrendered to a gang that is capable of taking advantage of that

---

[1] Harold Laski, *Reflections on the Revolution of our Time* (London: George Allen & Unwin, 1943), p. 135.

fact with the most refined, studied, and systematic brutality, with a tyranny of which the world has never seen the like. They saw that once freedom is lost, the tyrants are not to be shaken off again without endless suffering.

The military defeat of Fascism by no means signifies that the spirit of fascism is dead. Development curves from before the war drift freely through the air like steel girders in a shattered house. We shall again pick up the threads and feel our way forward. Is this way going to be a resumption and continuation of democracy, or shall we seek for new gods? This is the great question, and the destiny of our generation depends on how it is answered.

To be able to choose our attitude with responsibility and firmness, we must first of all know what are the alternatives before us, what the choice implies. What is democracy, and how does it differ from other forms of government? What are the human ideas and aims that most deeply bear the democratic meaning of life beyond the political forms of democracy? What are the forces and factors that operate for and against the development of a popular form of government, and how are we in a position to influence them? Do the traditional democratic forms require adaptation to new times and new tasks? It is these and similar questions on which this book will endeavor to throw light, and thus to provide everyone with the best foundation for making his own choice. We cannot free ourselves from the responsibility that every one of us has for whatever the future may bring. We are at once the forces and the pawns in the game. We must know what we are doing and assume the responsibility for it.

As an introduction to this reflection on the essence and value of democracy, it will be necessary first of all to look back and ask, "What can history teach us?"

II.

RETROSPECT

1. The Place of Democracy in the History of Mankind

If one were to mark on a map of the world all those states which, at the outbreak of war in 1939, had a democratic form of government, one would cover a considerable part of the earth's area but, even so, less than half of it. In Europe, the older democracies of the West and North were the Scandinavian states, Great Britain, Ireland, Belgium, the Netherlands, France, and Switzerland. Of the new (i. e., post-1918) democracies, only Czechoslovakia had maintained democratic government; the remainder had openly or covertly submitted to dictatorship. Outside of Europe, we find in the camp of democracy the United States and the British Dominions: Canada, Newfoundland, Australia, New Zealand, and South Africa. The non-democratically governed territories included, on the other hand, Central, Eastern, and Southern Europe, as well as most of Asia, Africa and South America.[1] Even if democracy was thus outweighed, it included in its ranks all the old and leading cultured countries, with the sole exception of Germany.

It is not easy to say at what precise moment democracy came about or was introduced into those countries. This is because, as is explained in Chapter IV, it is not possible to set up a sharply defined conception of what is to be understood by "democracy." Experience shows that, as far as political constitutions are concerned there is a sliding scale of transition forms, so that it may be at any time somewhat hazardous and

---

[1] In Central and South America a number of republics had introduced democratic institutions, even if their functioning was defective and often disturbed by military revolts and the more or less disguised dictatorship of generals.

precarious to decide at what stage in that development one may characterize what forms of government as democratic.

If only those states whose constitutions are based upon universal and equal suffrage, are to be called democratic, then the democracy of our own time is a very modern phenomenon, hardly reaching further back than one generation. This appears from the following survey of the year in which universal suffrage was introduced in the various countries:

Belgium	1919	(Women enfranchised in 1946)
Denmark	1915	
Finland	1905	
France	1875	(Women enfranchised in 1945)
Great Britain	1918	
Netherlands	1917	(Women enfranchised in 1919)
Norway	1898	(Women enfranchised in 1913)
Sweden	1918	
Switzerland	1948	(Manhood suffrage only)
United States	About 1820–1830.	

It would not, however, be right to regard those years as the birth year of democracy in those particular countries. In most instances, the granting of universal suffrage was the outcome of the gradual progress that had taken place over a long period of time within the framework of the so-called constitutional monarchy. This latter can fairly well be described as democratic government in so far as political power in the constitutional monarchies rested chiefly with the people's representatives, not with the monarch. On the other hand, democracy was not yet complete, since the people's representatives were elected by a limited franchise. Gradually, as that franchise was widened by degrees, government became more fully democratic.

Great Britain formed the prototype for the development along these lines. Since the Revolution of 1688 the Crown has had no appreciable influence in politics, the power resting entirely with the nation's representatives. But the House of

Commons was originally elected on a very limited franchise. Prior to the electoral reform of 1832 only 4 or 5 per cent of the adult male population of the country were enfranchised. Political power was in the hands of a small number of great landowners and rich merchants: this regime might be styled an oligarchy, or rule of the few. The reform of the franchise in 1832 extended the vote to the upper middle class, the well-to-do bourgeoisie, but without depriving the landowners of their leading position. The subsequent electoral reforms of 1867 and 1884 extended the franchise even further, so as to include, respectively, one-third and two-thirds of all adult males. Finally, the Representation of the People Act of 1918 granted universal manhood suffrage and enfranchised as well all women over 30. In 1928, this age limit was brought down to 21. Thus the British oligarchy gradually developed, within the framework of constitutional monarchy, into a democracy.

A similar development took place in a number of other countries. Constitutional monarchy was introduced in many states during the first half of the nineteenth century. While Denmark introduced at the outset a relatively wide franchise (which excluded only women and servants), democratic development in other countries moved more slowly. Thus for instance, in Belgium, in the 1830's, only about 1 percent of the population were given the vote for the Senate. In Sweden until 1907, only 20 to 30 percent of adult males had the vote.

The United States, Switzerland, and France occupy a special position. In those countries the development toward democracy did not take place within the framework of constitutional monarchy. The two former countries never experienced any monarchical government at all, and their democratic traditions go back a long way. In France, popular government was introduced by the great Revolution of 1789 (constitutions of 1791 and 1793), but could not maintain itself in the face of further historical developments—perhaps because it lacked traditions in the country's past. The libertarian ideas of the French Revolution remained the leaven that stirred the liberal-democratic development of the bourgeoisie in nineteenth-century Europe, but the better part of that century was to elapse before these ideas could become permanently the basis of the French constitution. After the 1789 Revolution, there followed a varied succession of regimes—Napoleon's Empire, the Bourbon Restoration under Louis XVIII, the bourgeois monarchy of Louis-Philippe, and Napoleon III's Second Empire—before finally the Third Republic could be established upon the principles of 1789, in 1875.

Even if we take into consideration the development of "relative" democracy, popular government is still a phenomenon of recent date, hardly more than a century old. But not even there can a fixed starting point be assigned to the history of democracy. Democratic *ideas* do indeed go back very much further than the institution of modern political democracy. As a matter of fact, they can be traced to the early Middle Ages.[1]

This background of modern democracy will now be more closely elucidated.

2. Democratic Ideas in the Middle Ages: Contract Theory, Popular Sovereignty, and the Right of Resistance

Though we lack precise information regarding the social and political structure of the old Germanic society, it appears that the population (apart from the serfs) during the Great Migrations and the Viking Age constituted a legally equalitarian and fairly uniform mass which, without being subject to royal or aristocratic power, managed its own affairs directly in popular assemblies called *things*.

It is hard to say how long primitive social and political democracy persisted in the course of time. Even in the days of the Vikings, the abundance of opportunity for acquiring

---

[1] This account bears only on the medieval and modern European scene. There is hardly any connection between the democracy of the Ancient World and later democratic development.

wealth in the form of booty and slaves led to the concentration of wealth, landed property, in a few hands. There arose a peasant aristocracy which, without legally or socially breaking the traditional framework and constituting a separate class, had in practice raised itself above the ordinary yeomen. The leaders of the Viking expeditions who assumed the leadership of the local levies certainly belonged to this peasant aristocracy.

What started an entirely new development and brought about a sharp division of classes into different estates was the improvement in technics and skills, the growth of international communications, and the division of labor thus brought about. Out of the old peasant aristocracy there developed a real nobility, whose status and legal privileges were linked to the possession of landed property and, together with it, were hereditary. After the introduction of Christianity the higher clergy, too, soon became a privileged order, owing, of course, to the fact that the church, because of royal endowments and private gifts and bequests, became a landowner on a large scale. At the same time, the power of the king also increased, often in sharp competition with that of the privileged orders, and assumed definite form through a series of legal enactments, becoming an institutionalized power. This development of aristocratic and royal power could not fail to change the position of the old popular organs, the *things*. The influence of the *things* decreased to the same extent as the old social and legal equality of the peasants disappeared, and their economic status deteriorated through their becoming largely copyholders, economically dependent on the privileged classes.

The dissolution of central state power that was peculiar to the Middle Ages, the process known as feudalism, contributed in the highest degree to the weakening of the old popular liberties. Feudalism was largely caused by the conditions brought about by the primitive state of technics and communications; the lack of easy communication impeded centralized government and resulted in the parceling out of authority among local landowners, who came thus to exercise royal sovereignty in their own name, in their own interests, often as a hereditary right, and who were subjected to the central royal power merely through a loose relationship of personal service and allegiance. These vassals largely passed on their power to subvassals attached to them in much the same manner as they themselves were to the king, through a personal link. Thus the direct subjection of the population to the supreme authority was broken and replaced by a hierarchy of overlords and lieges, with the king as the paramount lord. Since the vassal's duty to follow his overlord was gradually limited, very often to as little as forty days in the year, and since the duty of allegiance was not always taken very seriously, feudalism actually meant that the state had been broken up into a multitude of small units, in each of which the social power was exercised in an uncontrolled, arbitrary, and tyrannical fashion by the local baron. The great landowner was not merely, as the owner of the land, the economic master of the copyholder, but, as the feudal lord of the manor, he held absolute authority over his tenants. He had the right to prosecute, to sentence, and to punish. It was a situation similar to that which would obtain nowadays, if the average employer of labor possessed, besides his economic power as the employer, judicial and police powers over his workers, with no outside power to check him. This public dependence on a lord, to an even higher degree than the economic dependence, could not but kill the old peasant freedom and bring about a spirit of submission and cowedness. Thus we can see how feudalism, wherever it spread in Europe, soon put an end to the old, rudimentary democracy. Where the peasants' independence and liberties were already crushed, as soon as the rising monarchy was able in turn to crush the power of the feudal lords, the situation was ripe for unchecked royal absolutism. Only in those countries where the old peasant liberties were never wholly suppressed were the old traditions allowed to survive and to form a link between primitive and modern democracy. Such was the case of England, Sweden, Switzerland, Holland, and several others of the Netherlands Provinces, particularly Friesland.

So strong was the power of the old Germanic ideas that the political ideology of the Middle Ages is mainly based on the idea of the people's sovereignty, that is, the notion that the will of the people is the supreme source of all political power. Two political ideas govern medieval political thought: the theocratic idea of the divine right of kings, and the democratic idea of popular sovereignty. King and people are the two poles around which medieval thought revolves. It is remarkable that the Middle Ages, despite the emergence of a powerful aristocracy, never developed any theory in support of an independent right to rule for the feudal lords or barons. When the feudal barons, through their various institutions, took action against the king, it was always in the name of the nation, as a matter of principle. They represented the realm and not merely a single class. Even though the primitive democracy disappeared, the Middle Ages are nevertheless of decisive importance in the history of democratic ideas. It was in the Middle Ages that the idea of popular sovereignty was for the first time formulated in this cultural sphere. This idea has since, and right down to our own age, under many external vicissitudes but essentially unchanged, remained the fundamental idea of democracy.

The doctrine of theocracy, according to which God is the source of all political power, was the starting point of medieval religious thought. According to the typical medieval outlook, the whole universe makes up one living organism, the macrocosm, molded into a divine harmony, so that each of its constituent parts, the microcosms, itself constitutes an organism that reflects the essence of the cosmos. Within the universe, mankind constitutes a similar wholeness united in a kingdom of God, the *civitas Dei*, established by God himself, who is the supreme and sole sovereign. All power in heaven and on earth is therefore of God. Here on earth, power is divided into spiritual, which is administered by the church, and temporal, which is maintained by the state. Each of these forms, as parts of the whole, is a picture of the totality of the kingdom of God. Both are therefore monarchically ruled; the church is headed by the pope and the state by the king. Royal power therefore rests, directly or indirectly, upon divine authority, and is to be used for the fulfilment of the divine order in the temporal framework.

In accordance with these ideas, there was formulated the ecclesiastical doctrine of the divine right of kings, which gave royal power—after the old pagan belief of the divine descent of kings had died out—a new and valuable religious sanction.

This religious doctrine, however, never quite succeeded in supplanting the ancient Germanic idea of royal power as a national or popular office, but in peculiar fashion merged with it. The church itself opposed the idea that the king derived his authority directly from God, maintaining that it was rather the pope who, as Christ's vicar, had received all power, both spiritual and temporal, though he himself exercised only the former. Temporal power was left to the temporal authorities, whose power thus derived directly from the pope, and only indirectly from God. With reference to a biblical passage it was often thus expressed, that the pope had been entrusted with two swords, of which he kept one (*gladius spiritualis*) and handed the other one (*gladius temporalis*) to the worldly authorities, who were to use it, however, according to the instructions of the church.

Gradually, as a philosophical political theory developed alongside the ecclesiastical one, the democratic ideas gained further ascendancy, through the formulation of the theory that princely power originates in a contract originally drawn up between the prince and the people as a whole. This theory was, it is quite certain, formulated consciously and clearly only at the end of the Middle Ages, but it was nevertheless latent throughout medieval political theory. It was also the theory that reflected best the political realities.

The idea of the contract between king and people was most likely drawn by the medieval thinkers from their great treasure house of ideas, the Scriptures. The Old Testament is full of accounts of covenants concluded between God and men, such as those of God with Noah and with Abraham, and between king and people, such as the one that David made with the people of Israel before God at Hebron, when the people made David Israel's king.

In fact, the contract theory could be used to support princely power just as it could be quoted in support of democracy. Two theories oppose each other from ancient times. According to one, the contract implied an irrevocable, unconditional, and more or less complete transfer of political power to the prince (*translatio imperii*); according to the other, it implied only a limited and conditional grant of power to be used and administered on the people's behalf (*concessio imperii*). It was the latter theory that found the widest acceptance in the Middle Ages.

The contract theory presumably derives from the concept of popular sovereignty. The theory in both of its interpretations rests on the fundamental assumption that all rule ultimately depends on the consent of the ruled, that the people is itself the ultimate source of political power. According to the concession interpretation of the contract theory sovereignty is vested in the people, and the king merely exercises a trust power within definite bounds and under definite conditions. So long as he observes them, he has a contractual right to rule and cannot be deposed. But if he breaks the terms of the contract, he ceases to be a lawful king (*rex justus*) and becomes a tyrant (*tyrannus*). He is then subject to the people's judgement and punishment, that is, he is presently overthrown. This is the doctrine of popular sovereignty in a narrower sense, according to which the supreme power and control is vested in the people, while the king is only the holder of an office, subject to that power and control.

According to the transfer conception of the contract theory, the very substance of sovereignty has been transferred to the prince. This theory is therefore usually called the doctrine of princely sovereignty. But this interpretation of the contract theory still rests on the assumption that sovereignty is originally vested in the people, and it can, therefore, be classed together with the theory of popular sovereignty in a wider sense.

First and foremost of the ties that bound the king, according to the actual theory of popular sovereignty that prevailed throughout the Middle Ages, was the divine law, partly as revealed in the Scriptures, partly as it can be seen only in the light of reason as implanted in man's nature by God; this is the *lex naturalis*, natural law. It was this natural law that gave validity to the contract and was thus the source of all valid relationships within the state. It was raised above everything, it stood above emperor and pope, and no law, no act of government, no popular decision or custom could possess any validity whatsoever, once it came into conflict with those eternal principles.

But the king was also bound by the law of the land, that is, the traditional body of laws and legal principles, which he had confirmed in the coronation charters. The law stood above the prince and was the basis of his actions, and not the other way round.

If the king now broke those ties, he became a tyrant, and the population was no longer bound by any duty of allegiance to him. They had the right to disobey his commands and, if necessary, to depose him. This limited duty of obedience and the corresponding right of resistance are the essence of medieval democratic political theory. On that point all theories converged, whether they were based on a theocratic foundation or on the idea of a contract, and, in the latter case, whether they regarded sovereignty as finally transferred to the prince or not. In no case was the prince's power regarded as absolute and final, however different its limits might be construed to be.

3. The Reformation, the Monarchomachists, and Puritanism

In opposition to a widespread superficial conception of the significance of the Middle Ages and the Reformation for the ideas of freedom, it must be emphasized that the democratic ideas that had their roots in the Middle Ages were not taken over and continued by the reformers. On the contrary, the doctrine of popular sovereignty now recedes into the background, and the theocratic conceptions gain new ascendance and importance. The Roman Catholic Church had, if not out of love for the people, then for the sake of its own freedom and power, fought the theory of the monarchy's direct derivation from God, maintained that royal power was limited by divine and natural law, and supported the right of people and church to fight a king who becomes a tyrant. Luther, in his struggle against the pope, leaned upon princely power and accepted the supremacy of the state. The church became a state church and the work of man, whereas the prince's power derived from God.

Luther, Melanchthon, Zwingli, and Calvin were, for all their disagreement, agreed upon the divine calling of authority and gave the Pauline proposition that all authority is of God a new bearing. In the Middle Ages, as we have seen, the religious sanction had been closely connected with the democratic. The reformers pushed the idea of popular sanction aside. There was no question of the origin of state power. The authorities are simply those who in fact rule and govern, and their divine sanction directly attaches to that fact, for this fact—like everything else—reflects the will of God. The established order is the legitimate one. On this view the formula "King by the Grace of God" took on a new, antidemocratic meaning: the king is granted his authority directly by God, not by the church and not by the people.

The reformers were thus very willing to render to Caesar

that which was Caesar's, provided only that God received man's conscience and faith. It is clear that this blind submission to the powers of this world could not serve as a foundation for democratic trends in the struggle against aristocratic and royal power. The reverse was true: the theocratic ideas in their new form, and the denial of the age-old popular right of resistance, gave valuable support to the forces tending toward the absolute monarchy.

The experience of history also bears out that the Protestant Church, wherever it won the day and became the Established Church, became an instrument for the promotion of royal power. If there were certain Protestant religious movements that became the advocates of democratic ideas, indeed, that laid the foundations of democracy in the modern sense, it was because they were sectarian movements, and as such constantly exposed to persecution and oppression by the rulers of the state. Making a virtue of necessity, these persecuted people demanded tolerance and freedom of conscience, respect for the individual and the right of self-determination. In support of these claims, they went back to the traditional ideas of popular sovereignty and the contract of government.

That this change became possible within the framework of Protestant religion was due to the fact that ultimately Protestant submission to political power was not the expression of a genuine recognition of, and respect for, the intrinsic value of state power, but rather rested on the point of view that there is need for only one authority on earth. There lay dormant within Protestantism a dislike of all external authority, ecclesiastical and political alike, that came to a head in the sectarian movements' demand for personal fervor and piety. Respect for the individual, for his faith and conscience, recognition of his free association with others, were the ideas—however imperfectly understood—that inspired the sectarians, and they were bound to lead in the sphere of politics toward democracy.

Most important among the sectarian movements claiming religious and political freedom were the French Calvinists (the Huguenots) and the English Puritans.

It is customary to designate by the name of monarchomachists, or king-haters, a group of authors of the second half of the sixteenth century, mostly French Huguenots, but including several Catholic pamphleteers as well. These authors zealously defended the rights of the people as against royal power and made the right of resistance the focal point of their doctrine. Indeed, as a Protestant minority, they were the object of severe persecution by the state (the Massacre of St. Bartholomew in 1572 cost nearly 20,000 lives) until the Edict of Nantes (1598) granted religious toleration. They were therefore interested in asserting the individual's right to religious freedom and to set bounds to the expansion of state power. They published a number of fairly popular pamphlets, of which the best-known is Hubert Languet's *Vindiciae contra Tyrannos* (1579), published under the nom de plume "Junius Brutus."

After the Edict of Nantes had introduced religious toleration, the movement died away. France entered the seventeenth century, the golden age of absolute monarchy. In that century it was the English Puritans who, in opposition to the power of the state, took over the ideas of democracy and religious freedom, and handed them on, not only to an age to come, but also across the seas to a new continent.

The religious antagonisms played a decisive part in the political struggles of seventeenth-century England. It can be roughly regarded as a struggle between king and parliament for political supremacy. The monarchs—namely, the Stuarts, who had come to the throne with James I in 1603—attempted to free themselves from Parliament's power by an extension of the royal prerogative, and to establish an absolute monarchy. They secured the support of the Roman Catholics and the High-churchmen, who maintained the divine right of kings and the subject's duty of nonresistance. Parliament, however, denied the king's right to legislate or to impose taxation without its consent. It was supported by the Puritans, who based their political theory on popular sovereignty; they most certainly presumed the people to be adequately represented by Parliament, although according to the electoral regulations of that time only a small group of powerful landowners and wealthy merchants were actually represented.

The struggle was thus actually one between monarchy and oligarchy. But in that struggle there nevertheless came a moment when the radical Puritans, Independents, and other extremists played their part. There arose among the sectarian soldiers of Cromwell's army wild and bold dreams of how, once monarchy had been defeated, the time would come for democratic, radical changes in the social structure, politically and economically. These revolutionaries called themselves the Levelers, and were the first pioneers of modern democratic ideas. They were equally opposed to Parliament's upper-class rule and to absolute monarchy. However, they failed to obtain Cromwell's support. The movement was crushed, and it was the feudal and higher bourgeois upper classes who emerged victorious from that century's struggle.

The demands of the Levelers were set forth in a peculiar document called the Agreement of the People (1647), which was to be the basis of the future constitution. According to that document, Parliament was to consist of one chamber only, with 400 members freely chosen, in accordance with natural law, by all males over the age of twenty-one, with the exception of those receiving wages and the recipients of poor relief. Parliament was to possess legislative sovereignty limited only by a number of civil rights assured by the constitution. Thus it would not be able to legislate in matters of conscience, nor could it introduce monopolies or taxes on food. There was a demand for equality before the law, fixed punishment, and abolition of imprisonment for debt. Capital punishment was to be inflicted only for murder and attempts at overthrowing the constitution. All officials were to be locally elected and only for one year at a time. The armed forces were to be called up only with the people's consent. Parliament could not change the constitution.

It is surprising in our own day to read that seventeenth-century document, because it contains in so many respects quite modern points of view and expresses a demand for democracy that has been only partly fulfilled long afterward. The Independents' ideas were, in theory, based on the traditional idea of contract, which must have come to them naturally because the constitution of the church, in their view rested on a covenant. A new feature of essential interest, which was to be of great importance in the future, is the concept of *innate* natural rights, which are taken for granted on entering into a contract of government and make up the limits of the power that, through this contract, is transferred to parliament.

The document was called the Agreement of the People, because it was intended, in the spirit of the contract theory, that after approval by the leaders of the army it should be circulated among the people for signatures. But it came to nothing. Cromwell and his son-in-law, Ireton, opposed the idea. The leader of the Levelers, John Lilburne, was imprisoned and the revolutionary movement crushed.

But even if the time was not ripe for the radical ideas of the Levelers, this did not mean that the ideas they had fought for died away with the revolutionary movement that first advocated them. In a more moderate form, they have characterized British liberalism down to our own day. For a time it certainly appeared as though reaction would win. After Cromwell's death (1658), there was the Restoration of the Stuarts. Charles II (1660–1685) and James II (1685–1688) worked, covertly at first but later quite openly, for the introduction of absolutism and the promotion of Catholicism. But it was precisely in those years of reaction that the liberal Whig party was born, the party that carried the democratic ideas further. The Whigs were certainly not radical democrats like the Levelers, but they showed a far greater appreciation of the political reality of the time. They accepted the doctrine of popular sovereignty and favored a constitutional monarchy with a weak representative king and a strong parliament elected by the propertied classes. The Revolution of 1688 saw the definite triumph of these liberals. The Stuarts were banished, and with them the idea of the absolute monarchy disappeared forever from England. William of Orange became king of Great Britain as the result of the people's choice, and with him began the quiet development within the framework of constitutional monarchy that transformed English society from a feudal oligarchy into a modern democracy.

That turbulent seventeenth century, which everywhere on the Continent stood under the sign of absolute monarchy, had thus in Great Britain ended with the victory of Parliament. To be sure, Parliament was not democratic, in the sense that it did not represent the broad masses of the people of Great Britain. But for a historical estimate, taking the long view, this is not of decisive importance. The essential thing is that parliament was, in principle, regarded as the nation's mouthpiece, and sovereignty was thought of, in principle, as being of the people. This opened the possibility for a gradual development extending the franchise to ever-increasing numbers of people, bringing more and more sections of the population into the sphere of political activity. That victory for latent democracy was also of decisive importance in establishing a prototype, a pattern for the development in other countries.

The philosopher Locke, in his refutation of Filmer's and Hobbes's monarchical theories, defended the Revolutionary Settlement and formulated a theory of constitutional monarchy in his *Treatise of Civil Government*. He picked up the idea of innate, natural rights, which had been expressed by the English Puritans, and agreed with Milton that the power of the king was based not upon a binding contract but upon a freely revocable trust. Locke's ideas were not of least significance because of the influence his theory of the separation of powers came to exercise on Montesquieu and thereby on the entire body of new political theory.

Thus an essential part of the credit for the triumph of democratic ideas in England, and consequently later in Europe, is due to the seventeenth-century Puritanism. But Puritanism was also of fundamental importance for the New World. On the 11th of November 1620, the ship "Mayflower" arrived at Cape Cod, on the east coast of North America, and forty-one of its passengers—a group of Puritan emigrants who later passed into history under the name of "Pilgrim Fathers"—solemnly concluded, prior to landing, a social contract to set up the first English colony in New England. This event has become almost a legend in the American tradition, and the ship with the poetic name has become a symbol of the individualist puritan-democratic ideas that linked the New World to the Old and remained the foundation of American political development. This agreement of the Pilgrim Fathers reads as follows:

In the name of God, Amen. We whose names are underwriten, the loyall subjects of our dread soveraigne Lord, King James, by the Grace of God, of Great Britaine, France, and Ireland king, defender of the faith, &c.
Haveing undertaken, for the glorie of God, and advancemente of the Christian faith and honour of our king & countrie, a voyage to plant the first colonie in the Northerne parts of Virginia, doe by these presents solemnly & mutually in the presence of God, and one of another, covenant & combine ourselves togeather into a civill body politick, for our better ordering & preservation & furtherance of the ends aforesaid; and by vertue hearof to enacte, constitute, and frame such just & equall lawes, ordinances, Acts, constitutions, and offices, from time to time, as shall be thought most meete & convenient for the generall good of the Colonie: unto which we promise all due submission and obedience. In witnes wherof we have hereunder subscribed our names at Cap-Codd the 11. of November, in the year of the raigne of our soveraigne lord King James, of England, France, & Ireland the eighteenth, and of Scotland the fiftie fourth. Ano: Dom. 1620.

Even if the colonists thus did not in principle deny the sovereignty of the king of England, it is nevertheless clear that they wished by that compact to found a new society with its own popular legislative power based upon the voluntary combination "for the general good." The compact contains elements that anticipate the Declaration of Independence and the Declaration of the Rights of Man.

4. The Independence of the United States

After the first beginners' difficulties were overcome, the English colonies in America grew rapidly during the seventeenth century. While the number of colonists in 1640 was only 22,000, it increased to 290,000 in 1700. There were by then thirteen colonies. The oldest were Virginia and those colonies founded by the Puritans in New England (Massachusetts, New Hampshire, and Connecticut). Others were formed by new emigration from these; others again were Crown colonies. Most of them, in contrast to the mother country, had written constitutions that had their origin in the royal charters, in accordance with which the colonization had originally taken place. Under those constitutions, self-government in their own affairs was granted to the colonists, but the sovereignty of the British Crown was assumed. The British Parliament was the supreme legislative power for the colonies as well as for the United Kingdom.

Parliament's colonial legislation affected particularly the colonies' economic relations with the mother country, and was based on mercantilist principles. The colonies were to bring profit to the homeland by supplying it with raw materials, but must not be allowed to compete with it in the field of production. On the contrary, they were to serve as markets. Also, profit was sought through customs and navigation rules that compelled colonial imports and exports to go through British ports.

There was, however, no question of reckless exploitation. America was primarily a producer of raw materials, her economy being based on agriculture and the export of such staple goods as tobacco, rice, wood, iron, hides, sugar, and, later, cotton. The British customs regulations were to a great extent ineffective through large-scale smuggling, against which the British government did not take vigorous measures. Finally, the connection with the mother country offered considerable advantage, particularly the protection of the navy and the army in the fight against the Indians and competing colonial powers, particularly France. But even if the mercantilist commercial policy did not have such harmful economic effects as was once believed, there can be no doubt that it morally contributed to create bad blood against the home country by breeding a feeling of subjection and injury. Before the great colonial wars, however, there was no widespread discontent.

Things were quite different after that time. By the Peace of Paris in 1763, France had to cede the most important parts of her possessions in Canada and along the Mississippi, and was thus out of the running as a competing colonial power. Therefore, British protection came to mean less. Conversely, in order to cover the enormous national debt the war expenditure had entailed, Britain now embarked upon a more rigid policy in order to squeeze money out of the colonies. New customs and excise duties were introduced, and the control of smuggling was made more effective. Simultaneously, the population of the colonies grew much more numerous. The censuses for 1740, 1760, and 1775 revealed, respectively, 1 million, 1.5 millions, and between 2.5 and 3 millions. The population had reached one-third of that of the mother country. Besides, there was an increasing shift from agriculture to industry, which, of necessity, sharpened the clash of interests provoked by Britain's mercantilist policy. Finally, the war had strengthened the colonies' solidarity and the Americans' self-reliance. Vast new regions had been opened for colonization and called for initiative. The West began to play the part which, in the course of time, was to become more and more important.

All this led inevitably toward a collision, because the British were not judicious enough at the time to meet the young American urge for independence and expansion with understanding and sympathy. The excise on tea and the Boston Tea Party of 1773 were the spark that set off the Revolution. War began in 1775, and on the 4th of July 1776, the representatives of the thirteen states, assembled in the Continental Congress, issued the Declaration of Independence. In the following year, the states formed a Confederation which, after the war was won in 1787, was followed by the drawing up of the Constitution which united them in a federal nation.

These events were extraordinarily significant. For the first time in the history of European civilization democratic ideas had triumphed in practice. A people, relying on its right to decide its own destiny, had thrown off a yoke and drawn up its constitution on a democratic basis. The United States of America was the first modern democracy and within a century came to be the promised land of liberty. There is reason to examine a little more closely the principal ideas in the American struggle for independence and the formation of the new state.

The Declaration of Independence contains these words:

We hold these truths to be self-evident, that all men are created equal, that they are endowed by their Creator with certain unalienable Rights, that among these are Life, Liberty, and the pursuit of Happiness. That to secure these rights, Governments are instituted among Men, deriving their just powers from the consent of the governed. That whenever any Form of Government becomes destructive of those ends, it is the Right of the People to alter or to abolish it, and to institute new Government, laying its foundation on such principles and organizing its powers in such form, as to them shall seem most likely to effect their Safety and Happiness.

Here, in the first place, we find the old idea of popular sovereignty: all lawful authority is derived from the consent of the governed. That is the idea of the social contract, and from it derives the people's right, whenever a form of government becomes destructive of the people's happiness, to set up a new government. One cannot fail to notice that this is no longer based upon the medieval concepts of the right of resistance and the tyrant doctrine. With Milton, Locke, and Rousseau the concept of the contract of government which gives the ruler the actual right to rule so long as he fulfils certain conditions, is abandoned. Government is merely a trust which, in principle, may be taken back at any time, although prudence enjoins a people to do so only after a long succession of abuses and encroachments has occurred. This is the doctrine of full and undivided popular sovereignty: the right to rule is always and fully vested in the people. No contract can do away with it or diminish it, all other exercise of power is merely makeshift, and can be recalled at any time.[1]

But if sovereignty is always vested in the people, its content is nevertheless limited by the natural rights of man. Those rights are merely indicated in a very general way in the Declaration of Independence—the rights to life, liberty, and the pursuit of happiness—so vaguely, indeed, that the individual could not base upon them any legal claim against the state. That, of course, was due to the fact that Congress had no actual legislative authority. We find, on the other hand, a comprehensive list of concrete liberties included in the constitutions that the various states adopted in the years following 1776, at the invitation of Congress. These constitutions contained guarantees of religious freedom, freedom of speech, freedom of association and assembly, personal security and the right of property, and other rights, which were later regarded as typical and integral parts of any modern liberal-democratic constitution.

The roots of this idea lie in the religious idealism of the Puritan sects. Temporal power has no claim over spiritual matters. Freedom of conscience is not a right created by the political power, but is older than, independent of, and superior

---

[1] Compare the Constitution of Massachusets (1780), Art. V: "Since all sovereignty is originally vested in the people and derives from it, the different state officials and public servants who are given authority, be it legislative, executive, or judiciary, are the people's representatives and delegates and owe the people full account at all times."

to all constitutions and state power. This freedom of conscience had, in seventeenth-century America, its zealous apostle in Roger Williams, who founded the colony of Rhode Island, and it had been guaranteed in a number of state constitutions. From the sphere of religion that idea spread so as to cover a number of other demands for liberties as well, liberties that were regarded as warranted by human nature and raised above the sphere of political power.[1] In the language of the social contract the concept may be thus expressed: the fundamental contract is entered upon precisely in order to safeguard those original liberties.

The thirteen young states that had freed themselves from English supremacy were also liberal in the sense that fundamentally they regarded government as a necessary evil and every form of strong government as the germ of a new tyranny. The new constitutions which most of the states gave themselves in the period following the proclamation of independence are therefore marked by a division of power between the legislative, the executive, and the judicial authorities, according to Montesquieu's doctrine. In the same way, the confederation which, in the Articles of Confederation of 1777, was completed between the states, was determined by the fear of a strong central power. Mainly it merely aimed at coördination of the states' foreign policies, and congress, the alliance's common organ, was without legislative or financial authority to secure the internal provisions for a common policy (army, navy, finances) or in any other way to regulate the affairs of the states.

But even if in that way a strong individualism and liberalism excluded an extreme democracy after Rousseau's pattern, the leading ideology at the time of the Revolution was nevertheless thoroughly democratic. Men like Samuel Adams, Thomas Paine, and Thomas Jefferson were inspired by a belief in the people, and "the people" no longer meant, as had so long been the case, the propertied classes, but the great

[1] Georg Jellinek, *Die Erklärung der Menschen- und Bürgerrechte* (Leipzig, 1904), 2nd ed., p. 35.

masses. Accordingly, the hereditary idea of mankind's natural equality led, in practice, to a demand for economic equality. It was not by chance that Jefferson, in the formulation of the Declaration of Independence, replaced Locke's well-known trio, "life, liberty, and property," with "life, liberty, and the pursuit of happiness." Property was purposely denied the character of an inherent, inalienable right, a prerequisite and limitation of all state power. Not that Jefferson was a socialist who wished for the abolition of private property. All that was meant was that the existing conditions of property should not be held inviolable, but that it was up to the government to regulate these conditions. More radical demands for economic equality were also voiced, based on the idea that since all American property had been defended by everyone in common against British confiscation, it must accordingly belong to everyone.

However, these ideals of equality and this belief in the people and the rights of the common man did not impress themselves upon the American Constitution of 1787–1789.

The forces that were active in bringing about the new Union came from the well-to-do class, whose economic interests were based on capital; whose political philosophy was rooted in the postulate of men's inequality and the inviolability of the right of property, combined with deep distrust of a democracy in which the masses were able to arrogate the power to themselves; and whose political object, therefore, was a union that should be big enough and strong enough to create that community and that steady external and internal framework without which expansion of capital is impossible, but that should at the same time be provided with such conservative guarantees (especially by a complicated division of power) that an attempt on the rights of property could hardly be feared.

"Federalism"—as the political movement was called that opposed the "republicans" and carried out the constitution—cannot be understood except against the background of the economic situation immediately after the war for liberty. The destruction and the losses of the war, the exclusion from the British mercantile system connected with the ruling political disorganization, had led the thirteen states to something like economic chaos. The internal debt for financing the war amounted to $60,000,000, but the states were unable to pay either interest or principal, and the rate of exchange of public securities fell to one-tenth or one-twentieth of their nominal value. Paper money was issued, and quickly became worthless. In this mess, every one of the thirteen states tried to protect itself as best it might at the expense of the others. The result was a general worsening of the situation as a whole, following a pattern that has, unfortunately, become too wellknown in later days. The states on the coast tried to profit by their situation by increasing customs duties on goods that passed through their harbors on the way to other states. There was no common monetary system and the constant fluctuation of depreciated state currencies made commercial intercourse between the states hazardous or almost impossible. At the same time, of course, the single state was too small to form the economic basis for the growing industry (manufacturing) and trade.

Beard,[1] who was the first to undertake an economic interpretation of the constitution, has pointed out how this economic situation divided the population into different groups with opposite interests in regard to the prospect of a federation. On the one side stood the chief group of the population, the small farmers in the country and the small tradesmen and mechanics in the towns, who, as debtors, were satisfied with the devaluation and the paper money, and agitated for abolition of debt laws, bankruptcy laws, and other such arrangements for protection of creditors. They were against the plans of a union because they would more easily be able to bring their influence to bear through the local legislatures than through

[1] Charles Beard, *An Economic Interpretation of the Constitution* (New York: Macmillan, 1947, 1st ed., 1913.)

the Congress of the union. On the other side stood the interests of money and capital, bound to manufacturing, trade, shipping, and banking. The security holders took up a special position. Only a union government with authority of taxation would be able to lower the public debt and restore the value to the public securities. This would be the same as a profit for the security holders of about $50,000,000, or more than one-seventh of the value of all real property in all states.[1] Manufactures, trade, and shipping were interested in the destruction of barriers to trade between the states, a fixed monetary system, protection against English industry, and shipbuilding—in short, such orderly and stabilized conditions as could be established only in a community under a federal constitution.

The ideas that animated the Federalists were concisely expressed in *The Federalist*, a series of pamphlets written by Madison, Hamilton, and Jay in defense of the draft of the Constitution passed at the convention in Philadelphia in 1787, and as propaganda for the ratification by the individual states that was required to give the Constitution validity. It is clear that the wind now is in another quarter, only a decade after the Declaration of Independence. There is no longer talk about people being equal. On the contrary, Madison declares that men are born with "different and unequal faculties" which are the source of corresponding differences and inequalities in possession of property. On the other hand, he considers protection of these faculties to be the first object of government. On this basis, he gives a clear economic interpretation of the Constitution: "Those who own property and those who do not have always constituted different interests in society." The danger of democracy is that the unpropertied constitute themselves into a faction in order to become the majority, and thereafter to deprive the minority of its rights. The Union is already, by virtue of its size, a safeguard against such a con-

---

[1] In Article VI of the Constitution it was determined: "All debts contracted and engagements entered into before the adoption of this constitution, shall be as valid against the United States under this constitution, as under the Confederation."

tingency, since it will prove difficult to secure an absolute majority over such a great area. Besides, the Constitution ought to be based upon a sharp division of powers between different organs, which would be independent of one another and elected according to different procedures, in order to render any attack on the existing distribution of property more difficult.[1]

To this end four separate organs of government were erected: a President, a House of Representatives, a Senate, and a Supreme Court. For each a distinct mode of selection was provided. The President, who had the strongest position, was to be indirectly elected through an electoral college. The framers of the constitution wanted no popular participation in this choice. The House of Representatives was to be elected directly by popular suffrage; the Senate by the legislative assemblies of the individual states. Furthermore, the term of office was to be different for each of the organs of government: for the President, four years; for the senators, six years, and for the representatives, two years. Should an attempt at altering the economic principles nevertheless succeed, through legislation, then the Supreme Court with its specific right to declare any law unconstitutional, would represent an additional safeguard. Further assurance against future revolutions was sought by rendering any changes in the Constitution extremely difficult.

How the Federalists succeeded in carrying through the Constitution, when it may well be assumed that there was a majority opposed to it, is hard to explain. There was no resort to violence or economic pressure. The explanation is probably to be found in the use of tactical maneuvers (the delegates to the Convention at Philadelphia were elected by legislatures which had not themselves been elected for that purpose; the ratification of the constitution was, contrary to the articles of confederation, transferred from the legislative assemblies to special conventions), together with the fact that

[1] *The Federalist*, Nos. 10, 47, 48 and 51.

it was certainly the Federalists who commanded intelligence and capital whereby public opinion could be influenced. Among the men who gathered at the Philadelphia Convention in May 1787 there was not one who in his immediate personal and economic interests represented the small farmers and mechanics. The agrarian legislatures in part adopted the erroneous tactics of abstaining. A majority of the delegates were lawyers from towns on or near the coast (the Atlantic seaboard). Forty of the fifty-five delegates owned greater or smaller blocks of public securities. "The delegates differed only in the means of achieving their common ends. Not the conflicts and compromises, but the uniform distrust of democracy, and the universal desire for stability, stand out in clear perspective."[1] After these men had framed the constitution, great energy was displayed in ensuring its ratification. The debates in the ratifying convention often had to be suspended. Only four states ratified without any trouble; two (Rhode Island and North Carolina) ratified only after the federal government had been constituted and under pressure of the threat of isolation.

It would be useless to speculate about what would have happened had the Federalists failed to get the constitution adopted. It surely has to be recognized that, as it was, a constitution was adopted which happened to fit in perfectly with the capitalist-industrial development of the nineteenth century. It created precisely that constitutional freedom and elasticity which harmonized very well with the demand of capitalism for freedom of movement within a stable system of law, the safeguarding of property rights, and freedom of contract. The system was so firmly established that it could come to no great harm when the Agrarians, to the horror of the Federalists, won the elections and came to power in 1800, making their idol, Thomas Jefferson, president. Jeffersonian democracy, and later on (1828), Jacksonian, turned over a new leaf in the political history of the United states, but did not

[1] J. M. Jacobsen, *The Development of American Thought* (New York: Century Co., 1932), p. 169.

lead to the dreaded onslaught on the privileges of capitalism. Only in our own time, in the era opened by Roosevelt's New Deal, has it become a burning question, whether the American Constitution, with its markedly conservative elements, can also be fitted for a development that makes quite other and far-reaching demands on government and administration in respect of social adjustment and regulation of the powers of private capitalism within a framework of socially planned economy.

5. THE FRENCH REVOLUTION

The French Revolution is the second great event which at the close of the eighteenth century brought about the victory of democratic ideas. At one stroke the feudal absolutist institutions were swept away, and Rousseau's idea of absolute popular sovereignty was realised. But while the American emancipation was the result of a slow process of maturing as a people, a people constituted by an amalgamation of freedom-seeking immigrants whose faith in democratic and liberal principles was deeply rooted in religious convictions, the French Revolution was like a violent intoxication which is capable in a moment of tremendous enthusiasm of achieving extraordinary results, but ebbs away in a hang-over of reaction. Robespierre was succeeded by Napoleon, the Bourbons, the Orleanists (Louis Philippe), and the Second Empire.

When Louis XVI found himself compelled to summon the estates general (granting to the third estate as many representatives as to the two other estates together), with the right to authorize taxation, to meeting regularly, and to have a voice in matters of expenditure, the absolute monarchy may be considered to have in fact abdicated. Events were to gather momentum soon afterward.

It would be too much to recapitulate here the history of the French Revolution. I shall merely remind the reader of a few essential points.

The old feudal system was quickly liquidated. After the fall of the Bastille on July 14, 1789, the peasants were seized by panic. They threw themselves on the visible symbols of their oppression. They took the castles and seats of the nobility by storm and burned them to the ground, killing the lords who resisted, and—what was particularly important—destroying the rent rolls on which their feudal duties were listed. What was achieved by violence received legal sanction when the privileged estates, at the famous meeting on the night of August 4, at the suggestion of two young noblemen, the Duke of Aiguillon and the Count of Noailles, enthusiastically decided that all tax exemptions should be abolished, feudal duties done away with (though compensation was provided), villeinage abolished, and official posts opened to talent. With a clever gesture, which might have been dictated by the conviction that the battle was already lost, the privileged estates waived their own privileges.

The Declaration of the Rights of Man was also quickly adopted. The paths of two revolutions crossed in an interesting fashion. In 1789, Thomas Jefferson, the author of the American Declaration of Independence, came to Paris as the American ambassador. He was a close friend of the young Marquis de Lafayette, who was an enthusiastic supporter of libertarian ideas and had participated as a volunteer in the Revolutionary War on the American side. He had returned home inspired by the wish to transplant the idea of the rights of man to French soil. It is related that in his house in Paris he had two stone tablets erected. On one of them was engraved the American Declaration of Independence and the Bill of Rights. The other stood blank, ready to receive the French version. It was thus natural that it should be Lafayette who proposed before the National Assembly that a Declaration of the Rights of Man should be drawn up, and it is easy to understand that the French declaration plainly bears the stamp of the American model. Yet it was not the actual Declaration of Independence, which indeed contained only some highly abstract principles, that was taken as the model but rather the elaborate Bill of Rights, which was worked in as a constituent part of the constitutions of several states of the American Union.[1] It is therefore an established fact that even though French philosophy of the Age of Enlightenment has played a part in the growth of those ideas, the conception of the rights of man is essentially an American idea. The "ideas of 1789" could have been called more appropriately the "ideas of 1776".

The French Declaration of the Rights of Man and of the Citizen, which was passed on August 26, 1789, and taken to form the preamble of the Constitution of 1791, is typical of the attitude that prevailed in the first year of the Revolution. Liberal ideas blend with purely democratic ones. Every individual right is indeed a limitation of the absolute sovereignty of the people. The distribution of power is moreover specified.

The same moderate attitude is also expressed in the first French revolutionary constitution of 1791, which can be described as a cross between Rousseau and Montesquieu. It assents the principle of democracy: the people are the source of all power, which they exercise through their representatives. Yet it is still limited by the retention of a hereditary monarchy. The king is described as the people's representative alongside the legislature. Furthermore, the franchise depends on certain property qualifications, and is not granted to wage earners.

But in the period following 1791 Rousseau triumphed over Montesquieu. What was now aimed at was a strong concentration of power, and the liberal ideas receded into the background. The monarchy was abolished in 1792, Louis the XVI was executed in January 1793, and the second revolutionary constitution of 1793 was purely democratic. A republic was set up and the franchise made equal and universal. But this constitution, the most democratic one the world had seen up to that time, never came into effect. On October 10, 1793 it was indefinitely suspended and a provisional revolutionary

[1] See Georg Jellinek, *Die Erklärung der Menschen- und Bürgerrechte* (Leipzig, 1904), 2nd ed., pp. 15 ff.

government set up. The dictatorship of the Convention replaced democracy. The third revolutionary constitution, that of 1795, marked a reaction against the extreme democratic principles of the Revolution, but it did not last long either. After Napoleon's *coup d'état* of November 9, 1799, democratic ideas were either suppressed or disguised. Napoleon ruled as an actual dictator, first as the First Consul and later (after 1804) as Emperor of the French. The democratic episode was over, the enthusiasm had spent itself.

But although an end was thus put to liberty for the time being, the fruits of the Revolution were not entirely lost. The social gains were on the whole maintained. Napoleon did not aim at a Restoration. Progress went on in the direction of greater equality. To that extent, Napoleon remained the heir of the Revolution. The *émigrés* did not regain their feudal privileges. Equal access to public posts was maintained. Any talent capable of working its way up was given its chance. Simple soldiers became generals, and generals became kings of the newly created realms. Government was rationalized; the law was thoroughly reformed and set out in a major code, the Code Civil of 1804 (Code Napoleon). The form of government was an enlightened absolutism.

Again, one ought not to forget the aura that radiated from the French Revolution, which through the years had been persistently associated with the "ideas of 1789." The great reform work in Prussia associated with the names of Stein and Hardenberg was influenced by the Revolution. The same holds true of the Spanish Constitution of 1812 and the Norwegian Constitution of 1814. Even during the ensuing reaction, the ideals of the French Revolution survived in the people's minds, fostered by secret societies, like a faith that could not be eradicated. When the age of reaction took over and the Third Republic was set up in France in 1875, people looked back deliberately to the past. The ideas of 1789 were to a marked degree decisive, and still are, in the formulation of political opinion, whether for or against, in France. When

German barbarity in 1933 spread its shadow of horror over Europe, it was only natural that it was the "spirit of 1789" which was the first object of odium. Hitler was aware that the greatest threat to his Asiatic regime of violence derived partly from religious idealism and partly from the belief in democracy and human rights that was the ideal of the Revolution. It was equally natural for the French people, when, after years of humiliation, they were to give themselves a new political constitution, to look back to the tradition of 1789 and to mark it in the preamble of the Constitution of 1946 by a solemn confirmation of the Rights of Man.

6. Constitutional Monarchy

After the French Revolution, absolute monarchy came gradually to an end everywhere in Europe, except in Russia. That does not mean, however, that democracy carried the day. Reaction against the revolutionary adventure spread to all countries. After the Congress of Vienna (1815), which stabilized conditions in Europe after Napoleon's overthrow, it was Prince Metternich, with his Holy Alliance, who left his mark on developments.

In the ideological sphere the reaction expressed itself through the development of counterrevolutionary ideas which may be described as modern political conservatism. Romanticism superseded rationalism; the cult of history and tradition replaced the worship of reason. The leading idea of conservatism is: *that which has existed for a long time reflects the will of God or an inner, inherent reason, and therefore exists of necessity and by right.* The existing is the divine, the real is the reasonable. Tradition contains a wisdom that is greater than anything human reason can devise. History has its own, its inner, necessity which defies any shortsighted belief in world reform. A very essential element of conservative ideology is the mystical theory that state or nation is a living *organism* endowed with its own soul and will, which are not identical with those of individuals or with their sum total. The ideological purpose of that theory, which the Germans have particularly excelled in presenting with a mixture of devotion, mysticism, and confusion of thought, is the suppression of the bid for freedom and progress. By causing the people to believe that the individual is merely an unimportant link in the superindividual organism whose will and development are the state leadership's supreme law, those in power justify every claim to obedience; they veil the fact that their policy derives from the interests of individuals as such, and that this policy should be judged by the amount of happiness or unhappiness involved for every person. By emphasizing the natural differences between the links and their functions within the organism, they justify existing social inequality: everyone shall loyally obey and serve in the place that is assigned to him. It is easy to understand that the Nazi ideology has taken its best inspiration from that romantic, antirationalist, and antiindividualist conservatism.

Yet the Restoration did not mean a reintroduction of the *ancien régime*, that is, feudalism and absolute monarchy. True, the monarchical form of government was maintained or restored, but the king was no longer regarded as absolute. Absolute monarchy was superseded by constitutional monarchy, that is, monarchy in which the king's power is limited and precisely defined in relation to other state organs of popular origin by a constitution.

The essential point in this political type is the mixture of and conflict between two political principles: on the one hand, *the principle of monarchy* as expressing royal autocracy in continuation of the theocratic-autocratic ideas of absolute monarchy; on the other hand, *the principle of democracy* as expressing the idea of popular sovereignty The constitution is, as a rule, granted, that is, given to the people as a gift by absolute royal power or as a self-restriction of the absolute power. In this way it is established that the unity of state power rests with the king, who exercises it in accordance with the constitution. This presumes effective royal power: the king is the holder of all authority that is not expressly conferred upon others by the constitution. Popular representation consists usually of two chambers of conservative form. The upper chamber is composed of aristocrats sitting either by virtue of hereditary right or by royal nomination, or else by virtue of election by a very restricted electoral body. The franchise for electing the lower house is granted to only a minority of the population.

The model for the constitutions of the constitutional monarchies is found in the Bourbon Restoration's so-called Constitutional Charter of 1814, granted by Louis XVIII by virtue of his absolute power. This constitution, partly at once, partly later under the impact of the revolutions of February 1830 and July 1848, came to exercise a decisive influence on constitutional development in the rest of Europe. Constitutional monarchies, stressing now the monarchist, now the democratic principle, were introduced in most European countries in the course of the nineteenth century.

7. Modern Democracy

We have now come to the survey of the development of modern democracy, which was given in Chapter I and in the first section of this chapter. Constitutional monarchy in a number of countries passed by a gradual development into modern democracy, in which all political power really emanates from the people, and the king assumes the position of representative figurehead. The development took place partly through a steady extension of the franchise, partly through the democratization of the government, that is, the introduction of the parliamentary system of government, by which executive power is made politically dependent on popular representation. In accordance with the tradition, bicameralism was retained, which, on account of its origin, expresses a concession to aristocratic privilege. But the political power of the upper house was broken, either by the abolition of the hereditary principle, of royal nomination, or of a privileged franchise as the basis for holding seats, or—as in Great Britain—by allowing the upper house to continue in its old form but depriving it of its political influence (Parliament Act, 1911). The reform of popular representation was naturally brought about by the enactment of the appropriate statutory provisions, but the parliamentary system of government gained a firm hold through political practice and assumed definite form in legal custom and "parliamentary conventions," which vary greatly in character in the various countries. Sometimes, as in Denmark, for instance, parliamentarism emerged only as the result of protracted constitutional struggles.

As states that have undergone development from constitutional monarchy to modern democracy, one may name the "old democracies": Denmark, Norway, Sweden, England, the Netherlands, Belgium, and France. In the last-mentioned country, however, the transition did not go smoothly, but took place all at once through the proclamation of the Third Republic in 1875. Italy, too, in the years immediately before the First World War, was well under way toward the realization of parliamentary democracy, but war and Fascism temporarily put an end to that movement. In certain other countries, as for instance Spain, there existed on paper more or less democratic constitutions; however, owing to the people's cultural and political backwardness, they never actually meant anything.

On the other hand, there was also a group of states which, up to the First World War, stuck to the constitutionalist point of view and held fast to the conservative principles of an independent royal power, a government independent of parliament, an aristocratic upper house, a limited franchise, and so on. That was the case, for instance, of the German Reich and the individual German states, of Austria-Hungary, and of the Balkan states. The "new democracies" that arose after the First World War belonged especially to the latter group (see Chapter I).

III.

THE THEORISTS OF DEMOCRACY

1. The Doctrine of the Absolute Rightness of Democracy (Rousseau)

In the previous chapter we have dealt with the history of democracy and at the same time also touched on democratic ideas in so far as they have entered as dynamic ideas in the constitutional development. In this chapter, we shall discuss some of the main aspects of theories that have been put forth at different times as criteria for the excellence or defectiveness of democracy in comparison with other forms of government. We thus go from the sphere of political forces to that of pure thought.

We have seen in the historical part that all political thought throughout the Middle Ages and right down to the time of the French Revolution revolved around two ideas: the divine right of kings and popular sovereignty. The task in both cases was the same—to explain the origin of the actual political power's authority, that is, its power to bind legally and morally, and not only by physical might. The first idea traces authority back to divine sanction. The second, the idea of popular sovereignty, is the idea that all political authority ultimately is founded on the subjects' own consent. It operates, therefore, on the assumption of a *contract* of certain content, whereby the supreme power is set up, and presupposes a norm of natural law about the binding force of agreements. That the norm is of natural law means that its validity, independently of all human government and establishment, derives directly from man's spiritual nature.

It is now clear that from the idea of popular sovereignty

one could in practice obtain any kind of actual government, even the most absolute monarchy, according to the content one puts into the contract.

On the other hand, the road is clear for the basis of a real democracy, that is, a government in which the people's participation is not merely pushed into the background as the ultimate ground of legitimation, but is demanded constantly, actually as the basis for the conduct of government. It is only necessary to give the contract such a content that sovereignty does not pass from the people to a ruler. It must be remembered that the content of the contract was not restricted by historical realities. It was decided by considerations of what the people might reasonably be assumed to have entered into, and the function of the theory was—at any rate among the more advanced theorists—to give not a historic description of reality but a rational interpretation of the principles that can *justify* political power. Since now "reason" could be interpreted in more than one manner, there was freedom to fashion theories according to the ideas that animated the different authors.

According to the older theories, there was concluded between people and prince a submission contract, whereby the people transferred its sovereignty and liberty to the prince and thereby created—conditionally or unconditionally—a right for the latter to rule.

Already with Milton[1] (1649) and Locke[2] (1689) that idea is weakened in that political power is regarded as being based not upon a contract but upon a trust, which creates not an autonomous right but rather an obligation for the prince to rule, as a sort of defender of the people, in the people's name and interest. If the prince acts in a manner contrary to this trust, then he forfeits his office. But this idea had to wait for Rousseau to be brought to its logical conclusion. The ruler was now considered as nothing but a business manager or

---

[1] John Milton, *The Tenure of Kings and Magistrates* (London, 1649).
[2] John Locke, *Two Treatises of Government* (London, 1689).

servant of the people; and his mandate could be at any time freely and unconditionally recalled by the people.

Rousseau's theory—propounded in his well-known *Contrat social* (1762)—marks the climax but at the same time also the conclusion of the idea of natural law, which after his day gradually died away. He boldly used the arsenal of ideas of natural law to combat absolutism, which had for a time relied on these same weapons. But his theory also contained other conceptual elements, which were carried further in the nineteenth century.

Rousseau considers every contract of submission to a prince as incompatible with human reason, since man would thereby make himself the slave of another. If society is to be shaped in such a way that a social power is to be created while the individual still retains his freedom, it can only be done by the individual's submitting himself and all his rights without reserve to the *whole*, since he gains as a member of the whole a fraction of the social power and thereby regains the equivalent of all that he has lost. The content of the pact by which society is founded is, therefore, that everyone places himself, with his person and all his means, under the supreme direction of the general will.

By the act of union, there is simultaneously created a new moral or collective person, a common self, with its own life and its own will (*la volonté générale*). By obeying it, the individual retains his freedom, since he merely obeys himself as participant in the general will. Indeed, even if it becomes necessary to compel him, he is yet only forced to be free, that is, to obey his real self.

Sovereign power lies, therefore, indivisible and inalienable, in the general will. What it and it alone decides, is law. Legislative power thus belongs always, indivisibly and without any limits, to the people. For the practical carrying out of the commands of the general will, there can be instated a legislator; but the act by which this is done is not a contract. "It is absolutely nothing other than a commission, an appointment, according to which the legislator, as the plain servant of the sovereign, exercises the power that is set up to be administered, and, as the sovereign, the Will can at any time limit, change, or take back."[1]

What is new and characteristic in Rousseau lies in his remarkable and obscure doctrine of the origin and character of the general will. He departs from the assumption that naturally every individual always strives after his own private advantage without regard for others. But now, when a group of such egoists associates, the remarkable thing happens that the many wills, each itself egoist, offset and influence one another in peculiar fashion, so that there arises a new will, *the general will*, which is always and necessarily directed toward the common good, with equal consideration for each individual's interest, and which therefore, because of its nature, is always both useful and just. It seems as if Rousseau imagines the process to be almost wholly mechanical. The separate wills have, he says, each "some more" and "some less," and through their union they equalize mutually. Fichte gives a good illustration of Rousseau's thought. When two people deal with each other, says Fichte, each of them wishes to take advantage of the other. But neither of them wishes to be bested himself, so this part of their wills cancel each other out, and their common will becomes that each of the partners shall receive what is just.[2] Since the general will arises out of common interest and is directed toward the common good, it must also be general in form, that is, it must according to a general rule submit each and all to the same rights and duties. It must regard men and their actions in the abstract, never the isolated individual nor the individual action. This does not exclude the possibility that classes and privileges may be found. But it must always happen so that law by a general rule deter-

---

[1] J. J. Rousseau, *Contrat social* (Amsterdam, 1762), vol. III, ch. 1.
[2] I. G. Fichte, *Grundlage des Naturrechts nach Prinzipien der Wissenschaftslehre.* Sämmtl. Werke herausg. von I. H. Fichte (Berlin, 1845–1846), vol. III, p. 106–107.

mines who will be entitled to enjoy a privilege or belong to a class.[1]

The general will is therefore not only *legitimate*—since it is based on the individual's free approval—but *useful* as well—because it is directed toward the common good—and *equitable*, because it shows equal consideration for everyone.

In this curious play of ideas, two threads can be pointed out, one that connects Rousseau with the past and one that leads to the future. The former is the inheritance of the theory, derived from natural law, of a contract as the basis of state power whose actual nucleus is the conception that the "authority" or "ability to bind" of political power can always be traced back ultimately to the individual's free will, his consent or approval. The other trend of thought in Rousseau, which is quite new in the history of political science, is the theory of the origin of the general will and its necessary inherent righteousness, that is, its inherent utility and justice. Naturally this idea, too, in its absolute form, is somewhat a play with words (the general will directs itself toward the common good because "all" want the welfare of "all"; therefore in its form, too, it is general, etc.) which, in a cheap fashion, excuses Rosseau from speculation about the intricate problem of the powers of the majority over the minority. Who guarantees that the majority will not make a decision motivated by certain particular interests of the majority and therefore unjust to the minority? Here Rousseau has introduced a safety valve, but it is so elastic that it actually makes it impossible ever to confront his theory with reality (it has become tautological). Indeed, says Rousseau, the true general will, with its innate justice, is formed only if every individual feels himself spontaneously and vividly allied with every other individual in the community. On the other hand, if the communal bond breaks in the hearts, or if there arise connections, such as parties or associations of interest, among some in contradistinction to all, then the

[1] J. J. Rousseau, *Contrat social* (Amsterdam, 1762), vol. I, ch. 6, cf. vol. I, ch. 4, vol. II, ch. 11, and vol. III, ch. 16.

ominous particular interests gain prevalence and no true general will will emerge. "Then all are led by private motives and do not vote as fellow citizens, as if the state never existed, and in the name of law unjust decrees are fraudulently issued, the end of which is merely certain private interests."[1]

It is easy to see that, according to this way of putting it, it is always possible to explain away an "unjust" majority decision, by claiming that the formation of political parties has killed the true general will.

It may seem strange to a modern democrat that democracy's most famous theorist anathematizes all political parties and sees in them the source of democracy's ruin. This is connected with the fact that Rousseau was born in Geneva and, in his own words, always continued to love his fatherland's way of government. In the little Swiss Canton, where the adult male inhabitants gathered in primitive fashion to discuss common matters, where clashes of interest were few, the problems small, and the traditions strong, Rousseau saw an ideal that corresponded well to his romantic glorification of primitive man and the precivilization idyll. "When one sees among the happiest people on earth," he says, "a group of peasants attending to the affairs of the state under an oak and always behaving with sagacity, can one help despising the refinement of the other nations, whose misery shines through so much art and sham?" Accordingly, Rousseau did not conceive of the legislative power that belongs to the people in the same way as we do, that is, as a practical permanently functioning machine for social directions. "A state thus governed has no need of many laws, everyone realizes at once the need for them. He who first proposes them does nothing but to say what everyone feels, and there is never a question either of underhand dealings or eloquence in order to translate it into law, as everyone has determined to do."[2] Against this background, the abstract

[1] *Ibid.*, vol. IV, ch. 1, cf. vol. II, ch. 3.
[2] *Ibid.*, vol. IV, ch. 1.

concept of the general will and its inherent truth takes on living flesh and blood.

As mentioned before, the general will is always right in the sense that it desires the common good. Rousseau therefore recognizes no limits whatsoever to the legislative power, no separation of powers, and no personal liberties. Popular power is just as absolute as royal power has ever been. Every limitation would be tantamount to doubting the inner infallibility of the general will. But he concedes that the people can fail in the reasonable understanding of wherein the common good consists. Therefore the people stand in need of leaders who can formulate the laws and help the popular will to attain its end.[1] These leaders are best thought of as wise men of the type of the famous legislators of antiquity, such as Solon.

However, Rousseau rejects a legislative assembly composed of elected representatives of the people with the same definiteness with which he condemns political parties. The general will cannot be represented. This claim, so surprising to us, may be understood from Rousseau's conception of the almost physical, mechanical emergence of the general will through the mutual interaction and fusion of individual wills. This process cannot be transferred to a representative assembly. The people's representatives will invariably deceive it. "Every law which the people have not personally ratified is worthless, it is not a law. The English people believe they are free, but greatly deceive themselves. They are only free during Parliamentary elections, but as soon as the members of Parliament are elected, they are once more enslaved and are nothing."[2]

Rousseau's radical condemnation of representation and the party system appears to us dogmatic and exaggerated. On the other hand, one cannot close one's eyes to the fact that he has thereby put his finger on the very spots that have since become the object of much criticism. Instead of taking up the difficulties

[1] *Ibid.*, vol. II, ch. 3, 6 and 7.
[2] *Ibid.*, vol. III, ch. 15.

for sober consideration and possible solution, Rousseau ran away into his idyllic little world with its uncorrupted peasants around an oak, and constantly held up this primitivism as an ideal in contrast to civilization's unavoidable technique of representation—without possibly being ignorant of the fact that this idealization was and must be daydreaming. Rousseau clearly speaks here not as a social reformer, but as the apostle of a gospel.

Whereas the scanty legislation should always be made directly by the assembled people, the execution of the law, the governing power, can be entrusted either to the whole people or to a chosen circle or to a single person. The form of government is accordingly either democracy, aristocracy, or monarchy. Of these, "aristocracy" is considered normally as the best form. "Democracy" is regarded as suitable only to a people of gods.[1] But one must remark that the words "aristocracy," "democracy," and "monarchy" are used here in another sense than the current one, and that quotations without awareness thereof might give a quite misleading picture of Rousseau's ideas.

That Rousseau came to exercise such an overwhelming influence over both his contemporaries and posterity is not due to the clearness of his thoughts or their scientific worth of truth. It was, on the contrary, rather their obscurity and semipoetic elaboration that made it possible for different schools of thought to find in Rousseau what they were looking for. But the decisive factor was actually not the theories at all, but the passionate force with which, for the first time, the common man's dignity and rights were proclaimed and held up as ideal as against the wise and rich, barons and kings. "All contribute," says Rousseau, "to deprive of uprightness and reason the man who is educated to command over others."[2] It was such words that inflamed. One must consider that they were uttered in 1762 in the times of absolute monarchy. But they could, for that matter, be equally well said in 1949.

[1] *Ibid.*, vol. III, ch. 324.
[2] *Ibid.*, vol. III, ch. 6.

2. Bentham's Utilitarian "Proof" of the Absolute Rightness of Democracy

In the nineteenth century, one may still come across traces of the social-contract theories of natural law, but the trend in the treatment of political as well as legal and moral problems now points in a diffierent direction. This does not mean, however, giving up the belief that from man's nature there derive certain supreme, obvious principles for the rightness of all human actions. The point is that those principles are no longer expressed in terms of right (and duty). The leading idea is that the value or rightness of human action never depends on the action itself and its immediate conformity to a commandment, but rather on the effects it calls forth, measured in relation to the sum of human happiness as the good in itself. It was regarded as a self-evident principle that an action must be approved or condemned in relation to its tendency, through its effects, to increase or diminish the sum of happiness in the world. The best action is that which produces the greatest happiness for the greatest number (the utilitarian principle).

On the basis of this principle, Jeremy Bentham (1748–1832) thought himself able to produce nearly a mathematical proof that democracy is the only right form of government. The end is, according to the principle, to find the organization of the state that creates the greatest possible sum total of happiness. How can this happen? Unfortunately, men are so made, according to Bentham's view, that they always seek their own happiness or advantage without regard for those of others. If, therefore, the power of government is given into the hands of one or several persons, the result can only be that the holders of power take advantage of their position to pursue their own particular interests and not the common good or the happiness of all. The task must therefore be to find a system whereby agreement is brought about between the rulers' interest and the general interest, and this can be done only by giving the supreme political power to the people, to all; for then the measure will be the happiness of all, and the government will thus be in agreement with the principle of the greatest happiness.

In the absolute monarchy, the state institution serves only one end, says Bentham, namely, the greatest happiness of the one individual into whose hands power has been put.

In the limited monarchy, the state institution serves the greatest possible happiness of the monarch and the small circle of aristocrats with whom he shares the power.

Only in democracy is the aim of the constitution to realize the greatest happiness for the greatest possible number, and this proves that democracy is the only right form for the constitution of the state.[1]

It is evident that this train of thought recalls much of Rousseau's. Bentham, too, starts from the assumption that man is an egoist who seeks only his own advantage; yet he assumes the miraculous, that when these egoists act together they suddenly begin to seek an end that lies beyond their own particular interests, namely, the common good, the happiness of all. But whereas Rousseau, after all, attempts to give a certain explanation of that miracle through his theory of *la volonté générale*, no hint of explanation is to be found in Bentham. As far as I can see, the fact is that Bentham has been blind to the contradiction. He has let himself be deceived by a crude sophism: when every individual seeks everyone's happiness, then all seek the happiness of all!

On another point, too, Bentham is more shortsighted than Rousseau. The latter realized that the general will could err rationally because it did not understand what the real common good was, but it never occurs to Bentham to doubt that the people always possess the right insight into what serves their interests.

On this sketchy, slender, pseudo-logical foundation, Bentham then erected a radical democratic constitution, which he

---

[1] Jeremy Bentham, *Constitutional Code*, Works ed. by John Bowring (Edinburgh, 1843), vol. IX, especially pp. 10, 47 and 127.

elaborated with prodigious industry into many hundreds of articles—covering over five hundred double-column foolscap pages printed in brevier—in the naive belief that the states, once the righteousness of his basic principles had been realized, would accept that monster as the law of the land.

The essential features[1] of Bentham's scheme are worth noting. Supreme power is vested in the people, but, on practical grounds, they must exercise it through representatives. All state representatives are freely dismissible, since they have only an entrusted commission. Moreover, they are to be criminally responsible if they seek their own interest at the expense of the community.

The franchise for parliament is universal, equal, by secret ballot, and annual. It is particularly emphasized that the poor ought to have the franchise, since their happiness is just as much a part of the universal happiness as that of the rich. Womens' franchise is advocated, too, even though Bentham realized that, on grounds of prejudice, it would not be possible to grant it immediately.

The legislative assembly consists of one chamber only. An upper house would either be superfluous or an impediment to the carrying out of the people's will.

Elections are to be direct.

The competence of the legislature is unrestricted by previously granted civil liberties, which have meaning only in a state in which the government is not vested in the people but is despotic. For the same reason, Bentham also rejects every thought of separation of powers after Montesquieu's model.

The supreme executive power rests with a prime minister. Monarchy is categorically rejected, since the monarch always seeks his own advantage and is an enemy of the people.

This radicalism, in so far as constitutional law is concerned, does not correspond to a similar attitude in the realm of social policy and distribution of property. Here Bentham is definitely a conservative. The aims of government are defined more

[1] *Ibid.*, pp. 96–145.

precisely as maintenance of security, prosperity, and equality. Of these, security, i. e., of the existing rights, is the most important; equality is the most conditioned, and can be considered only in so far as it is compatible with security. Greater equality can be brought about only through a series of continual interferences with the property owners' rights. This interference will, in itself, partly mean the disappointment of expectations, partly undermine industry and zeal. Bentham is therefore no supporter of any equalization but that which takes place of itself when the legislator lets things take their own course and does not create artificial monopolies. Compared with the feudal era, there has been great progress toward equality. The pyramid of feudalism has been destroyed, to the advantage of the many. Thus a conservative liberalism resulted.[1]

It may appear odd that this conservatism could unite with radicalism, as far as constitutional law is concerned. Strangely enough, Bentham entertains no fear that political rule by the masses might be used to deprive the property owners of their advantages. This optimism is based on a few abstract arguments of a kind typical of Bentham's schematic psychology: the mass cannot rob the rich with violence, for thereby all property, even that of the poorest, would be ruined; no more can it be done by means of taxation, for the well-to-do cannot be taxed without taxing also the less prosperous. The worst that can happen to the influential and ruling few, if power is given to all, is that they will be put on an equal footing with others in every respect with the exception of property.[2]

For all his many and voluminous works, Bentham has not exercised an influence comparable to that of Rousseau. Whereas Rousseau appealed to the emotions, Bentham spoke exclusively to reason. Few philosophers have shown so little understanding

---

[1] Alf Ross, "*Kritik der sogenannten praktischen Erkenntnis*" (Copenhagen: Munksgaard, 1933), p. 137–138.

[2] Jeremy Bentham, *Constitutional Code*, Works, ed. by John Bowring (Edinburgh, 1843), p. 143.

of the obscure, the irrational, the urge- and habit-determined in human nature as he. On the other hand, his belief in the power of reason was unlimited. It was to him literally a mystery that statesmen did not rush eagerly to light their torches at the fire he had kindled, or that his principle could even be looked at with distrust.[1] With his plain, intellectualist psychology and his absolute lack of historical sense, Bentham belongs typically to the eighteenth century. He is one of the great, naïve planners who believe that what matters in social problems is the devising of a rational scheme; it will then be up to the legislator by his sovereign decree to transform it into reality.

Within his limitations, however, Bentham possessed a penetrating analytic faculty, and his critique of British social conditions was often biting, striking, and fanatical. He therefore found many supporters, among whom was a little group of eminently gifted, radical minds, that came to put their impress on the trend of the times. Even if Bentham's "proof" of the infallibility of democracy did not lead to its immediate introduction, all the same the great British electoral reforms of the nineteenth century (1832, 1867, 1884) were undoubtedly under his direct or indirect influence.

3. The Aristocratic-Conservative Critique: The Fear of Mass Tyranny

After Rousseau and Bentham, no more abstract "proofs" were adduced in support of the absolute rightness of democracy. The utilitarian trend is continued—that is, the tree is judged by its fruits; but a few abstract principles about the structure of human nature are no longer taken as a basis for judgment. The experience of history and of the present is appealed to, democracy is studied as it develops in practice, and its relative advantages and shortcomings are discussed. Only during the

---

[1] Alf Ross, *Kritik der sogenannten praktischen Erkenntnis* (Copenhagen: Munksgaard, 1933), p. 147, note 24.

nineteenth century, as democracy won out, did it become clear what it was that was being discussed.

The essential feature in the development is that the dogmatic belief in the infallibility of the popular will has disappeared. Even the stanchest supporters of democracy realize that the system is not without certain drawbacks, which have to be overcome. Popular government is not so simple and perfectly ideal as its first theorists believed. It is not a system that can readily be derived from a few basic principles, but a task that must be carried out with constant regard for the demands and problems of the time. Some saw democracy's possibilities in a brighter light and others in a darker. During the whole time from the French Revolution down to the modern dictatorships, there was hardly anyone who, on principle and definitely, rejected the idea of popular representation.

The criticism that is advanced in different disguises and with different force is chiefly the expression of a conservative fear of the consequences of full democracy. It is feared that power in the hands of the broad masses will lead to class rule and mass tyranny—dictatorship of the majority, as we would say in our own day. Therefore, brakes of various kinds on popular government are required: limited franchise, royal privileges, an aristocratic upper house. This is a theory that very well reflects the limited, constitutional monarchy that was typical of the actual political development in the nineteenth century.

In its cruder interest-determined form, the fear of the people is simply the propertied classes' fear of being deprived of their privileges. This side of the question stands out clearly in the reaction against pure democracy that characterized the American Constitution of 1787. In *The Federalist*, Hamilton, Madison, and others stressed the danger of entrusting the legislative assembly with unlimited power. If all power is gathered into one hand, the result can only be a new, "elected" despot who can be just as dangerous for freedom as any hereditary monarch. Pure majority government leads to class rule and mass tyranny, by which the rights of the minority are pitilessly sacrificed. It is therefore necessary to protect the propertied minority against the majority. This task the Fathers of the Constitution sought to perform by a finely attuned distribution of power which was to insure that no individual population group could ever be in possession of the entire state apparatus (see Chapter II, Sec. 4). The American Constitution therefore provided for a democracy with pronounced conservative guarantees.

The egoist interest of the upper class in preserving their privileges is obvious in this conservatism, and its ideological rationalization was mediocre. When the majority's tyranny over the minority is anathematized the obvious question arises whether that would be a lesser evil than the minority's tyranny over the majority, which seems to be the alternative. When the broad masses' conquest of power is labeled class domination, one feels tempted to ask in turn whether the exercise of power by the upper class is not also the rule of one class over another. Yet those men were certainly not hypocrites. That they could in good faith defend the minority's right against the "encroachment" of the majority is explained by the powerful grip the established order and customary prejudice have over the human mind. They were not able to understand that the given distribution of property and the existing "rights" are nothing but reflections of a certain legal order created in defense of certain interests, and that therefore a change in this order for the purpose of creating another and more equalitarian distribution of property cannot be referred to as an "encroachment." To them the given distribution of wealth was right in an absolute sense, and the claims of the underprivileged therefore appeared to them as "encroachments" based on "class domination" and "majority tyranny."

The fear of the people could also assume another and more sublimated form, connected with the belief that the important factor is quality, not quantity; that there will always be a minority elite which, by reason of outstanding faculties, culture, education, or the independence that is the fruit of the aristocratic tradition and way of life, is more than others suited to govern and rule; and that the people, therefore, in their own interest, would do better either to leave all the power to the selected few or, at least, to grant them a place of precedence above others. The danger of democracy is that the people, because of lack of judgment and small-mindedness, will destroy the conditions of life of the elite who are, in reality, the basis of all progress.

No one has more clearly stated the significance of the intellectual elite for a society than John Stuart Mill (1806–1873), and his word carries particular weight because he, better than anyone before him, saw where the greatest value of democracy lies.

In defense of democracy, Mill points out first that one is oneself the only reliable defender of one's own rights and interests and that the rights and interests of any person are secure against being disregarded only when the person interested is himself able, and habitually disposed, to stand up for them.[1] In this line of thinking it is obviously presupposed as a demand of social justice that equal consideration shall be given to the interests of each and every person, and Mill expresses here in psychological and relative terms the same idea that lay behind Rousseau's dogma of the absolute rightness and justice of the general will.

But the essential and new in Mill is his eye for democracy's indirect importance for general education and the development of character. How would it help to transfer the power to an individual, asked Mill, even if it were possible to find a man with superhuman strength and wisdom? What human beings would be educated under such a rule? Both the intellectual and the moral qualities would be blunted and decay. To leave everything to the government is, likewise, to leave everything to Providence, which is tantamount to political indifference and the decline of community feeling and consciousness of responsibility, which inevitably lead to national decay. "Everyone is

[1] J. S. Mill, *Essay on Representative Government* (London, 1861), p. 55.

degraded, whether aware of it or not, when other people, without consulting him, take upon themselves unlimited power to regulate his destiny."[1] "Any education which aims at making human beings other than machines will in the long run make them claim to have control of their own actions."[2] The value of democracy consists, therefore, in great part in respect for the personality and the possibility it assures the latter of growing and developing. One must take into consideration how little is found in the usual life of most people that can give their ideas and feelings any greatness. Through participating in public political life they are raised above the narrower sphere of private life and educated to a common spirit and solidarity with others, to the enrichment of the individual and the strengthening of the nation. "It is a great discouragement to an individual and a still greater one to a class to be left out of the constitution; to be reduced to plead from outside the door to the arbiters of their destiny, not taken into consultation within."[3]

Mill therefore agrees with Rousseau and Bentham that the highest political power should rest with the people and that no social group should be excluded from sharing in it. Nevertheless, Mill fears that the unlimited power of the majority will lead to abuse and tyranny against the minority, both in the intellectual and in the economic sphere.

In the intellectual respect, this is bound up with Mill's deep respect for the intellectual elite, the few who are the salt of the earth and the source of all that is great and valuable among men, together with his belief that this elite can develop and thrive only in a world that understands the value of individual peculiarities and grants them the greatest possible scope for free development. What Mill feared was the spiritual tyranny of the masses which would demand uniformity of all according to the standard of collective mediocrity. The average individual, who constitutes the material of which the majority is built up,

[1] *Ibid.*, p. 166.
[2] *Ibid.*, p. 52.
[3] *Ibid.*, p. 66.

lacks inner intellectual freedom; he is ridden by social prejudice, codes, and conventions which reflect his surroundings, and he is an easy victim for press and propaganda. On the other hand, such a man, when he is raised to power, will have a tendency to intolerance while demanding recognition and respect from all for the beliefs and the customs that rule him. A slave himself, he will demand that all others shall wear the same chains.[1]

This compulsion in the intellectual domain, however, is exercised not so much through state power as through public opinion, the moral police. In the actual political domain, it was more the exploitation of political power to further certain class interests that Mill feared. Suppose the majority to be of whites, the minority negroes, suppose the majority Roman Catholics, the minority Protestants—is it likely that the majority would allow equal justice to the minority? The same applies with regard to a majority of the poor in relation to the minority of the rich.[2]

To avoid the abuse of class domination and to counterweigh the popular instincts, Mill thought it necessary to give the enlightened minority a relatively greater influence in the government of the state. From that point of view he first of all recommended proportional representation, which assures the minority a proportionate voice. Next, he advocated a system of plural votes in favor of those whose intellectual superiority rendered them particularly qualified to govern. Here a difficulty arises for Mill, as for all those who wish to build upon qualified intellectual competence, when the practical criterion has to be found, and he is obliged therefore to fall back on occupation as an indication of higher capacities. He thinks that a banker, merchant, or manufacturer is likely more intelligent than a tradesman, because he has larger and more complicated interests to manage.[3] In this way Mill's

---

[1] These thoughts Mill developed in his book *On Liberty* (London, 1859).
[2] J. S. Mill, *Essay on Representative Government* (London, 1861), p. 120.
[3] *Ibid.*, p. 175.

aristocracy of the intellect assumes a dangerous similarity to the more common conservative desire to protect the property-owning classes' economic privileges. His appeal to enlightenment and culture, seeing that these qualities in his day particularly were reserved to the owning classes, actually amounts to a masked form of conservative guarantees.

Nor can one avoid asking the question: Is the primary problem actually whether the majority of the poor under full democracy will grant fair treatment to the rich minority? Is it not rather, whether the wealthy minority will, under another system, grant the poor majority full equity? Is not Mill's point of view the expression of the fact that he himself, in a certain respect, is bound by prejudice and convention, namely, the prejudice that the rich have a *right* to their wealth which the poor are bound to respect? Only on this premise is the talk about majority tyranny fully understandable.

The two leitmotivs in the critique of democracy in the nineteenth century are (i) the assertion of the masses' ignorance, unreason, and instinctive passions, which make them the victims of demagogic leaders and render them unfit to participate in the government of the state; and (ii) the assertion that the party system necessarily involves corruption and divisions and makes party interests, not the welfare of the state, the highest norm.

Both motives, which can be performed in a great number of variations, gain particular strength and foundation in connection with the conservative ideology which, after the French Revolution, was developed in England by Burke, in France by the Traditionalists, and in Germany by the Romanticists, and the basic features of which have been discussed above under the description of constitutional monarchy (Chapter II, Sec. 6).

The claim that the people lack intelligence, judgment, reason, and knowledge is developed to the extreme by the French writer Emile Faguet, who would make the cultivation of ignorance, the lack of respect for knowledge and competence, into the very principle of democracy and the cause of the decay not only of political life, but also of culture and the forms of social life. Democracy is the confusion of the political functions, the destruction of social differentiation and organization which are based upon nature-given inequalities. He and others stress particularly the lack of real candidates for leadership in popular government. Mediocrities that dominate the masses are not capable of electing leaders of higher caliber because they are involuntarily attracted by those people who reflect their own pettiness. Nobody is allowed to raise his head above the crowd. Expert knowledge, too, which of necessity must play an increasing role in the modern complex society in which the state takes over more and more tasks, is pushed aside because the common man lacks understanding of it and believes that he can decide everything in his own way.[1]

The drawbacks that are in many ways connected with the party-system are discussed most exhaustively by Ostrogorsky.[2] He makes the party system responsible for the deterioration of the work of legislation, corruption in state and borough, the lack of public responsibility and adequate leadership. The parties have a tendency to distort public debate by setting up party advantage and not the common good as the highest aim. In connection with private money interests, sharing out of offices and soft jobs to party members, and other forms of corruption, the party machine develops into an organization which, instead of serving the political life, preys on it. The party becomes an instrument for the interests of private capital, a gigantic organization for corruption and bribery. Such a development, which is particularly evident in the United States, can, however, take place only in a country where money and respect for money rule public opinion, and where corruption is tolerated so long as it does not bring about personal loss.

[1] Emile Faguet, *Le Culte de l'incompetence* (Paris, 1910).
[2] M. Ostrogorsky, *Democracy and the Organization of Political Parties* (London, 1903), abridged into *Democracy and the Party System* (London, 1910).

The hidden influence of financial power in a democracy is precisely one of the complaints most frequently stated.[1] Everything can be bought for money, even political influence. Even though the phenomenon is not specific to democracy, the danger is perhaps the greater, because the poor allow themselves more easily to be tempted into selling themselves than the well-to-do. Of the methods whereby money can assert its influence, the illegal form, bribery and other forms of punishable corruption, is only one among many. Direct buying—of electors, people's representatives, administrative officials, or judges—no longer plays a great part in the advanced democracies except, perhaps, the United States. The same cannot be said about patronage, that is, the giving away of offices and soft jobs to political friends. But there exist legal methods, which are more difficult to do away with. The most important among these is the power of money via the press and other channels of information to influence public opinion. The respect the press entertains for the big advertisers is well known.[2]

The objection is also common that politics is irreconcilable with honesty. It is not only the party spirit, corruption, and professionalism that are the cause. Even the parliamentary system, it is said, of necessity requires that the honest man leave his honesty at home when on his way to parliament. Here all ideas undergo a process of stultification; here trading and bargaining go on. Agreement is incompatible with clear party lines. All great thoughts end as planless compromises, all real ideas are betrayed in order to curry the favor of the electorate. The fight becomes a fight for votes and not for principles. People talk "through their hats" to catch votes for the electoral campaign; hackneyed slogans that appeal to the masses' instincts supersede real arguments and objective explanations. In short, in parliamentary life all greatness is drowned and

---

[1] See, for example, James Bryce, *Modern Democracies* (London, 1921), vol. II, p. 522, cf. ch. VI, Sec. I.
[2] Cf. Sec. 5 and ch. VI, Sec. I.

true personality founders in a sea of degradation, trafficking, and professional play acting.[1]

Among the authors of this period James Bryce takes a special place. He is at once one of democracy's warmest champions and its most sympathetic critic. His two monumental works[2] are based upon a thorough study of the practice of popular government in six countries (France, Switzerland, the United States, Canada, Australia, and New Zealand) and contain a wealth of facts and observations that are indispensable to any thorough study of the problems of democracy. Bryce has given up every attempt at arguing about principles. Without setting up certain ideals, without becoming aware of his implicit basis of valuation, he judges the advantages and drawbacks of democracy in relation to the ability and effectiveness with which democracy has been able to solve what he regards as the natural tasks of the state: protection against external enemies, internal order, equitable administration of justice, efficient administration and assistance to the citizens in their various occupations. History shows that these functions can be fulfilled as well by democracy as by any other form of government. Moreover, popular government produces a very valuable by-product: the social education, a widening of the horizon and the range of interests, the identification of oneself with the community and its problems, which John Stuart Mill had already pointed out as being to the credit of popular government.[3]

James Bryce's great work on the modern democracies appeared in 1921. It is the finale in the theoretical development of an era that ended precisely with the apparent victory and culmination of democracy immediately after the First World War. The following years brought the crisis.

---

[1] Cf. below, page 119.
[2] *The American Commonwealth* (London, 1903), *Modern Democracies* (London, 1921).
[3] *Modern Democracies*, vol. I, pp. 161–169; vol. II, pp. 580, 583 ff.

4. THE FASCIST-NAZI CRITIQUE OF DEMOCRACY

With the Fascist[1] dictatorship ideology, a new era set in for the problems of democracy. Certainly it is partly the old well-known arguments of the ignorance of the mass and the misery of the party system, which are advanced anew. But the spirit and the tendency are different.

Conservative criticism of earlier days was advanced to warn against supposed abuse and dalliance. It was rooted in fear of the consequences of total democracy for the existing institutions and established rights. It pointed backward to monarchy and aristocracy, culture and property as factors of state-preserving importance alongside the popular will. But seldom or never had the conservative critics attacked the idea of representation or the parliamentary idea themselves; they still believed that the national will ought to be formed on the basis of representation of and debate among the interests and ideas of the different population groups. Even if the critics could be severe, the criticism was yet objective and sincere. Its aim was to castigate in order to improve, to limit in order to secure the best balance between purely democratic and conservative forces in the community.

It was different now. Fascist criticism of democracy's weaknesses and defects is not objective but perfidious, because it aims exclusively at discrediting the system itself and paving the way for one party's absolute mastery. No exaggeration or distortion is shunned if only it is suitable for serving as a means to this goal. Party dissensions and lack of political tradition and training, together with the chaotic social, economic, and national conditions, made the new democracies formed after the First World War the easy butt for a scorn and a ridicule that were wrongly directed against democracy as such.

In accordance with this aim, the very foundations of democracy—the ideas of representation and debate—are now also

---

[1] I am using here and from time to time in the following, the word "Fascism" as generic term for Italian Fascism and German Nazism.

attacked. The individual's claim to be heard is rejected because there is no longer a belief in the dignity and the moral autonomy of man. The idea of reaching rational solutions through discussion is rejected; there is no longer a belief in any reason. Tolerance and respect for others are branded as cowardice, compromise as moral weakness and spinelessness, because only power and the right of the strongest is believed in. There is nothing but contempt left for parliamentary debate. Discussions, negotiations, and compromises are regarded as idle detours, impediments to the powerful will. After all, the parliamentary system is only a show, a pious fraud in honor of the naïve. Actual power has always lain with a small minority of rulers, the active heroic natures, the clear-sighted and open-minded, who love power and do not let themselves be hampered by any consideration. For them, ideologies are instruments used to satisfy the great masses' urge for rational motivations and to give their politics an appearance of honesty.

The spiritual source of dictatorship's political mentality is, as was shown by the Swedish investigator Herbert Tingsten, to be found first and foremost in the antiintellectualism that emanated from such men as the German philosopher Nietzsche and the French authors Maurice Barrès and Georges Sorel. Tingsten sums up the psychological scheme of development thus: A critical analysis of the current moral ideas and systems of valuation leads to universal relativism or nihilism. There remains only the belief in life itself as a value, and this belief in life is transformed into a romantic worship of action, strength, self-assertion—activity without goal. At that stage appears the insight that the ideologies, regardless of their content of truth, can serve as incitement to a life of action, and this leads to a willingness to accept even the most primitive beliefs if only they give value and content to life. Relativism can thus change into a "faith of second degree," a faith that is on principle regarded not as truth but as stimulus, and that therefore from the ontset is immune to every rationalist criticism.

Such pragmatic belief is also called a myth. Sorel, the great theorist of syndicalism, sought in the myth of the general strike the vitalizing belief that was to give the life of the toiling masses moral firmness and dignity by constantly stimulating their desire for struggle, heroic effort, and self-sacrifice. Fascism took over from syndicalism the worship of violence and uncompromising struggle, of vitality as the supreme and only value, but altered the myth's content to the nation, the people, or the race.

Bound up with vitalism is antihumanism. The struggle and the unfolding of life are the supreme values, not life as such. Man is not sacred. The weak is the victim of the stronger. The doctrine of compassion is slave morality. Christianity is the religion of the weak. Man is a pawn in the struggle for power and nothing else. Freed of all taboo attached to the idea of the sacredness of human life, the struggle for power becomes pure and simple unrestrained technique. The cynical and methodical destruction of men in their millions in German concentration-camp gaschambers and giant crematoria is the consistent development in practice of a mentality that has cast off all humane restraints.

Intellectual and moral nihilism, worship of pure vital force, of the superman of genius, of brutal and unrestrained violence—these are the marks of the mentality that created the modern dictatorship.

But in order that the strong may reach their goal, conquer power and keep it, an ideology is needed for the broad masses, a myth that can satisfy the slaves and turn them into a willing tool in the ruler's hand.

For this purpose the dictatorship used the national consciousness. Germany's defeat, and Italy's feeling of having been cheated of the fruits of victory, created in those countries the ideal ground for a morbidly swollen national urge for self-assertion. With unfailing instinct, the champions of dictatorship found their way to the same fundamental urge in man, which was their own paramount law: the lust for power. The secret of how the people could possibly be made to renounce all their rights to personal freedom and self-assertion is that they were promised in exchange power and glory as members of a victorious nation. Fascism created the myth of the chosen people, the *Herrenvolk*, blood and race. In the legend of the resplendent past of his people, his race (the Roman Empire for the Italians and the cultural achievements of the Germans) and in the dream of ruling other peoples in the future, the common man found an outlet for his repressed lust for power. Herein lay the deepest sounding board for the appeal to national unity, efficiency, discipline, and regimentation under the Leader's almighty will, which is to lead the people to the new Jerusalem. In its ready susceptibility to the gospel of power and the myth of the master race, in the dissolution of all humane ideals, which rendered possible Hitler's gangster politics, lies the basis of the German people's coresponsibility for its fate.

With this is closely bound up the fact that dictatorship, in order to justify itself in the eyes of the multititude, kept on hammering upon democracy's failing effectiveness. Nothing, from the standpoint of the lust for power, could better legitimate the dictatorship than its effectiveness, that is, its greater expediency in the struggle for power with other nations.

The passionate fascist attack upon the fundamentals of democracy was in a curious way not without value for democracy. By attacking the principle of mutual understanding, by preaching the brutal gospel of violence, and by demonstrating in practice what consequences this will lead to, it awakened the adherents of democracy to an understanding of the fundamental human values on which the democratic system builds. Self-reflection gave the old and usual a new living value and awakened in the democratic people the will to fight for the human ideals of democracy.

5. The Communist Critique of Democracy

Common to the different socialist schools within the workers' movement of recent times is the opinion that private capitalism means the exploitation of the broad, laboring population and that the aim must therefore be to overcome that system.

But the great problem that divides the different schools, primarily social-democracy and communism, is how far political democracy is a suitable means for reaching this goal. Since the exploited, propertyless proletariat is said to constitute the great mass in relation to the minority of capitalists, and since political democracy, at any rate in its well-developed form, aims to put political power into the hands of the majority, one might believe from the outset that the question should be answered in the affirmative. Nevertheless, it is denied by the Communists. They maintain that so long as capitalism as an economic system remains in existence, it will have such advantages on its side that it will be impossible within the framework of parliamentary democracy—despite the apparent freedom of every opinion to assert itself and put itself through—to reach the point of abolishing the system. Therefore, there is no other way than violence. The proletariat must through revolution smash the bourgeois state machine to pieces and create a new state in which the proletariat rules and holds down with violence the previous oppressors. This is the dictatorship of the proletariat. According to the theory, it is to be superseded, at some time in the future, by a state of society that is not at all based upon violence and oppression, where there exists no state apparatus whatever, for the state withers and dies away.

The most obvious feature of this critique is that it goes in the very opposite direction to the bourgeois-aristocratic conservatism discussed above in Section 3. While the latter feared that absolute democracy would lead to tyranny of the masses, encroachment of the lower classes upon the upper class, the idea of the former is that the broad masses are unable to satisfy their demands within the framework of democracy. The accusation directed against democracy is this, that it is not effective in the special sense that it cannot fulfil its own claim that the will of the majority shall be the law of the land. The reason for this is that there are certain economic structures and forces which are stronger than all legal conventions. Capitalism lives, so to say, in an underground shelter which is inaccessible to the parliamentary political fighting. These economic forces may well alter the conditions on the surface but they can never reach deep and transform the existing economic foundation of society, capitalism. Therefore the political struggle by parliamentary means for the economic interests of the working class can never be anything but feints and make-believe, and the workers' economic bondage will continue to the day when they violently overthrow the capitalist state, the dictatorship of the bourgeoisie, and in its stead set up their own dictatorship.

Neither is it possible, from the standpoint of the proletariat, to attribute great value to the democratic institutions of political rights, freedom of expression, etc., as ends in themselves. The formal liberties are not of much value for him who is economically dependent. The right of free criticism is a luxury for the underfed worker which he cannot afford to think about. What he craves is a full stomach, not a free tongue. Without the former, he has no strength to avail himself of the latter. This is sometimes bound up with the belief that the formal political liberties not only are of secondary importance, but may even be directly dangerous from the point of view of the proletariat's interests. These political liberties, in reality illusory, create an appearance which, just like religion, is a kind of opium for the people, lulling the revolutionary consciousness to sleep. Participation in parliamentary debate for the attainment of the small, partial progress that is possible in that way, rivets the attention on day-to-day measures and leads it away from the great aim.

What testimony of experience and what arguments are now adduced by communism in support of the far-reaching claim that it will never be possible within democracy to achieve a real economic emancipation—an assertion which, in consideration of the great changes that it has actually been possible to carry through in the parliamentary way, must at first appear strangely exaggerated and improbable? As I am presently going to show, it advances some few, rather superficial, general considerations, part of which, at any rate, are obviously untenable. One gets the impression that in reality it has *never examined seriously and thoroughly* whether or not the parliamentary method is adequate. The crux of the matter seems to be that the will of communism to use violence and revolution is founded on other grounds. Chief of these is probably, that the demand for a change in the situation is so well justified and so pressing that communism does not wish to put up with the waiting time and the difficulties that are bound up with the parliamentary method. It seeks to justify this point of view, furthermore, by maintaining that under no circumstances can the parliamentary procedure lead forward. If this psychological interpretation is correct, it cannot surprise anyone that the communist critique of democracy is superficial, summary, and actually based more upon postulates than upon facts and well-founded arguments.

To illustrate this, I quote at some length one of the most important passages from Lenin, where the question is discussed.

> In capitalist society, under the conditions most favorable to its development, we have more or less complete democracy in the democratic republic. But this democracy is always restricted by the narrow framework of capitalist exploitation, and consequently always remains, in reality, a democracy for the minority, only for the possessing classes, only for the rich. Freedom in capitalist society always remains about the same as it was in the ancient Greek republics: freedom for the slave-owners. Owing to the conditions of capitalist exploitation, the modern wage slaves are also so crushed by want and poverty that they cannot be bothered with democracy politics: in the ordinary peaceful course of events the majority of the population is debarred from participating in social and political life . . . .
>
> Democracy for an insignificant minority, democracy for the rich—that is the democracy of capitalist society. If we look more closely into the mechanism of capitalist democracy, everywhere, in the "petty"—socalled petty—details of the suffrage (residential qualification, exclusion of women, etc.),

and in the technique of the representative institutions, in the actual obstacles to the right of assembly (public buildings are not for "beggars"), in the purely capitalist organization of the daily press, etc. etc.,—on all sides we see restriction upon restriction on democracy. These restrictions, exceptions, exclusions, obstacles for the poor, seem slight, especially in the eyes of one who has never known want himself and has never been in close contact with the oppressed classes in their mass life (and nine-tenths, if not ninety-ninehundredths, of the bourgeois publicists and politicians are of this category); but in their sum total these restrictions exclude and squeeze out the poor from politics, from taking an active part in democracy.

Marx grasped this *essence* of capitalist democracy splendidly when, in analyzing the experience of the Commune, he said that the oppressed were allowed, once every few years, to decide which particular representatives of the oppressing class should misrepresent them in parliament!

But from this capitalist democracy—inevitably narrow, tacitly repelling the poor, and therefore hypocritical and false to the core—development does not proceed simply, smoothly, and directly to "greater and greater democracy," as the liberal professors and petit bourgeois opportunists would have us believe. No, development—toward communism—proceeds through the dictatorship of the proletariat; it cannot do otherwise, for the *resistance* of the capitalist exploiters cannot be *broken* by anyone else or in any other way.[2]

In this passage a number of different ideas can be found.

One of the points of view is that the poor are unable to plead their own interests because there exist, to their detriment, a series of *legal restrictions* on democracy, each in itself "insignificant" but in their sum total very conclusive, particularly the restrictions on the franchise. This is, however, only a sign that political democracy is not fully carried through in accordance with its own idea, and there is no basis for the assumption that such a completion of democracy would not be possible. Even when Lenin wrote the above-quoted passage (in 1917), certain states had already introduced universal and equal suffrage, among others Denmark, and later the development went further in the same direction. That the restrictions of the

[1] Lenin, *State and Revolution* (London: Lawrence and Wishart, 1933), p. 79–80.

franchise should be an insurmountable barrier to the advance of democracy is obviously quite wrong.

Next, we are referred to different *actual restrictions* upon democracy, namely, situations that prevent the proletariat from using effectively the political rights formally granted to them. It is pointed out that the poor are so crushed by their poverty that they have neither the time nor the strength to bother about politics, that they have no access to suitable meeting places, and so on. Stalin supplements this by saying that, under capitalism, there do not exist and there cannot exist any real rights for the exploited, because all public buildings, all printing houses and stocks of paper, and similar requirements for the exercise of civil liberties, are the privilege of the exploiters.

Can anyone who knows the conditions in modern democracies really believe that the progress of socialism has been prevented by the workers' lacking meeting places and paper?

The most important point, which Lenin just touches, is undoubtedly the power of capital over the press and other means of communication, and thereby over public opinion. Even if Lenin's statement is very much exaggerated, it touches a sore point to which democracy's own critics have for a long time called attention. They are concerned not merely about direct, venial political influence, the power of capitalism behind the scenes, but also and mainly about the diffuse, suggestive influence which is all-pervasive, penetrates the people's consciousness through thousands of hidden channels—school, press, church, film, theater, radio,—and influences the general mentality in the spirit of the existing capitalist society. Through the relative breakdown of class barriers, the more highly paid workers, clerks, and civil servants become *petits bourgeois*, whose outlook, ideals, and habits to an increasing degree are cheap copies of the upper-class prototypes. Thus it happens, it is claimed, that important population groups are influenced in a conservative direction toward an attitude that is not in accordance with their true interests. The "white-collar proletariat's" false distinction and emotional dissociation from the working class is quoted as a typical instance of this. It is maintained more especially that the working class's own leaders, when they attain leading positions in the bourgeois state, become so infected by the ruling class's views and ideas that they—perhaps without being aware of it—are absorbed into the bourgeoisie and become traitors to their own class.

One cannot, to my mind, deny these considerations a certain importance. So much is certainly true, that the existing system possesses an element of sluggishness, which acts conservatively against every tendency to abolish the system. This, one may also say, has a certain capacity of forming people's mentality in its own image. The capitalist system has the capacity of making all of us into small capitalists in the same way as the communist system has the opposite capacity of making people, once they live under it, into petty communists. Every system, in short, has a certain faculty, through influencing the mentality of the people, of stabilizing itself. A radical change of system pressupposes, therefore, an excess of strength.

But this by no means indicates that it might not be possible, by continuous, purposeful work, through enlightenment and agitation, to bring about the consciousness and energy necessary for a change in regime. Nothing says that there should be any absolute bounds to what can be achieved within the framework of democracy. Every thoroughgoing social reform must of course take its time. Democracy is still very young. The fact that social reform has not yet been fully carried through by parliamentary methods does not, therefore, prove that this is due to an inner impossibility. Experience shows at any rate that much can be achieved through peaceful and continuous development. Compare present-day conditions with those obtaining 100 or only 50 years ago, and see what extraordinarily far-reaching changes have taken place on the political, social, economic, and cultural levels. To him who doubts the possibility of social reform through parliamentary means, it seems obvious that the upper class will never, of its own accord, give up legal political power, and that the latter can therefore be conquered only through revolution. Yet history shows that in many countries, Denmark and Britain for instance, political democracy was introduced in a peaceful way, through a number of successive and gradual reforms. Continual criticism from the dissatisfied, continual appeal to reason and justice, together with fear of what would be the consequences of denying the fermenting forces a legitimate outlet, have brought it about that the politically privileged themselves, in virtue of their own privileged franchise, have limited and gradually abolished their own political privileges. The same holds true in other spheres: the standard of living of the working class has, during the last generation, improved not only absolutely, but also relatively to those of the other social classes. Both economically and spiritually a certain stabilization has taken place. The upper class has to a large extent simply lost its faith in its right to exploit others. No one now would offer a domestic servant or a farm laborer the same conditions as were current a generation or two ago. Should an employer in our day allow a child to slave for 10 or 14 hours a day, this—which once was quite a matter of course—would rouse the most vivid indignation among his own fellow employers. Sickness and accident insurance, old-age pensions, unemployment relief, progressive taxation, and other aspects of social and financial legislation have brought about important social and economic progress. Every one of these advances, won by parliamentary methods by radical and socialist parties, refutes the communists' claim that capitalism is able to hypnotize the lower classes into marching with its own oppressors. Everywhere one searches in vain for valid arguments in support of the belief that it is no longer possible to continue this evolution by constant appeals to reason and human feelings.

That this is nevertheless denied with so great assurance by the communist theory is presumably for two reasons. The first one, which has already been discussed, is that by this means an attempt is made to set up a further justification for the violent revolution, which has already been decided upon on other grounds. The second one is the mistaken belief that a change in regime can consist only in a decision whereby capital is transferred *once and for all* from private to public ownership. That something of this kind is most unlikely is undeniable. The fact, revealed by modern development, is that the deciding factor is not the formal right of property in itself. Property is not something absolute. It is a well-known phenomenon that often the owner of real property is in reality nothing more than a trustee for the mortgage holders. In the same way, it is possible, through a continual undermining of the very substance of the property right, by constantly extending public control, to change the capitalist from the real owner of an enterprise into a mere manager. Thus it is possible gradually to liquidate the system of private capitalism, and this makes it more probable that radical changes may be brought about in a peaceful manner through steady development. (See Chapter VII, Sec. 4.)

IV.

WHAT IS DEMOCRACY?

1. The Approach to the Problem

The word "democracy" is used in everyday conversation in many different senses. First and foremost, it is the designation of a certain *form of government*, that is, of the manner in which a state is organized, which finds expression in its constitution. The question is: what are the rules that determine by whom "public authority" may be exercised, and how? In every state it is indeed thus that—through legislation, administration, and dispensing of justice—a number of decisions are made which are regarded as universally binding. This presupposes rules regarding those persons who—as state "organs"—have "power" or "competence" to exercise public authority and the manner in which they may do so. These rules are called the state's constitution and they lay down the organization of that state. A distinction can now be made between various forms of constitution or organization, and the word "democracy" is used to designate one of these, namely—to put it roughly for the present—an arrangement of the state according to which the people as a whole, and not just a single individual or a smaller or larger group of individuals, possess the supreme or decisive influence over the exercise of public authority. This may also be expressed by saying that "sovereignty" rests with the people; in this way democracy—government by the people—is distinguished from monarchy or autocracy (government by one man) and from oligarchy (government by the few). Taken in this sense, "democracy" is a legal and formal concept. It indicates how political decisions are made, not what these decisions are in substance. It designates a method for the establishment of the "political will", not its object, end, or means.

But the word "democracy" is also used in a different sense, as relating to content. Economic or *real* democracy means something in the nature of an economic order which has in view a leveling of economic privileges and class-determined economic inequalities, to the advantage of those sections of the population that are now regarded as economically underprivileged and dependent. Economic democracy is in this way closely connected with the concept of planned economy. This requires that the leading motive in the organization of production must not be the interest of one particular class, the private capitalists, in the highest possible profits, but on the contrary, the interest of the total population in the most effective production and satisfaction of needs. Whence again ensues the demand that the highest control over production should pass from the private industrial owners to the public and be exercised according to a plan for the common good, in order to reach the most rational utilization of the factors of production.

Finally, the word "democracy" is used in a yet more comprehensive sense, as an *attitude* or a *way of life*, which appears not only in the political and economic spheres, not only in public life, state and society, but also in international affairs, in family life, in social relations, in the upbringing and education of children, indeed, in every contact between man and man.

One can therefore, on the whole, distinguish between democracy in a political (legal) sense, in an economic sense, and in a human sense. These different meanings of the word are, however, not of equal and independent originality; they are mutually connected by a derivative relation. The nucleus in this entire field of ideas is political democracy. The legal forms of the political organization offer the most tangible and precise material for examination. Hence the concept has been enlarged to include also other related phenomena. I am therefore convinced that it will be worth while to start from here. Once it is established what ought to be understood by democracy in this original and narrower sense, a basis is created from which one can seek to advance toward an interpretation of the purpose and ideals that animate political democracy and give it its meaning, and a definition of democracy as a way of life. When the way is thus indicated, there is hope that the inquiry may progress in good order and avoid the arbitrariness and looseness into which an interpretation of the human essence of democracy will otherwise fall quite easily. It will then also be possible to decide whether there is a reasonable basis for an economic interpretation of the concept (See Chapter V, Sec. 9).

In thus turning the spotlight for the time being on the concept of political democracy, we must from the outset realize what the task is that we set ourselves. To define a concept means to specify the sense in which the particular word is to be used. Since a word naturally does not in itself possess from the Creator's hand a certain quite definite significance but has no other meaning than that which men attach to it, it is open to everyone to declare what he understands by the word in question, as long as there is coherence and clear meaning in what he declares. But if this declaration is not to be arbitrary and without interest to other people, if the purpose of the definition is to reach mutual understanding, especially in scientific work common to many peoples, the definition must satisfy two important demands.

First, the definition must to a certain extent be related to the present linguistic usage. To define a word in a way that has no connection with what generally, in a linguistic community, presents itself to people's minds when they use the word is an absurdity that cannot expect support. Second, the idea, which indeed is intended as an instrument of human thought, whereby it may penetrate into the coherence of things and grasp their regularity, must be formed in such a fashion that it comprehends within itself essentially related phenomena and distinguishes them from essentially alien phenomena. The conceptual distinctions are artificial ones we humans draw up in order to facilitate our survey of the phenomena and to render possible a penetrating understanding of their nature. These distinctions are not, however, taken from nature. Scientific progress rests to a great extent on skill in finding out precisely the conceptual differences that prove fertile for scientific research. Here often an interaction occurs. A more fruitful conceptual technique renders possible a deeper recognition, which in due course leads to a refinement of the conceptual apparatus.

These two considerations, of traditional usage and of the fruitfulness of distinctions, can sometimes lead in the opposite direction, and it depends then upon scientific tact and discretion how much weight is to be ascribed to each of them.

It is plain from what has been said that it is a mistake to believe that there is a single clear definition of an idea which is the only true one, or that a definition can be proved. A definition is not proved as true, but is *justified as expedient* on the assumption of the two considerations mentioned, which may also be called the demands for *adequacy* and for *relevance*, respectively. This is overlooked when the task of definition, say of the concepts "state," "justice," or "democracy" is thought of as a matter of finding out the "true essence" of these things. "State," "justice," or "democracy" have no "essence" in themselves that can be the object of true recognition. It is we ourselves who decide what meaning we shall put into these words. It is only a question of doing so in the scientifically most appropriate manner.

Often the solution of the task of defining is distorted because one is led by other than scientific considerations. It may happen, for instance, that, for political reasons, in order to exploit the emotional goodwill that among the population attaches to a certain word, one desires to extend its sphere of meaning, regardless of whether such an extension is scientifically appropriate. By this means it is possible to cover up essential differences and to mislead public opinion. Such a tactic is particularly obvious and dangerous in the field of social science. For example, the Nazi propagandists were masters in the art of giving old words, words of good repute, like "democracy," "liberty," "constitutional state," and "socialism" such an extension of meaning and such misinterpretation that they were able to present the Nazi regime as the true democracy, the true freedom, the true constitutional state, and the true socialism. But the very existence of that little word "true" as a qualification is the external sign that the whole thing is a lie, in the sense that there is a politically motivated distortion of ideas, putting them in conflict with the traditional meaning as well as with scientific relevance.

It is important in future to keep these criteria of method clearly in mind.

2. The Customary Idea of Political Democracy

Democracy is usually defined as the form of government in which the political power (sovereignty) rightly belongs to the population as a whole and not merely to a single person or a particular limited group of people.

This definition suffers from the short-coming that it is not clear. The characteristic which, according to this definition, should be decisive for democracy is not described in such a way that it is clear what facts are intended. If, therefore, the definition is applied to an existing constitution, it will often not be possible to decide whether it should be regarded as democratic or not. I shall now show more precisely how the concept in different directions is lost in vagueness.

(*a*) That which according to the definition rests with the people as a whole is defined as "the political power" ("sovereignty," or the like). It is not quite clear what is meant by this. Political power is not something tangible, which it is easy to grasp. What we can comprehend is the individual acts of authority that are ascribed to the state,—legislative acts, administrative ordinances (and decrees), judgments, and the like. When all of them in their variety are ascribed to one and the same power (the state), it is presumably because they constitute an organized whole, created through the rules that coördinate the different political acts into a series of superior and inferior instances. But in what sense can the government, as an expression of the organizational unity of all the individual official acts, be said to rest with the people as a whole or with certain particular persons? It is certainly not the people as such who, for instance, lay down the content of the laws, arrest a criminal, or condemn him to imprisonment. These acts of authority are carried out respectively by the Congress or the Parliament and the King jointly ("the King-in-Parliament"), by the police, and by the judges. What can be the meaning of maintaining nevertheless that in a democratic state the power that is exercised by those different institutions still rests with the people as a whole?

The crux of the matter is this: the exercise of authority by the police and the courts takes place in accordance with the law. They do not act on their own discretion or in their own interest, but carry out the law. The power they exercise is regarded therefore only as derived from and subordinated to the legislative power. The same applies to that power. The legislative body (Congress or Parliament) elected by the people is considered to be their representative, and for that reason political power is considered to rest, in the last analysis, with the people.

We conclude that government is regarded as resting with the people as a whole if the organ of government that lays down the content of the national will in its supreme and most general form (the legislative organ) is regarded as the people's representative.

But what is needed for the supreme organ of state to be regarded as the people's representative? There are difficulties in this question that threaten to render the concept of democracy quite blurred.

In all democratic countries at present, the idea of representation is based on the regularly recurring parliamentary elections. But one can visualize the election period gradually extended or even the mandate given once and for all; and in the same way the number of representatives might be reduced to one. An extreme instance is the form of government in which the people have transferred the supreme power once and for all to a single person and to his successors, as fixed by specific rules. This is still spoken of as democracy because the supreme power is still sanctioned by a popular mandate, which is consequently regarded as the basis of "sovereignty."

Thus all delimitations of the idea of democracy seem to vanish —even as the historical factual basis of claims for popular representation often becomes very precarious or is simply replaced by arbitrary postulates which neither allow of proof nor can be refuted. This ambiguity of ideas is not gratuitous speculation, but is confirmed by experience. In Denmark, for instance, the absolute monarchy was based upon the popular mandate given by the Assembly of the Estates in Copenhagen in 1660. Supreme political power rested with the people and the people authorized the absolute king to exercise it on their behalf—just as the people today authorize Parliament to exercise power for five-year periods. The difference is merely one of degree, and the conclusion seems to be inescapable that the absolute monarchy also belongs under the heading of democracy when the king's power is sanctioned by a popular mandate.

From this same point of view of representation and sanctioning, the modern Fascist-Nazi dictatorships have claimed to be democracies. On the basis of a more or less real or fictitious mandate it is asserted that the dictator represents the people. Why should not the people equally well decide to let themselves be represented by one man for life as by several individuals for a four-year period? Must one then not admit that dictatorship likewise is democracy? Moreover, the construction of legitimation may also tend toward the opposition direction, since government in a state with more or less democratic institutions is, on the whole, considered to rest with a single person. Thus, in the constitutional monarchy of the nineteenth century (See Chapter II, Sec. 6), power was typically ascribed entirely to the monarch, since the democratic institutions and the constitution that had been granted were regarded as voluntary limitations which the monarch had imposed upon himself by virtue of his absolute power. Princely sovereignty was therefore constantly the ultimate source of legitimation of government.

A notion that becomes thus blurred obviously needs further clarification.

The source of confusion lies in the following situation: The content of the national will is directly laid down by others than the people—the parliament, the absolute monarch, the dictator. We may still, by virtue of the ideas of representation and legitimation, arrive at the conclusion that actual government, "sovereignty" itself, lies with the people, but this is because, by a mystical, metaphorical mode of thinking, we imagine a "power" to create law which originally lies with the people, but which, in one or another period of time, through some act of transfer, is handed over to the authority that now directly governs. This abstract picture of transfer of power may, with the same right, be applied in all cases from parliamentary government to absolute monarchy and dictatorship, all of which thus come without exception under the heading of democracy.

The task must be, instead of thinking in terms of semi-mystical metaphors of power, to seek for the actual legal-functional relations which are hidden by the metaphors of representation and transfer of power. We shall then see that there are great differences among the various types, so that they cannot be classed together under the same concept.

The idea of representation is a tangible thing to the extent that the representatives' freedom of action is legally bound by the wishes of the represented (i. e., the electorate) and the represented possess legal means of enforcing respect for these wishes. This is the situation in a private relationship such as that of a proxy, which has provided the model for the train of thought. He who gives power of proxy instructs his representative (proxy) how he is to behave, and he has various legal means to assure that the proxy abides by those instructions. The parallel in political life would be that the people, at the time of electing their representatives, should lay down certain directives which the representatives would have to follow in the exercise of their task (as was the case with the medieval Coronation Charters), and, moreover, that there should exist means of control whereby the people could at any time assure themselves that these instructions were not being disregarded. From this extreme case as starting point, one can imagine a sliding scale with the idea of representation constantly decreasing in actual substance. It may be, for instance, that the mandate is unrestricted, but that control may still be exercised at any time either in the form of legal responsibility of the representatives or by discretionary means open to the people of removing such representatives as do not act in accordance with the people's wishes. It may be that the control cannot be exercised at any time, but only at regular intervals. The rarer or the more uncertain that opportunity becomes, the further away we get from the starting point. The form that is prescribed for the exercise of control is also of significance. According to medieval political theory (see Chapter II, Sec. 2), the people had a constitutional right to rebel against the king who infringed his mandate and became a tyrant. But it is clear that the decision whether such a condition exists is so vague, and the mode of procedure itself so uncertain and hazardous, that the "control" here considered as legal remedy is not of great value. It provides no certainty that the majority opinion will assert itself. For the ultimate in meaninglessness, we come to the absolutist monarchy and dictatorial forms of government, where the popular mandate without any limitations is given once and for all (or perhaps is purely and simply a fiction), and where the people do not possess any means whatever of exercising control in any form.

The actual facts behind the idea of representation are thus highly varied, extending along a sliding scale from one pole to the other. The difference lies in the effectiveness with which the people are able to make their influence felt in political life.

This effectiveness is greatest, moreover, when there is hardly any question of representation, that is, when every act of state, every exercise of public authority, is decided directly by the people as a whole, so that not only every act of legislation, but also every administrative act and every judicial decision, requires the holding of a direct popular consultation (plebiscite).

It is evident that nothing like this has ever existed in actual political life. Even in primitive conditions it would not be possible. The nearest approximation to it was certainly the state of affairs in primitive Germanic society, where legislative as well as judicial power was directly exercised by the whole people at the *thing* assemblies (see Chapter II, Sec. 2). But here, too, certain administrative functions were left to certain individuals. In more developed conditions the people's influence is exercised exclusively, or at any rate mainly, through representatives, and the effectiveness of popular power lies then in the control that the people are in a position to wield over these representatives.

(*b*) Otherwise, too, there is a certain vagueness and relativity in the definition's statement that "government" in a democracy rests with the people. Here one can think of a sliding scale, since in certain areas of political life the people are displaced by other political forces, or at any rate must share power with them. The ideal is that legislative power and executive power, as well as the judicial authority, are under the people's command. Qualifications may occur in particular, either when the legislative body is composed in such fashion that nonpopular elements also enter into it, or when a nonpopular government exercises independent and competitive power collaterally with a popularly elected legislative body, or, finally, when a combination of the two occurs.

The first obtains when the popularly elected representatives have to share the legislative power with the king. Under the parliamentary form of government, however, there is no political reality in this state of affairs. The same thing also holds true when the legislative body is composed of two chambers, one of which has an aristocratic character in so far as its membership is based on aristocratic birth or on a privileged franchise.

The second is the case when the king has the power to issue on his own certain edicts (prerogative ordinances) or to carry out certain acts of government without the sanction of parliament.

Both of these occur typically enough in the constitutional monarchy without parliamentary government (see Chapter II, Sec. 6).

A privileged upper house and an independent executive are the two factors that in recent historical development have stood in the way of democracy. The struggle for parliamentary government is tantamount to the struggle for the democratization of the executive by making the cabinet politically subordinate to parliament. The struggle against the upper house meant struggle for the complete democratization of the legislative body. Only when both ends have been reached is democracy complete in the sense that popular influence is absolute over the creation of the supreme national will.

With regard to the subordinated administration and judicial power, the question has not the same importance. These are, according to their nature, closely subordinated to the legislative power and are not normally, or at any rate are only to a small degree, political factors of importance in the life of the state. Therefore the indirect power over the administration and the judiciary which lies in the popular control of legislation will often be felt to be adequate. A purer democratic form of government exists when the people have direct power over these organs through appointment and control. This is particularly important if popular power over legislation and government is limited. A more moderate tendency in the same direction exists as a result of the introduction of juries and lay judges as participants in the administration of justice.

(*c*) What in the last analysis is implied in the idea that the people as a whole, according to the definition, shall be in possession of political power? Here, too, we find all possible transitions. The logical extreme that every human individual, without exception, as a member of the people shall be given voice and vote on an equal footing with all others is in practice impossible. A line must of necessity be drawn with respect to a certain intellectual maturity (the voting age). It is possible, moreover, gradually to get away from pure democracy, partly through increasing exclusion of certain population groups from the electorate, partly through increasing inequality in the importance that attaches to the vote. However, one cannot as a matter of course assert that the degree of undemocratic character of the system stands in direct ratio to the numbers excluded. On the other hand, the political relevance of the exclusions is conclusive. Thus it will be, for instance, more undemocratic to disfranchise persons with an income below a certain limit than to exclude women, even though the latter constitute the larger group. The disfranchisement of women is certainly arbitrary and unreasonable. It obviously rests upon the wrong conception that women are not full-fledged human beings and lack the ability and the interest to devote themselves to politics. But the distinction between man and woman is not politically relevant in nearly the same degree as a distinction according to the size of income.

In this way, instances can be ranked from pure democracy (in this regard) to more and more aristocratic forms.

3. Democracy Defined in Relation to an Ideal

The preceding considerations have shown that the concept "democracy" does not allow of definition as a class concept, that is, in such a way that certain characteristics are indicated which set a certain class of phenomena apart from other similar ones, so that one may say: a form of government possessing these characteristics is democratic, others are undemocratic. In this manner we can define, for instance, the concept "mammals" as all those animals among which the mothers suckle their young. But the same kind of definition cannot be given of democracy as a form of government, because the transition here is gradual. We have seen how one passes, in different respects, from something that is pure democracy over into other forms.

Under such circumstances, it is wise to apply another logical technique. One sets up a concept that denotes the most extreme, pure democracy one can imagine, and indicates the line along which the forms can move further and further away from the paragon in order to arrive at last at its diametrical opposite, in a certain respect. This pure fundamental concept, or paragon, is called an *ideal type*. This term must not be misunderstood. The ideal type is not something good that one ought to endeavor to realize. The idea is merely that this type is something imaginary, a thought construction in which the various characteristics that actually occur to some degree are combined in their highest conceivable form. The ideal type thus depicts hardly anything real. Its value for comprehension is that it, together with concepts derived from it, offers the possibility of characterizing the real constitutional types "topographically" according to their position along the lines that branch out from the ideal type of democracy. It will now often happen that even if all gradual transitions can be imagined, the actual transitions nevertheless cluster around certain definite points in the topographical outline. These "clusters of reality" are called *real types*. We may then also say that the ideal type with its various "dimensions" (the respects in which the characteristics may vary) constitutes a basis, a center, a measuring rod for the description of real types. The relation can be made clear from the diagram, in which I stands for an ideal type with four dimensions, and R_1 and R_2 two different real types put into the outline, determined in each direction by their closeness to or remoteness from the ideal type. There is naturally nothing to prevent that a certain real type, say R_1, lies closer to the ideal type in one direction than the other, R_2, while in another direction it is farther away.

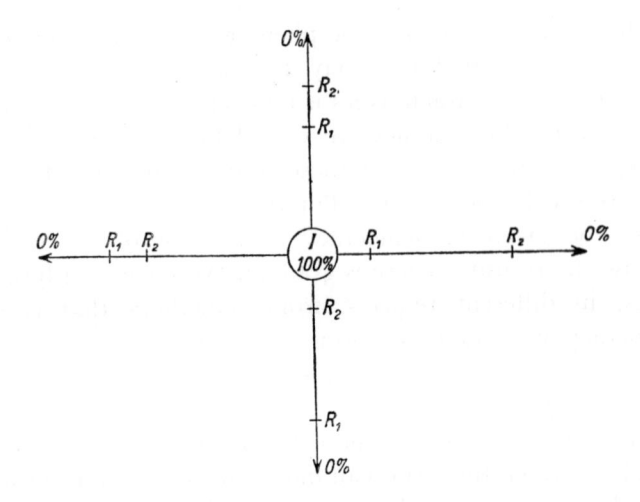

Thus, one cannot simply say that a form of government is democratic when political power rests with the people, for it is not a simple either-or relation. It would be better to say that a state is democratic to the extent to which political power rests with the people. But even this is still too vague. The point to be clear about is in what different ways there can be more or less democracy. When this is clear we may reach the construction of the ideal type.

What has been explained in the preceding can be systematized as follows: The democratic factor, the people's influence over the exercise of public authority, can vary with regard to:

(1) *Intensity*, that is, the size of the group of people who are given the right to participate in voting and election. The clearest instance is equal and universal franchise for all adults. The more the real type deviates from this, the more it becomes a *moderate democracy* with increasingly oligarchic form. Britain

under the greatly restricted franchise in the eighteenth and nineteenth centuries may be given as an instance.

(2) *Effectiveness*, that is, the degree to which the people are able to assert their points of view. This is greatest in direct democracy, in which the people themselves, through the referendum, decide on all affairs. In so far as the people act through representatives, the effectiveness depends on the strength of the control the people are able to exercise over their representatives, the organs of state, which again is particularly dependent on the frequency of the elections (the period of the mandate). The more that control is weakened, the more the form of government changes into a merely *nominal democracy*, where the power is certainly exercised in the name of the people but lies in reality to an increasing degree with the representatives and not with the represented. This is, for instance, the case in the Soviet Union. The undemocratic element here is not represented by the decreasing of the electorate, as in the preceding case, but in that latter's loss of control over the representatives. The Soviet Union is undemocratic in a different way from nineteenth-century Britain.

(3) *Extensiveness*, that is, the extent to which popular influence and control are extended to include more or less of the various ramifications of government. The extensiveness is greatest when popular power controls not only legislation but also the executive and the judiciary. If this is not the case, democracy is more or less partial. A typical example is the constitutional monarchy where legislative power is partly under aristocratic and partly under monarchical, and the executive under monarchical, influence.

In short: Democracy means popular government; but that which is thus designated may, in the first place, be more or less *popular* (intensity), and in the second place, more or less actual *government* (effectiveness and extensiveness).

When we have said above that the people make decisions, exercise power, and so on, we meant that the idea of the majority wins out. This can only be ascertained by voting in the parliamentary manner. If violence is resorted to, the will of the strongest is decisive. But the strongest need not be the most numerous.

Accordingly, the *topographic diagram of political democracy* can be thus defined: *The ideal type is the form of government in which the political functions are exercised by the people with maximum intensity, effectiveness, and extensiveness in the parliamentary manner.* In these three respects the type tends, respectively, toward *moderate, nominal,* and *partial* democracy.

We refer for other applications of the term "democracy" to Sec. 9 of the following chapter.

V.

THE IDEAS OF DEMOCRACY

1. Introduction

As we have seen, democracy is essentially a form of government, that is, a form of political organization, a political method. The word "democracy" indicates a procedure that is followed in the development and exercise of political power and that regulates the social life within the framework of the state. On the other hand, the concept does not *directly*[1] tell us anything about the actual substance of the policy carried out according to that method. Democracy indicates a *how*, not a *what*.

It may well seem surprising, at first glance, that the struggle between the defenders and the opponents of democracy has been capable of rousing as strong passions as it actually has. One might, perhaps, have thought that most people would be more interested in the substance than in the form, more in the actual living conditions than in the procedure by which those conditions were to be laid down. Nevertheless, two revolutions of world importance and two world wars have been fought in the name of democracy.

The explanation is, of course, to be found partly in the realization that the means are of essential importance for the end in view. When two children set out to share an apple, the result depends on the procedure adopted for the actual sharing. The same holds true in political life. Nor is this the whole story. The problem of whether there is to be democracy or not reaches beyond the sphere of political decision. Even if democracy is but a means, a method, it still can be valued

---

[1] But it does so, indeed, indirectly; see Secs. 5–7.

for its own sake, or, more correctly perhaps, for its effects beyond political decisions. The form of government under which we live will, directly or indirectly, set its mark upon our personality and upon our way of life in all its ramifications. The political method of shaping social life is not a specialty which can be isolated from our life, for that matter. It reflects and is itself reflected by fundamental human characteristics and reacts in turn on character formation. It is deeply connected with our feeling of human values, with our attitude to life and our moral faith. It is a common denominator into which enter many human ideas.

When we wish to sum things up, we must of course, first of all, be clear ourselves what democracy and autocracy *are*, that is, we have to decide wherein lies the fundamental difference between these two political systems. That is exactly what I have attempted to do in the preceding chapter in setting up a definition of the concept, democracy. But that is far from sufficient. In order to adopt a point of view, it is necessary to know also the *meaning* of democracy and autocracy with regard to the effects these political systems have, and how these effects influence our standard of values. Why do some people value democracy? What qualities inherent in that system have those people in mind? What values do they find realized in that form of government?

In this chapter, I shall deal with the ideas of democracy, by which is understood merely a short formal expression of the values connected with that system of government. It is difficult, but also very important, to state the task thus set, how it may be dealt with scientifically, and how the results achieved are to be interpreted.

First of all, I wish to make it clear that I intend to refrain from every attempt at making my readers believe that it is possible to ascertain scientifically what is the absolute good and therefore entitled to our love and fidelity. If a person dislikes democracy, liberty, or peace, I am unable to prove logically to him that he is making a mistake and that I am right.

In the last analysis everyone has to make up his own mind, and many are prepared to risk their lives in support of their belief, whether or not it may be proved to be true. The truth has a claim to respect. Its essence is to be valid for all. Therein lies its authority, which scientists are supposed to administer. For that very reason it is so serious a matter, a misrepresentation of facts and a leading of people astray when, in the name of truth and with the authority of science, someone tries to make it appear that he is capable of proving what is good in itself and therefore has a claim on our love and must be the goal of our actions. Unfortunately, a number of scientists still assert that they are able to do this. I do not actually doubt that they are acting in good faith, even if they are bad scientists. But the pleasant feeling of being able to appear as judge and authoritative guide in burning questions of practical politics may still play a part in the subconscious.

The only thing one can say in the name of science to an opponent who, for instance, disputes the value of democracy is to ask him if he has also realized quite accurately what democracy *is* and *means*; thus we may find out whether we are actually talking about the same state of affairs and whether he fully realizes what effects are due to it in different ways. The points of view themselves cannot be discussed, but the understanding of the facts that constitute the prerequisite for the points of view can be.

Therefore a scientific elucidation of the question of the value of democracy can consist only in clarification of what democracy actually involves of significant consequences for the lives of people. I may try to track down and unravel these consequences as well as I can, contrast them with autocracy and its consequences, emphasize the values that I for my part see in them, and, for the rest, leave it to everyone ultimately to settle with his own conscience and take his own choice. Science cannot make the final choice. But it can make the choice easier by bringing to the consciousness as clearly as possible what it is one may choose from. I wonder whether there are not many who declare themselves for or against democracy but who really have no clear idea of what it is they are making up their minds about?

It may be objected that anyone who, in this fashion, denies that values can be determined scientifically thereby cuts himself off from making a choice between good and evil and must end up in an indifferent passivity, but this objection is foolish. Because a point of view is a point of view and not a scientific truth, it naturally does not follow from this that one cannot have some point of view. I know very well what I shall stand for and fight for. Only I do not imagine myself, or try to make others believe, that it can be scientifically proved that my point of view is the "right" one.

But even if this is an established fact, there are difficulties. When I set out to clarify the important consequences of democracy, which ones are then "important" and which are not? Indeed, that selection itself will be conditioned by subjective valuations which perhaps are not shared by others so that the account will be without interest to them. The mode of procedure must therefore be to start from the available historical valuations that have actually been held by large groups of people. Of course, this does not preclude the possibility that a certain person may for his part adopt other qualities and construct other standards of values. But the chances of encountering something that commends itself to many are increased. It is not possible to do better.

In the next place there arises the question what exactly it is that forms the object of the examination and valuation. Indeed, democracy indicates, as we have seen (Chapter IV), not a quite definite form of government having definite characteristics but something fluid determined in relation to an unreal ideal type. The answer must be that we attach ourselves to the principle that is the measure of the degree to which a form of government is democratic; this is the principle that political decisions are determined by the will of the majority as expressed through the vote, or in short, *the majority principle.*

The opposite to this is not simply the minority principle; there is no form of government that rests on the absurd idea that the opinion of the minority, as determined by a vote, should prevail. The opposite is the *qualified minority principle*, that is, the principle according to which political power is vested in a precisely determined minority pointed out by certain characteristics, for example, the rich, the intelligent, the noble, the strong. When now the choice between democracy and nondemocracy is to be considered, it is clear that the issue is to stress those values which are *specific* of democracy, that is, those which—necessarily or, at least, typically—are connected with democracy but not with its opposite. It is not an uncommon mistake to refer in support of democracy to values that are either not necessarily connected with that form of government or, at any rate, can also be found in connection with autocracy.

It is common in the enquiry so far under consideration to set up a single principle as the idea of democracy. Some have wished to find it in "the idea of freedom," others in the "idea of equality," others again in various other ideas. Any such procedure involves a fallacious simplification of the problem. What we see in democracy cannot thus be reduced to a single formula. The factual situation is that we value democracy for different reasons corresponding to its typical effects in different situations.

What is now finally the consequence of this discussion if I succeed in explaining a number of specific democratic values that also find response in the reader's mind? Does it mean that we are agreed that a form of government with complete democracy is desirable and the goal of our strivings? By no means. The great and good things that we see in democracy are pointed out, and this is in itself a significant step in the direction of the final decision. But it is not the whole matter. From other points of view there may possibly be disadvantages attached to the principle of democracy that render certain modifications desirable. Indeed, it might even be thought that the negative aspects are predominant, so that, in spite of all positive values, an autocratic form of government would be preferable. This aspect of the matter will be dealt with in a later chapter.

2. Democracy and the Resort to Force

It is natural to assume that the most important democratic value consists in the adoption of peaceful discussion, rather than force, as a means of solving political conflicts. So Hal Koch, for instance, defines the "essence" of democracy with the slogan, "Word or sword?" There are on the whole, says Koch, only two ways to the solution of disagreements: (i) one can fight for one's right, which means that it is the will of the stronger that prevails; (ii) one can talk oneself to one's right, which means that through a discussion the disputing parties seek to get the matter elucidated from all sides, and that they really strive to reach through discussion a right and more reasonable understanding of the problem. It is the discussion and the mutual understanding and respect that are the essence of democracy. If these fail, the disputants will inevitably slide back into the struggle for power.[1]

Nevertheless, this contrast is not so absolute as it might seem to be. It is certainly true that the democratic method rules out the use of force. This means, in a state where the democratic ideology controls all its members, that violence is not used as a means to the establishment of the substance of the state will. But this is not in reality anything specific to democracy. The same holds true also of a state whose members are all ruled by an authoritarian ideology, for instance, the belief that all decisions rest with a certain person by virtue of his divine sanction, exceptional qualities of leadership, or the like. In such a state, a man will neither fight nor argue to get his right but he will, so to speak, obey to get his way. All conflicts will

---

[1] Hal Koch is a Danish author. His book to which I refer is available only in Danish.

be submitted to the authoritarian ruler and the disputants will bow to his decision. Consider, for instance, the Danish absolute monarchy. It was not democracy, but one cannot very well assert that the decisions in that state were reached through battle.

The true situation would be rather that the struggle for power is characteristic of neither the democratic nor the autocratic state, but occurs in the state where the official ideology, whatever it may be, actually does not govern all the members of the community. If, for instance, the idea of democratic mutual agreement breaks down among a certain group of citizens, there arises the possibility that they will seek to further their ideas in opposition to the system, through rebellion or through force. The democratic state may then also resort to force, if it does not wish to sacrifice its own existence.

Although there is important truth in setting up democracy and force as opposites, this is because the democratic ideology —particularly in our own day, when religious ideas have lost their power over men's minds—presumably is the only one that has a chance of winning universal recognition. It is difficult to get the great majority really to believe that the few or the one has a right to rule the many. There will certainly always be important circles that do not share that belief, circles that are so important that the ruling minority regards those dissenters as a potential enemy who must be fought with force. The ruling minority dare not rely only on ideological power. It dare not allow ideologies in conflict with the system to arise and to make themselves heard but must combat them at the outset by means of repression (censorship) and, if necessary, force.

The question presents itself differently for democracy. Just as two children can more easily agree to divide an apple equally than to recognize a title of one to a greater share, so the people in fact can also more easily agree that the majority shall rule rather than recognize a title for a particular minority. Democracy dares therefore to rely only upon voluntary, that is, ideological, support. It dares to allow conflicting ideologies to arise and find expression. Democracy is not afraid of free discussion and need not resort to repression and force, because it has confidence that the majority will remain supporters of the majority principle. Should this trust be at last betrayed, should it really turn out that the majority of the population desires an authoritarian regime, then indeed democracy has nothing to gain through violence. As I shall later show in more detail (Chapter VIII, Sec. 6), the idea of imposing democracy by force against the wish of the majority is an absurdity. A people cannot be forced to be free and independent; they can only be educated to it. The weapon of democracy against the ideology of dictatorship must therefore be education and enlightenment, not force.

But this does not mean, as has already been said, that democracy may not be compelled to resort to force. If the democratic state is to subsist, it must with every means at its disposal defend itself against forcible attacks, and in doing so it in no way infringes on its own principles.

When it appears superficially that democracy and the use of force are opposites, this is because one subconsciously thinks of antidemocratic movements in a democratic society, that is, just such an ideological conflict as leads to struggle for power. But a quite corresponding situation is found again when, conversely, democratic movements fight their way in an autocratic society. In such a case, it is the democratic movement that resorts to force (or the threat of force). As is well known, democracy has been introduced in some states by means of revolution.

The difference between autocracy and democracy, as regards their relation to force, is clear enough in principle: autocracy relies on force against those having other views; democracy uses force only in defense against attack by force. It may also be expressed by saying that *the democratic state is one in which political power—to a high degree, if not absolutely—is based upon ideological support*, that is, on the idea of law and not on fear.

A democracy is a state based on law to a higher degree than is autocracy. *He who prefers peace and law to struggle and force has therefore to that extent a reason to prefer democracy to autocracy.*

In practice, however, there may arise difficult problems when it is a question of deciding when the democratic state may resort to force. It is true enough that democracy offers everyone freedom of expression as a means to peaceful mutual understanding. But if speech is used not for this purpose but as preparation for the use of force against the state, the promise no longer holds. The democratic freedom of expression cannot be made to include the call to rebellion and revolution. There may arise through the application of this principle a question of doubt, which I shall refer to later (Chapter VIII, Sec. 6).

3. The Concept of Liberty

Liberty! There is hardly another word so extravagantly used, praised, and sung about, yet at the same time so bare of clear and definite meaning, as the word "liberty." The two things, however, belong together: just because the meaning is so fluid, it allows of so wide an application. Liberty is one of those suggestion-loaded, resounding words that is used more in order to awaken feelings in the breast than thoughts in the head.

I shall start my analysis of the idea of liberty by saying that it seems to be a *negative* concept: it indicates the absence of something that is regarded one way or another by the acting individual as a fetter, a limit, a restraint. He who acts freely feels, as it were, that the action, unrestrained and harmonious, appears out of himself. He can fully accept it as his. He who acts under compulsion thinks, on the contrary, that the action is forced on him, as it were, by factors outside of himself. The task must be to find out what are the circumstances that condition the feelings of freedom and of compulsion.

We may at once dismiss the thought that the decisive fact is whether or not the will is subject to the law of causal relation, in the way that an act is free when the will is undetermined.

Also, the free act is born of circumstances and motives. It is only that we feel in those cases as if the causes lie wholly within "ourselves," in our "own will," as something that develops according to its own sovereign law and is not woven into nature's great coherence. Indeterminism is a primitive attempt at directly interpreting the feeling of liberty in metaphysical ideas. The issue is, as has been said, to decide which circumstances actually determine the experience of "liberty" and of "compulsion."

Let us consider a typical compulsion situation. A Gestapo man demands, with the threat of torture, that I shall disclose a secret of military importance. If I now, out of fear of the threats, hand over my knowledge, people will say that I have been forced to it. But if, on the other hand, I hold out, I can also be said to have been forced, namely, to submit to torture in order not to disclose the secret. It is the very *situation* that is one of compulsion. I stand before a choice, and however I choose I act under compulsion.

The decisive element in this situation seems now to be the conflict between incompatible wishes. I wish at once both to preserve my secret and to avoid torture. These wish-aims are in the given situation incompatible and I know it. I know that, however I act, I must, in order to fulfill one wish, act against the other, thus acting against my own wish and to that extent against "myself."

So far as I can see, every other compulsion situation is similar. The essential is always a conflict between incompatible desires. There is nothing remarkable in that. Whatever the outer circumstances are that press on my action, it must always happen that they appeal to a motive within me. The opposition between "the compelling" and "myself" must psychologically of necessity consist in an opposition between different motives within me.

The incompatability of my wishes may depend on different circumstances, so that different types of compulsion correspond to it.

In the first place, the incompatability may be a simple effect of nature's arrangement. I cannot both eat my cake and have it. Nor can I at the same time be at home for lunch and go to a concert. If I want to do both at once, I must choose, and one of my wishes forces me to act contrary to the other. My fear of the unpleasantness of hunger compels me to give up the concert.

In the next place, incompatability may be due to other people's reactions to my actions, that is, to *social* conditions, as in the above-analyzed instance. The same applies in all cases of individual or collective "commands," "orders," or "demands" which meet the individual from the social surroundings, particularly in the form of conventional norms and legal rules. Incompatibility means here that I cannot perform a certain action, for instance, steal, and at the same time avoid my fellows' disapproval or yet more unpleasant reactions. It is clear that these are mainly cases which interest the social sciences.

Lastly, the incompatibility may be due to something within myself. The odd, peculiar impulse to do what I call my "duty" is often incompatible with my "inclinations." In such a case I am compelled either by the duty to act against my inclinations, or I am also compelled, as the slave of my vices, to act against "my better self."

We can now differentiate between *nature's* compulsion, *external-social* compulsion, and *inner-moral* compulsion. At all events, the feeling of compulsion or obligation arises because the situation is such that my action necessarily, whatever I choose, is an action that goes against something within myself, against my own wish. I cannot fully acknowledge it as "mine" because partly it goes against what I wish. Therefore, I am involved in the circumstances that give rise to the conflict and regard these as the actual "compelling cause" of my action. The feeling of liberty arises, conversely, in a situation where all motives tend harmoniously and unimpeded in the same direction. If, for instance, I can give to my fighting fellow countrymen important information, the desire to further the common cause unites with the desire to make myself deserving and to win recognition. I do not act in any way against myself, against my own wish; I can therefore fully acknowledge my action as "mine," as deriving wholly and fully out of my own "free will."

The conception of liberty that I have here explained I shall call the *material* concept of liberty. It means general absence of compulsion (incompatibility of wishes) and, in the social sphere especially, absence of such "demands" on the part of society as may collide with the individual's wishes. Since it is now obvious that absolute social freedom never exists—since all social life involves a certain binding and integration of the lives of individuals—the material freedom dissolves itself into a series of individual liberties, that is, special, precisely delimited spheres in which no claim is made by society that can collide with the individual's wishes. Among such liberties we shall discuss in particular freedom of expression and organization (Sec. 5) and the personal freedoms (Secs. 6 and 7).

But the word liberty is also applied in another sense, corresponding to another and narrower meaning of the word compulsion. The qualified form of compulsion comprises only those instances in which I am forced to act "against myself" in a quite particular sense, against "my better self," my "true" or "real" self (I), and not merely against my inclinations of the moment. With this, one thinks of the opposition between the central and permanent element of the personality, which is the expression of valuations and attitudes that hold true "in the long run," and the inclinations and impulses that, perhaps during an outburst of passion, take control for the moment but are not permanently approved by the person. Thus one says, for instance, that the person who follows the command of his conscience maintains his freedom, regardless of his having to curb certain desires. He feels all the same that the action "at the bottom of his heart" is his. The compulsion is only superficial; seen more deeply, it is carried out by his "true" or central self over his peripheral self. He who obeys his own conscience obeys only his "better self." He is his own master and therefore free. Only he who is compelled to act by his inclinations against "the best within himself" is a slave.

The concept of liberty corresponding to this I shall call the *formal* concept of liberty, which thus means absence of compulsion as above qualified. In the social sphere, liberty in this sense means that the person is not subject to other demands or obligations than such as he himself "at the bottom of his heart" can approve—regardless of whether at the moment he is perhaps urged by his inclinations to infringe them. This liberty is also called *autonomy* or self-law: the law that binds the individual is his own.

4. Democracy and Political Liberty: Autonomy (Self-Government)

With special reference to the legal nexus, the concept of autonomy is modified so that a person is said to be free, or autonomous, when he is bound only by those legal rules to which he himself has agreed. Autonomy means freedom from external rule, freedom from bonds that are imposed by others which have no root in the bound person's own mind and conviction. He can quite certainly not unilaterally abolish the system, once he has entered it. To that extent he is bound by external will. But he still feels himself free in the awareness that he himself has participated in making the resolutions which regulate his life, and that he is therefore the master of his own fate.

For the person who has achieved mental maturity and freed himself from the fear of existence and from the dependence on father, mother, and other protecting authorities that characterizes the child, this autonomy, this self-control, is a fundamental moral value, the basis of his perception of himself as a human personality. There may be authorities that are wiser than he himself and that, in a certain sense, could perhaps guide his steps with greater security and guarantee him greater happiness. However, the happiness he could achieve in this way would never have for him the same value as that which he achieves for himself. It would have been bought at the expense of that which would give him confidence in life and courage to face all difficulties, the consciousness of being a man in the fullest sense, who bears the promise of his life in himself.

Such a man is also possessed by the wish to see the same inner strength develop in others. As he himself abhors alien rule, neither does he wish to rule over others. He is pleased to see life unfolding itself free and strong in his fellow humans. He finds himself happiest in a circle of equals, not surrounded by slaves. In education, his aim is not to exact submissive obedience, but to foster young individuals who in due course will themselves be able to form their own lives with freedom and responsibility.

There are undeniably many people who never reach an understanding of this point of view. They remain all their lives like children, themselves bound by authority and domineering towards others. They fear liberty and feel at home only in a world where the decision and responsibility may be thrown on others. I cannot prove that they are wrong, but can only be sorry for them. Those who are themselves free men, or are on the way to being free, will understand me; others will not. I believe, however—although I cannot scientifically answer for this assertion either—that every normal person treated in the right way has the possibility of growing up to that human ideal, and I see a goal to work for, that this may be realized in as high a degree as possible.

Now, what has autonomy to do with democracy?

The connection lies in this, that democracy is the form of government which gives the maximum of political freedom in the sense of autonomy for the citizens. This maximum is obtained precisely by the majority principle. If a qualified majority or even unanimity were required, there would very likely also be fewer persons bound by the introduction of a measure they could not approve. On the other hand, the amendment or repeal of the measure introduced would be dependent on a corresponding support. Thereby the will of the minority would become predominant over that of the majority. This consequence is avoided only by the majority principle.[1]

This indeed does not exclude the possibility that a certain group of people may be subject to a rule of which they cannot approve. But those who in this fashion are subject to alien will, according to principle, always constitute a minority. Add to this that the minority in a democracy, as will be fully discussed later, is not altogether without influence on the final decision. The more democracy is exercised in mutual understanding, in the spirit of amicable settlement and compromise, the more the parties will feel themselves sections of a community, the more the individuals will identify themselves with the whole, the less will even the outvoted minority feel the control to be alien. They will feel that they have been heard and have had a certain share in the result, which they can approve at any rate in the sense that it harmonizes with the fundamental democratic principle, which also has the minority's support.

Everyone who has had the opportunity of working in a college with people tied together by their interests will be able to understand the reality that lies herein. The outvoted also normally identifies himself with the decision of his colleagues. He subordinates his particular point of view in the interest of serving the common cause and therefore also accepts the majority's opinion as the basis of continued coöperation. This is what Rousseau expresses in an exaggerated, paradoxical way when he says that the fellow citizen agrees to all laws, even those that are instituted against his will. When a proposal is submitted to a vote, the question that is asked is not whether the individual person approves or rejects it, but whether it is in agreement with the general will or not. By giving his vote, everyone expresses his opinion about it, and, if he is outvoted,

[1] Following Hans Kelsen, *Allgemeine Staatslehre* (Berlin, 1925), p. 322–323.

nothing more is shown than that he was mistaken in his idea of the substance of the general will.[1] The fundamental thought in this peculiar formulation is precisely that the individual in an intimate community of interests feels himself more attached to the general idea than to his own particular point of view.

Now, it will be willingly admitted that the situation is different in the state, particularly since the larger and more complex the state, the greater the opposition of interests that clash. These conditions bring it about that the individual, even as a member of the majority, cannot feel himself a party to the political decisions in the same way as in the narrower circle of interests. Nevertheless, in political life also, a tendency asserts itself in the direction described.

Democracy is the form of government for mature and grown-up peoples who demand that their fate be in their own hands. Autocracy, on the other hand, means, so far as the majority is concerned, submission to alien will. Autocracy at best, namely, if the few really exercise power for the benefit of the many, is political tutelage. At its worst, namely, when the power is mainly used to serve the interests and lust for power of the ruling minority, it is exploitation and oppression. At all events, it destroys the individual's chance to develop himself to a full, autonomous personality.

Naturally, it must be admitted that democracy makes great demands on the human material it is working with. Self-government, moral and political, not only demands a certain ripening of character, but also a certain development of the intellectual faculties, which again are dependent on a certain economic standard. The ignorant has not the faculty, the starving not the time or the strength, to engage in politics. A people that has not a certain living standard, a suitable general education, and moral training, is not ripe for democracy. It must for the time being live under political tutelage. The historical exposition has shown what a great role a people's political tradition plays. Democracy cannot be "introduced"

[1] J. J. Rousseau, *Contrat social* (Amsterdam, 1762), vol. IV, ch. 2.

ready-made overnight. On the other hand, experience has shown that the best education for democracy lies in the gradual attainment of democracy.

This is due to the fact that democracy not only assumes a certain development of personality, but itself contributes to bringing about this development. Thus Mill pointed out the importance of democratic life for the education of the people and the development of the character, in that it widens the individual's range of interests and teaches public spirit, fellow feeling, and responsibility (See Chapter III, Sec. 3). Conversely, autocracy leads in the direction of political indifference and the personal irresponsibility of which the German dictatorship has given so lamentable an example. All responsibility was handed over to Hitler; all the others felt merely like puppets in his hands.

Usually when one talks about political liberty, one thinks in the first place precisely of freedom as autonomy. As we have seen, this can only be ascribed in a limited measure to the individual. On the other hand, we can without reservation attribute to the people as a whole political freedom, to the extent that they govern themselves, that is, live under the democratic majority principle. A free people means precisely a people that is subject only to its own "will," not to alien rule, by which is here meant subjection to either an autocratic ruler or to the will of a foreign state. It is in this sense that one says, for instance, that Denmark received in 1849 a free constitution, or that after the German occupation Denmark regained its freedom.

It will be seen that there is a close connection between political freedom as self-rule and law and order in contrast to force. It was pointed out in Section 2 that the democratic state is the state in which political power is to a high degree (though not absolutely) based on ideological support, that is, on the idea of law and order, not on fear. But it means the same as saying that democracy is the form of government in which voluntary support rooted in the individual's autonomy is greatest. Liberty and the rule of law belong together as two aspects of the same thing. Recognition of this relation is the essence of truth which can be found in contract theories of natural law, when the fundamental idea of these theories tends to show that a political power is felt to be legitimate or lawful power only to the extent that it has its root in the individual's voluntary support, his autonomy (See Chapter III, Sec. 1).

Democracy is thus the form of government that offers the urge for freedom, in the sense of self-rule, the best conditions; and he who loves the free unfolding of the personality under self-responsibility, and abhors the ties of authoritarianism and imperiousness, has to that extent cause to prefer democracy to autocracy and to aim at bringing about the conditions that are the prerequisites of the democratic state.

5. Democracy and Political Liberty: Freedom of Expression and of Organization

Democracy, as we have seen, is a political method expressed through the majority principle. It is therefore necessarily connected with freedom in the formal sense of the term, that is, autonomy. On the other hand, there is not directly included in the concept of democracy any indication of its content, that is, of the ordering of the conditions of social life. Democracy is, as the Swedish author Tingsten expresses it, a supra-ideology. One is a democrat, but then also a Conservative, a Liberal, or a Socialist besides.

When we turn to examine the concept of *material* freedom, or, more correctly, the various liberties, the starting point will therefore have to be the fact that according to its very concept democracy does not necessarily mean greater freedom of action for the individual than that conceded by any other form of government. The political trend that aims at the greatest possible legal freedom for the individual and thus by the same token at minimum state intervention and regulation is usually called *liberalism*. The essence of liberal government is freedom of contract and the right of private property. The task of government is limited to guaranteeing the unhampered development of the freedom of private contract and to protect property rights and other basic rights against encroachments. Nineteenth-century democracy evolved along with the liberal ideas. At its beginning, democracy was naturally allied with them in protest against the benefits that the upper classes gained from the privileges of the absolute monarchy. The young democracy was a middle-class movement and what was demanded in the first place was freedom for middle-class initiative, freedom for the economic activity of merchants and manufacturers. They wished to sweep away all the artificial restrictions and ties and all remains of feudalism and of the privileges that in the class state were attached to landed property and birth. But this historical parallelism should not veil the truth that democracy and liberalism are different concepts and are not interconnected.

The development of democracy proceeded then in a direction away from liberalism. Gradually, as popular influence grew and consolidated itself, the inner logic of things brought it about that people once again asked of the state something more than passivity and the enforcement of the law. People came to see that prosperity and progress, or merely tolerable living conditions for the mass of the population, are not achieved just by abolishing the old class privileges. Unlimited freedom, which is merely the law of the jungle, assured the strong, that is, the capitalists, of excellent living conditions, but not the weak. If the interests of the latter as well were to be looked after, then it would be necessary to demand that positive measures be taken by the state, such as intervention to prevent the oppression and exploitation of the weak which are the invariable result of the jungle law of everyone fighting everyone else.

In its historical path, democracy has everywhere long since overtaken orthodox liberalism. That which today goes under the name of liberalism, the New Liberalism, is to a great extent a compromise. Social-political reforms, such as labor legislation, social insurance, progressive taxation, and the like, have been accepted as necessary. Freedom of contract is largely supplanted by collective agreements. Behind it all there is still the core: the demand for free trade on a private capitalist basis.

The great problem today is whether this development is to continue, whether democracy is to develop into socialist democracy. The difficult problems this involves will be considered later (Chapter VII, Sec. 3). Here it will be enough to put forward the general point of view that even if the idea of democracy is equally compatible with socialism and with liberalism, there can be no doubt that a development toward socialism will put the institutions to a hard test. There is no doubt that democracy works more easily under a liberal economy. So long as liberal ideas prevail no great difficulties arise, because of the unobtrusive position of the political power. In the laissez-faire state there is no reason for a major dispute as to who is to be the caretaker and how the caretaker shall go about his job. But as the demands of the state increase and as the state is expected to regulate the economy, or even to direct it, the struggle for political control becomes more intense and the differences of political opinions become more violent. But democracy, that is, peaceful compromise through debate and vote, can stand only so much strain. When the strain reaches the breaking point, there is open conflict. In a liberal Britain, the Whigs and the Tories could regularly alternate in office, as in a play or in a parlor game. Still everything continued unchanged. It was the same upper class that ruled the same lower class. Only the setting changed. But when it so happens that socialists and liberals seriously compete for power, then it is an altogether different story. Then it becomes a question of whether the democratic supra-ideology can stand the inner tension or whether the antagonisms become so irreconcilable that the whole framework breaks up.

But even if we assume that democracy does not guarantee

the individual any definite freedom of action, there are still certain liberties that are inextricably bound up with democracy, for without them the majority principle would lose its meaning. There is first of all the freedom of expression and association, the freedom of citizens in speech and in writing to express their opinions on political questions and to form associations for the purpose of seeking to realize these opinions. This is the second meaning usually given to the term political liberty. It is easy to understand that without that freedom the majority principle loses its meaning. A vote that does not arise out of free debate but in which only certain groups of the population have had an opportunity to assert their point of view can naturally not be taken as an expression of the people's will. The bogus plebiscites whereby the dictators at all times have sought to gloss over their regimes of coercion have nothing in common with real democracy.

The majority principle is the formal, the legal, criterion of democracy. But it is impossible to understand the deeper "essence" or "idea" of democracy without linking up that principle with the idea of debate, or parliamentarism in its wider sense.[1] This idea is so essential that it is not uncommon for people simply to define the essence of democracy as discussion or debate in order to reach a common understanding with mutual consideration of the opinion and wishes of others. Since in the meanwhile this idea, from the nature of things, does not allow of formulation into a legal claim, it appears to me most obvious to define the concept democracy merely in terms of the majority principle, and transfer the idea of discussion to the methods by which the ideals of democracy may be realized.

According to this idea, the vote whereby the majority imposes its will upon the minority is only a makeshift. The goal is in the first place to bargain for agreement, to meet and discuss things in order to reach a common understanding. It is

---

[1] In contrast to the parliamentary system of government, which means the government's political identity with the majority of the people's representatives.

thus assumed that every single party is willing not only to tolerate the points of view of others but also to understand them and allow itself to be influenced by them, so that its own final view is based also on a fair regard for what others think and wish. Every party at first expresses a view determined by its own particular outlook. In the free and friendly debate these points of view meet and the idea is that they should be made to influence each other and to harmonize and fuse, so that there arises a common outlook in which all can share. If this does not succeed, it becomes necessary to resort to the vote, and let the will of the majority have precedence over that of the minority. But even then the discussion has played its part, for it may be assumed that the majority's decision has not been unaffected by that debate but has been influenced by the minority's opinion and wishes, so that the debate has contributed to reconcile and compose originally existing differences. In this way the outvoted feel themselves to a lesser degree disregarded and subjected to external will, and political freedom in the form of freedom of discussion acts increasingly on political freedom as autonomy.

   A Danish author has illustrated this point by a good example. Somewhere in Denmark there is a parish council in which there are two groups, a majority group of seven members and a minority group of four members. The majority is thus solid, and there is no reason to believe that it could be shaken within the next few years. It often so happens at the meetings that the majority summarily set out the proposal that they are agreed upon. Thereafter, the opposition is given the floor. It is indeed a democratic assembly! The opposition makes a long and often well-founded case, pointing out the difficulties of the matter. While the opposition has the floor, no one can tell whether the members of the majority group are listening or sleeping, but we must assume that they are listening. When the opposition has formulated its objections, it may happen that the chairman or someone else says a few words—preferably fairly caustic words. But it seldom takes long before the majority group move putting the question to the vote. Further discussion is as a rule found unnecessary. For the majority have decided the matter beforehand and do not care for the opposite party or its point of view. But the meeting always ends with a good democratic vote which, remarkably enough, always turns out to be seven to four, after which everybody goes home convinced of having done a good democratic job. Has not the debate been free? Has not the matter been decided by vote, and has not the majority been allowed to decide? What more is wanted? Everybody would be most surprised—the minority, however, perhaps pleasantly—to hear it alleged that this state of affairs is undemocratic to the highest degree.

A state with an autocratic form of government, that is, a state in which the will of a certain minority is politically supreme, as we have seen above (Sec. 2), cannot afford the luxury of granting general freedom of expression. Discussion and debate, for the rest, do not amount to much, when the ruling minority has decided beforehand to impose its will. Autocracy is based on the attitude, "We alone know," and thereby it assumes the character of dictatorship. The concept "autocracy" means the denial of the principle of majority rule, and with it the denial of political freedom in the sense of autonomy, and thus stands in opposition to the concept "democracy." The concept "dictatorship" means the denial of political freedom in the sense of free debate and thereby stands in opposition to the concept "parliamentarism." These two sets of opposites are in actual fact so intimately connected that, in the general opinion, they often are merged.

In the nature of political affairs there are forces which—fortunately—bring it about that the demand for consideration of and respect for the minority becomes more than merely a moral idea. If people in a democracy behaved as a rule in the same way as in the parish that has been described above, that democracy would soon be in danger of undermining itself. If the majority, in blind faith in their own right, ruthlessly carry out their own policy without any form of obligation toward the opposition, it must be prepared to find that the latter will gain in strength and retaliate when the majority and government swing over to them. Experience shows that change in government involves only to a surprisingly small degree the repeal of the measures enacted by the opposite party. This continuity in politics proves that the demand for amicable settlement and compromise is more than a beautiful thought.

Free debate is thus not merely a necessary prerequisite in itself for democracy, if the majority principle is to be established as the rightful expression of opinion. It involves, in addition, effects in the way of compromise and unity that place democracy under a new set of values.

People have often formed exaggerated and dogmatic ideas of the happy effects of free debate in this connection. In Rousseau we have met the idea (Chapter III, Sec. 1) that the general will, arising as it does out of free discussion and vote without the formation of parties, has an inner justice because it is necessarily directed toward the common good, so that the different special interests cancel out one another. Apart from the untenable in the idea of "the common good" as an objectively recognizable aim, it is clear that this faith in the mystical union of all individual wills into a higher unity that is necessarily good and just to all is a dogmatic idealization which does not hold true in reality. There is nothing to prevent the majority from one-sidedly pursuing their own interests at the expense of the whole. But behind Rousseau's absolutism there lies the relative truth that the individual is the most dependable defender of his own interests, and that therefore a system which allows everyone to raise his voice to express his wishes makes it most likely that the decision arrived at expresses a reasonable consideration for all, which is in harmony with the idea of fairness prevailing in the community in question which goes under the name of "equity." Even if "equity" is not something given a priori or objectively recognizable, the moral feeling of right and reasonableness is, nevertheless, a social-psychological reality which causes the political decision that satisfied this feeling to be more easily accepted by all parties as binding and not merely as a decree imposed from above. In this way, free discussion tends toward "equitable" solutions and thereby again toward the strengthening of the ideological ties or legal ideas, in contrast to mere submission out of fear of violence. In the autocratic society, on the contrary, the compromise between the interests of the different social groups depends solely on the idea that the rulers have of the power and justice of those interests. That dissatisfaction cannot find expression does not mean, of course, that it does not exist. Adjustment is thus rendered difficult, but the chances are great that important groups of the population feel the existing order to be "unjust" and therefore do not accept it ideologically but merely bow to force. This undermines national unity and increases the risk of a violent upheaval.

There can be no doubt, for instance, that if the Danish peasants during the later Middle Ages and right to the end of the eighteenth century had been allowed to state their case freely before the rest of the community it would not have been so long before it came to be realized that reform was necessary, both on practical and on ideal grounds. The justice that one receives as the result of other people's efforts in the name of humanity most certainly comes later than that one achieves for oneself.

Among the nineteenth century's Utilitarians, there is also found a remarkably exaggerated faith in the absolute and infallible value of freedom of discussion as a means to the solution of all political questions. This is due to their one-sided intellectualistic conception of social life as well as of human nature. All political problems, according to this conception, are arithmetical problems of concrete measurable units of magnitude ("pleasure") which can be solved with the help of a table of logarithms, and Man is a rational being who only requires clear arguments, evening classes, and enlightening literature in order to understand his true interest and to act accordingly. The obvious goal of all social action is the common good defined as the greatest happiness for the greatest number, which can be calculated like an arithmetic magnitude. The task is to find, through proper insight, the means that serve this end best. The Utilitarians had no doubt that this task could be solved by rational deliberation, nor had they any doubt that, once the right way was found, it would be possible, merely by virtue of rational argument, to convince everyone of the correctness thereof and to induce him to accept the true solution. For just as every individual seeks his own happiness, so all seek together the greatest possible happiness for all. The citizens are spoken of as though they were a little group of philosophers who gather in order to solve an abstract problem and after an hour's debate are convinced by knowledge and penetration.

To this blind faith in the ability of reason to dictate to people a common social goal, as well as to find the way leading to it and to impel the individual to act in accordance with it, free debate among enlightened intellects must have seemed the panacea that was to bring light into the darkness, create unity out of chaos, and show the way to the right solution of all problems. The force of truth is boundless if only the freedom to seek and express it is not limited. Freedom of thought is the only guarantee for the victory of truth. Every attempt at suppressing false opinions runs the risk of being itself based on error and thereby of preventing progress. Delusion and fanaticism should not be repressed. If left alone they are harmless as a germ which will be destroyed or purified in the fire of free criticism. Therefore there must be freedom for evil as well as for good. "Freedom," says Renan, "is the great means of destroying all fanatical opinions. When I demand freedom for my enemies, freedom for him who would like to oppress me had he the power, I actually present him with the smallest of gifts. Science can bear the virile force of freedom; fanaticism, superstition cannot bear it."

Considered in the light of the ideas of our time, this appraisal of the value of debate is based on a number of fatal illusions. It is a mistake to believe that a straightforward common goal may be set for all social endeavor. "The common good," "the general interest," "social usefulness" are only labels people stick on what they regard at the time as right and reasonable. It is an equally great mistake to believe that even if a certain common final goal, such as the greatest happiness of the greatest number, is generally professed it should be possible to prove rationally which is the right way to reach it. It is too far removed and too intangible. Such airy phrases set no bounds to anyone's freedom to choose his own way in the direction he believes to be the right one. In the last analysis it would be most shortsighted to believe that man is so rational a being as alone to strive toward an absolutely rational goal and to let himself be swayed by nothing but rational insight and reasoned argument. We have learned to realize that "reason" is, to a great extent, merely the surface, the cover of the innermost, irrational forces acting within us. Accordingly, political problems assume actually a character that is essentially different from what meets the eye. When everything that is based upon the objective knowledge of technicians and other specialists has been explained, there still remain fundamental divergences of opinion, resting on differences of interest, valuation, temperament, and judgment, differences of a volitional rather than intellectual order.

On the basis of that assumption the judgment of the significance of debate must also change its character. The essential value of discussion lies not in its being the way to truth through the combining of arguments, but in its being the way to *compromise*, by causing wills to yield to one another. At best, the result of discussions between parties is recognized by each of them as better and more reasonable than its own original proposal (synthesis). This may occur because the discussion has stimulated interests or considerations that the opposing party had not at the beginning allowed for, but the justification of which is now conceded. It may also happen that the parties' original proposals, precisely because of the possibility of being able to yield later, appeared more extreme in character than was actually intended. It is most common, however, that the compromise is accepted by the parties only with resignation, yet is accepted because understanding and peace are valued more highly than uncompromising insistence on their own demands. A particular form of compromise is the so-called "horse trade." Here the settlement takes the form of a combination of the solution of two or more technically unconnected problems so that one party yields on one point in order to obtain satisfaction on another. A concession over the defense problem, for instance, is compensated by a concession over fiscal policy. A Swedish author aptly characterizes the three forms of a compromise with the following economic comparison: "While the synthesis can be compared to a purchase in which both the buyer and the seller find the price fair, and compromise with a transaction where, after various offers and with a mixture of satisfaction and irritation, the parties agree on an intermediate price, the horsetrade reminds one of a barter between a European mariner and an African Negro chieftain, in which each one—he who has got the cotton goods and he who has got the ivory—thinks he has done good business."

Compromise—as a common designation for the various forms of settlement—is the essence of democracy. Willingness to compromise presupposes a complex psychic attitude, which it is not easy to define. There enter into it tolerance, respect for others, willingness to give and take, prizing of peace and understanding rather than subjection and war, together with a belief in some common humanity, which unites and which is stronger than the particular that divides. The essence of the spirit of compromise is connected with the respect for the autonomy of others. However convinced I am of the correctness of my own point of view, however anxious I am to reconstruct the world in accordance with it, yet I recognize that the decisive prerequisite for the realization of my ideas must be my ability to get other people to support them. I prefer an actually worse world to a better one that can be maintained only through oppression, dictation and force. Yet the Swedish author, Tingsten, is certainly right in saying that the parliamentary idea of discussion and compromise is not necessarily bound up with a universal relativism or skepticism with regard to moral philosophy and outlook on life. The sinister examples of Fascism and Hitlerism show precisely that a far-reaching antiintellectualism and moral nihilism can be related to the most reckless will to dictatorship. And conversely, there is nothing to prevent opinion of an absolute, metaphysical-dogmatic nature, such as certain Roman Catholic or natural-law political doctrines, from being compatible with democratic tolerance and recognition that the only way of realizing them is to secure other people's voluntary support.

Compromise has, on the other hand, nothing to do with indecision or slackness of will. For the democratic way of thinking there is nothing compromitting in compromise—quite the contrary. The excited talk about the paltriness of parliamentary politics, its spineless compromising, its haggling and bargaining, its incompatibility with honesty and virile uprightness, evinces the spirit of Nazidom. The demand for responsible, ruthless action without any attempt at currying the mob's favor is also to be found in Hitler's *Mein Kampf* (see Chapter III, Sec. 4).

But compromise has, of course, its limits. All discussion presupposes that the participants speak the same language. Every compromise presupposes a certain community of valuation and attitude which may form the basis of an understanding. Divergences may become so fundamental that the parties can no longer compound them. Even for the most loyal democrat there may come a time when he has to pass. Democracy is a method, not an only and absolute value. If this method comes into conflict with other fundamental values and interests, it may well be that a weighing may lead to the sacrifice of democracy. Should it happen, for instance, that it is democratically decided to exterminate the Jews, suppress scientific research, or introduce concentration camps for political opponents, then, as far as I am concerned, my loyalty to democracy will have reached its limit. The rights of the majority are not absolute. Such a democracy would have betrayed ideals on which I cannot compromise. For some people, the conditions that capitalist democracy offers the broad working population are so unacceptable that they are already on that score willing to sacrifice democracy. Such a point of view in itself allows neither of proof nor of refutation. Those who think otherwise, whether they themselves have also sufficiently realized what values they are hazarding—this book will serve to elucidate this—and whether they are quite sure that what they want to put in place of the present system offers such great advantages, may only expostulate with the revolutionaries on the ground that the revolution is not bought too dearly.

Also, with regard to the technique of creating public opinion, the rationalist conception of human nature prevented the older theorists from reaching a realistic understanding of the nature and problems of political propaganda. Since it was assumed that man is a rational being whose actions are determined by clear, rational consideration of his interests, the technique of propaganda could not, according to their views, consist of anything other than appeals to reason and insight, to convince through arguments. The modern technique of publicity and propaganda has taught us how far that idea is removed from reality. Emotional suggestion, in accordance with the laws of mass psychology, has shown itself far more effective than objective appeals to reason. Arguments are more harmful than useful from the point of view of effectiveness. Arguments may be criticized and awaken doubt. Propaganda appeals straight to the instincts. It works with promises and threats which tempt and flatter, which appeal to hatred, vindictiveness, the lust for power, vanity, which, coldly calculating, cynically disillusioned, use every means to spiritual violation. Repetition, slogans, incitement, and lies are the weapons it prefers to use.

Experience, especially in Germany, has shown what astounding results can be achieved when a skillful and reckless propaganda is let loose on a spiritually defenseless population. Similar methods characterize the political propaganda in the democracies, although to a lesser degree—owing to a certain decency and to the facility for criticism, and particularly because here there have never existed to quite the same extent the fear, insecurity, and nervous excitement that, as experience shows, are the best ground for terror propaganda. To the same extent, debate loses its actual meaning and degenerates into a struggle with means of propaganda technique. We are faced here with a serious problem. If the politics of the democratic state are to be the expression of a popular will that is "true" in the sense that it derives from opinions based on factual knowledge and understanding of social facts, and not of a synthetic popular will based on misguidance, misrepresentation, and intellectual violation, it is necessary to take measures to counteract the power of propaganda. Since it is now hardly possible to distinguish demagogic propaganda from honest agitation and to regulate the matter through prohibitions, the best safeguard against the influence of suggestion is to make the population propaganda-proof, that is, to develop the critical sense which is the best immunization against the spiritual infection of suggestion. (See Chapter VII, Sec. 2).

Thus it comes about that public opinion and debate assume a somewhat distorted character, and that the democratic regime cannot unreservedly be approved of as the expression of the people's "actual" will based on its "true" interests. There is reason to believe that important population groups, under pressure of tradition, sluggishness, conscious propaganda, and the influence that is in the air, allow themselves to be led and misled by an ideology that is not in their "true" interest, which they would experience and follow were they not exposed to this pressure but had instead a genuine insight into the political possibilities and their consequences.

The reformist parties must therefore be especially interested in educational work, and the political debate assumes a new task and meaning alongside of compromise. Compromise is the function of debate in relation to actually conflicting interests, as between labour and capital, or between free traders and protectionists. Its aim is to realize democracy by reconciling the conflicting wills so as to allow a common will or a majority will to arise, and to prevent the whole from drowning in a chaos of incompatible wills. Compromise imbues the formation of opinion to all its levels; it is not only a compromise between parties but also within the parties and their sections. At all levels there is a demand for a mutual adaptation and integration and this process of integration continues right up to the "people's will" as the expression of the final and total integration. The will of the majority is then attributed to the whole "people," in the same way as the management of a society is said to speak on behalf of the entire society, regardless of whether there is an outvoted minority opposition. This imputation has meaning only on the assumption that the minority feels itself bound by the majority's decision, hence on the assumption of democracy. The concept "popular will," therefore assumes democracy—and not the other way around!

When the political disagreement, on the other hand, is not based on actual clashes of interests but on faulty adaptation of political ideology to a group's actual social position, then the task of political propaganda is to educate and reëducate, or, to put it in another way, to awaken to class consciousness. Its aim is to realize democracy by bringing the "real" popular will to expression. Education to a critical sense of reality is the weapon that the democratic reform parties will use instead of revolution. The future of democracy depends on the degree to which such education may be realized.

Free debate has yet a third and essential function, namely, in relation to government. Effective democracy assumes that government is controlled by the popular will. According to the majority principle this control is exercised in its legal form when the people, at certain intervals through elections, are given the opportunity of approving or disapproving, and thereby dismissing, the existing government. In this respect, public debate not only is a prerequisite for the democratic function of the vote, but also supplements it. Public debate creates a *public opinion*, which is of the greatest importance as a continual control and inspiration of government.

The debate on the settlement of accounts with traitors in Denmark after the occupation presents a good example of what is here discussed. The sense of justice is not something inherited or given a priori. It has its root in familiar reactions to well-known types of crime. The disloyalty during the occupation toward the national solidarity presented the conception of justice with new and unknown types of crime. The result had necessarily to be uncertainty of reaction. The new situation demands an adjustment which does not come about all at once. In such a situation, public debate plays a decisive role. By reflecting the way in which the problems of the settlement of justice are regarded by the citizens, it contributes to readapt the general sense of justice and to create a public opinion that can influence the policy of the government and the legislature. Debate on a problem of change of frontier affords another example. Here, too, a new reflection and a new adjustment of the demands of justice were needed. In both instances, there was a certain change of attitude under the influence of public debate. In neither case was the formation of opinion without influence on the response of public bodies.

Political freedoms, such as freedom of expression and of organization, and the parliamentary ideas connected with them are the nerve of democracy, and that is precisely what many of democracy's most serious problems are about. There is the question whether freedom of expression is to be absolute, or whether it ought to be limited for the self-protection of democracy ("active democracy"). There is the question whether a development toward socialism is in practice compatible with the preservation of political freedom. If it is not, one is forced to choose between socialism and freedom. Such a choice would be a particular illustration of the universal problem, touched on in the preceding passages, of the tension between the formal democratic supraideology and the economic and social ideas that are to reach a balance within the framework of democracy. If this tension becomes too strong, democracy is threatened with destruction. What particularly concerns the parliamentary ideas is the question of the distortion by propaganda of the "real" popular will and the fight against it by means of information and education. The parliamentary idea of willingness to compromise and regard for the minority raises the question whether democracy can degenerate into "majority dictatorship" or whether there are, on the contrary, certain decisions of such an either-or character that the above mentioned idea cannot find application. I shall come back to these problems later (Chapters VII and VIII).

Here the task is merely that of clarifying the ideas of democracy. In this connection, what does political liberty, such as freedom of expression and of organization, mean? In part it is only the prerequisite for the realization of the majority principle. To that extent it serves and strengthens the ideas of autonomy, law, and peace, which are already contained in it. But beyond that, freedom of expression has its own relevance of value. To be able to talk freely, to be able to protest against injustice, to mold and be molded in a free disputation with others, is for many people an essential component of their feeling as free personalities. Certainly there are also those who turn up their noses at it and think that a full stomach is more important than a free tongue. It may well be that freedom of expression is a cultural advantage, the appreciation of which presupposes both a certain material welfare and a certain intellectual development. It has to that extent the character of a luxury good. In Denmark, with our developed social life and lively public discussion, I should think that most of us possess the necessary prerequisites for the appreciation of this freedom. The occupation gave us a taste of what it means to have to whisper in corners. My own point of view is that I should feel it a spiritual mutilation to lose this freedom. For him who agrees with me in this, there is further reason to prefer democracy to autocracy.

6. Democracy and Personal Freedom: Intellectual Freedom

As has been said, democracy and liberalism are two different things which do not of necessity belong together. If personal freedom is understood to mean that the greatest possible scope is given to the individual to tackle his personal affairs, freedom to get drunk, to gamble, and to visit night clubs, freedom for sexual and other eccentricities, it cannot be claimed that personal freedom is in any way guaranteed by democracy. On the other hand, democracy is no more essentially inconsistent with personal freedom than are the autocratic forms of government. The trend away from liberal ideals that has been taking place for the last hundred years was not brought about by the form of government. We can generally say at most that the mixed form of government, partial democracy (Chapter IV, Sec. 3) based on the balance of power which prevents the rise of a strong government, is the one that harmonizes best with liberal principles.

On one point only, but a very essential one, namely, where the branch of personal freedom called intellectual liberty is concerned, is democracy by its nature necessarily liberal. Freedom of expression guarantees the individual against the systematic stunting of his spiritual personality that is brought about by political regimentation, the typical feature of modern forms of autocracy. Even if the freedom of expression in a democracy is thought of mainly as freedom of political expression, still the coherence of all intellectual manifestations, and the impossibility of setting up rigid limits between political ideas on the one hand and art, literature, religion, science, and philosophy on the other, demand that the same freedom must reign in all spheres. We cannot give a man political freedom of expression and at the same time forbid him to express his opinions about Christianity, economics, the Materialist conception of history, free will, Plato's philosophy, Einstein's theory of relativity, or the problems of education. It cannot be laid down a priori for any sphere of intellectual activity that it is without any significance for the formation of political opinion. Nor may it be lawful for a man to make a speech and at the same time unlawful for him to express himself in verse or pictorial arts. Intellectual freedom must necessarily be *total*, and must therefore also include those manifestations which apparently have no political relevance, direct or indirect. The majority principle necessitates freedom of political expression, and freedom of political expression in turn demands, if it is not to be indirectly curtailed, full intellectual liberty.

This indirect effect of democracy's political structure rendered necessary on technical-legal grounds is of the greatest importance. Perhaps not everybody experiences intellectual freedom as a fundamental value and condition for the development of the personality. This naturally presupposes that we are possessed of a mind and seek to develop it. But regardless of that everybody who believes that the human mind holds unused possibilities of new realization for the promotion of human progress and happiness must be interested in that freedom. For it is a very ancient experience that the mind thrives only in freedom. Every canonization, whether of St. Paul's, of Hitler's, or of Marx's scriptures, leads to stagnation and decay. Every orthodoxy is incompatible with the dialectic development of the spirit. The motto of orthodoxy, "Now truth has been found and the point is to preserve it," is incompatible with continued progress. My idea is not to glorify truth seeking for itself. If anyone actually offered me in one hand "truth" and in the other, the search for truth, I would

—Lessing to the contrary notwithstanding— choose truth. But the fact is that such a choice is unthinkable if man does not accept revelation. All orthodoxy, including the Communist, presupposes a belief in revelation.

Democracy and intellectual liberty thus belong together. If future developments within democratic society may possibly nevertheless involve a danger to intellectual freedom, it will be due not to the democratic institutions themselves but to the trend toward standardization inherent in the mass production, rationalization, and mechanization of modern technology, and in the systematic mass propaganda that these make possible. However, it is only the last that can represent a serious danger. The spirit that is killed by walking in utility shoes, driving in *Volkswagen*, or living in prefabricated houses does not in itself amount to very much. The sinister effects of a standardized mass propaganda must be met by education for critical independence.

Therefore, everybody who values intellectual liberty as an indispensable personal and human good, as the basis of all culture, has to that extent, too, reason to prefer democracy to dictatorship.

7. Democracy and Personal Freedom: The Idea of Public Security

The expression "personal freedom" is also used in another sense, in which there is no actual question of "liberty," that is, free scope for the individual, unimpeded by state control; in this sense the term means security of the individual against arbitrary encroachment on his person by the government, that is, public security.

The demand that everybody who is deprived of his personal liberty shall be immediately brought before a judge so that it may be legally ascertained whether, according to the law, there is reasonable basis in his deeds for imprisoning him, may seem to be a safeguard of secondary importance, since this does indeed not set any limits to the conditions under which imprisonment may be authorized by law. If the law sanctions the imprisonment of everyone who is a communist, the right to be brought before a judge is of little comfort. Nevertheless, it is a guarantee of procedure of fundamental importance. The point is that it is far more difficult to corrupt the law than individual acts of administration. The law must in all circumstances have a certain relation to the people's conception of justice, but what is done by the secret police escapes public criticism.

From the democratic point of view, public security must be an absolute necessity. Indeed, it is the guarantee of political liberty (freedom of expression). Arbitrary imprisonment, the Bastille, concentration camps, are not used against rivals in love, but against political opponents. Freedom of expression is not worth anything if it is not combined with the security that expression of political opinion not agreeable to those in power does not involve the risk of a visit early in the morning by the secret state police. Personal freedom is merely a new expression of the idea of law and order, as opposed to government by coercion.

Autocratic government, on the other hand is, as has been pointed out earlier (Sec. 2), if not in theory yet in practice, inseparably connected with repression and violence. Only a metaphysical ideology can, in an era in which religious ideas hold sway over the mind, create so strong a legitimation for an autocrat that he dares to overlook occasional criticism and desist from violent methods. But this is more of a theoretical possibility. Normally, the ruling minority is afraid of every criticism and eager to nip in the bud every attempt. It is itself guided by fear and rules through fear. Precisely for that reason, terror, that is, the ever-present threat of secret, arbitrary violence, is its favorite means. But repression naturally does not have to go to that extreme. The decisive thing in this respect is the tension that exists between the rulers and the latent resistance groups, and the extent to which repression is legalized so that legal forms can be used. The settlement with the Trotskyites in Russia went on in a somewhat more civilized manner than the Nazi St. Bartholomew's massacre (of June 30, 1934).

Personal freedom is the cornerstone of public security but from that corner the idea radiates to other aspects of life. Every arbitrariness, every highhandedness, holds a threat to the independence of the citizens, a danger of the abuse of state power. The ideal of public security includes therefore what the British call "the rule of law," that is, the idea that all administration is exercised in accordance with previously established legal rules and subsequent control by the law courts. Police, price-control agencies, ministries, and all other administrative organs are not popes on their own authority, but servants carrying out the directives of the representatives of the people. Their authority over the citizens is laid down and limited by the common rules of law and they, like everyone else, are responsible for their actions before the independent law courts.

Now it must be admitted that the principle of lawful administration thins out to the degree that the sanctioning legal rules lose their concrete substance and become extensive, discretionary norms of authority. It is difficult for a businessman in Denmark to be right as against the Price Control because the rules of the price law give so wide a scope to the administration's discretion. The modern development in the direction of state control undoubtedly renders unavoidable an increase in the state organs' discretionary power, and it is a problem how this can be brought into harmony with the traditional ideals of public security, a problem that will become more and more urgent as the contrast between the private-capitalist sector in business life and social control becomes greater. I shall refer to this later (Chapter VII, Sec. 3).

The same applies to public security, especially personal freedom, as to the freedom of expression: it is not merely a technical condition of democracy but also something that may be valued in itself. The feeling of security, order, and humanity which it promotes will surely be regarded by most as a blessing. Those who are in agreement with this have again a new motive for preferring democracy to autocracy.

Summing up the relation of democracy to the manifold ideas of freedom, we can establish that democracy gives man the maximum of *freedom from domination by others, freedom from intellectual oppression, especially freedom of political expression,* and *freedom from fear* (personal freedom, public security). Otherwise, democracy is not necessarily connected with liberal ideas. It no more sanctions free enterprise than it guarantees freedom from want. This latter is the goal of socialism, not of democracy.

8. Democracy and Equality

While the connection of democracy with the idea of freedom in its different ramifications is clear and straightforward, the situation is quite different with regard to the idea of equality. This is partly because the latter is in itself even more indefinite and ambiguous than the idea of liberty.

We speak about equality when burdens or advantages are to be distributed among a group of people. Yet equality does not by a long way mean that the shares given to every individual shall be identical. Equality does not exclude the possibility of differences. Equality before the law does not mean that everybody has the same rights and duties. Nobody would regard it as an infringement of equality if a difference were to be made between married people and single, or between majors and minors, or if different rules were to apply to bakers and to blacksmiths. Only a very few will also think that equality in taxation should mean that everybody pays the same amount in taxes. Some will think that equality demands that taxation shall be proportionate to the size of the income, others that it should correspond to capacity to pay and therefore be progressive. Neither does the socialist ideal of equal distribution of the national product preclude differences. One definition of socialism says, "to each according to his needs"; another, "to each according to his work." The idea of equality precludes only *arbitrary or unreasonable* differences. The former means that the treatment does not follow a general rule but quite extraordinarily violates otherwise recognized principles, as would happen, for instance, if the tax-assessing authorities were to give a personal friend a preferential position. The latter means that differences in procedure indeed follow a general rule but that this rule is one which cannot be sanctioned because it is based upon criteria that are considered inadmissible, as if, for instance, the Jews were to be outlawed, or taxed more highly than others.

One may therefore say that *formally* the demand for equality amounts to nothing other than a demand that a certain common rule be followed, regardless of what it may be. Equality before the law means in that sense that the law is purely and simply applied regularly according to its content; formal inequality or injustice means that a decision has been taken for irrelevant reasons, such as bias, or political favoritism. Materially, the demand for equality means that the rule which is followed shall, in its substance, be in keeping with certain values, so that it does not make the differences conditional on criteria whose importance cannot be recognized. In this sense, equality before the law means, for instance, that Jews may not be placed below others because one cannot recognize that race is a well-founded criterion for difference in legal status; material inequality or injustice, that the rule which would sanction it would be in conflict with certain valuations and ideals.

It will be understood from this that either the demand for equality (in a formal sense) is fairly meaningless, or that it is (in a material sense) just as variable as people's valuations and ideals and only a derivative expression of those.

If we now turn to democracy in order to examine its relation to the idea of equality, then we must distinguish between political equality on the one hand and economic, social, and cultural equality on the other.

Politically, the principle of majority rule is the expression of an absolute, material equality of all adult individuals with regard to voting. Democracy denies every criterion in support of granting political power to certain persons in preference to others. It denies the absolute king's divine right and the leader's "call to leadership"; it denies aristocratic privileges whether these be based on birth, education, possession, or party allegiance. Naturally it does not deny that those qualifications—except the divine right and perhaps the "call to leadership"—do in fact exist, but it denies that any of them or any other criterion may be the basis for a claim to political power. This is not the place to discuss the "correctness" of this point of view. The question here is only one of showing that there lies in democracy a recognition of the ideal of equality, in so far as the principle of majority rule gives to every single citizen exactly the same possibility of exercising political influence to the extent of participating in the elections.

All the same, there is no complete political equality in democracy, either in the legal or in the actual sense. It is true that political power through the elections *derives from* the people, but it is not *exercised by* the people, but by a little group of elected leaders. It would be a fiction to deny that cabinet members or ministers, members of Congress or of Parliament, and party leaders exercise both legally and actually greater political influence than the common man. Democracy too has its leading elite, its generals and privates. Where it differs decisively from autocracy is only that democracy's "general staff" is appointed by election, enjoys the people's confidence, and is under their control. Even if the political power of the leading elite is therefore greater than that of the common man, it is not "alien" rule. Equality can indeed be deviated from, but not freedom or autonomy. Already this shows that equality is not as important for democracy as liberty.

It be added that political equality is not something specific to democracy. Equality includes equality in political power as well as in the lack of it, equality in freedom as well as in bondage. Even the many who are without any rights whatever are subjected to an authoritarian government, are still equals.

From this it appears that equality is a democratic idea of a subordinate and dependent character only. The leading idea is freedom, political and personal. It is further assumed that this freedom is to be granted to everyone and, in so far as democracy demands equality, equality in freedom. But it is freedom that is the end in itself; the demand for equality has only the relative meaning that the benefit of freedom should not be withheld from anyone. It is true that democracy demands equal franchise for all. But the stress here is not on equality, for that may be also obtained by granting nobody the franchise or else only one of limited political importance in relation to an autocratic monarchy. No, the stress lies on the fact that the full franchise, autonomy-liberty, is a most desired benefit and desired therefore by everybody without exception. Democracy therefore can be entirely consistent with such limitations of political equality as do not encroach upon freedom, whereas autocracy, on the other hand, is equally consistent with a political equality that is equality in bondage.

Next we shall talk about economic, social, and cultural equality. Here, equality does not mean absolute identity of the allotted portion but distribution according to certain rules which differ from those now in force. There is disagreement and confusion as to how these rules shall actually be formulated. The core of the demands for equality is presently stated in the negative, in the form of a denial of certain of the criteria that now decide the size of the share of economic, social, and cultural advantages allotted to each person—especially one's own or one's parents' possession of capital. It is this situation which in today's society primarily determines class divisions, as an expression of the differences in economic, social, and cultural positions. The striving toward equality therefore coincides with anticapitalism or socialism.

Is there now any connection between this demand for equality or socialism and political democracy? None whatever. Democracy (in the political sense in which we are at present using that term) is a political method, a supraideology, not a norm for the substance of the system of social conditions. One can be a democrat without being a socialist. Of course, one can also be both: a Social Democrat. But the combination is not a necessary one. The idea of socialism is not included in the idea of democracy, and socialism's idea of equality is different from democracy's idea of liberty (political and personal). Democracy is no more necessarily bound up with socialism than with the latter's opposite liberalism (capitalist free enterprise), but is, according to its concept, equally consistent with either of these substantial ideologies.

If, nevertheless, democracy is often interpreted in terms of equality,[1] this is no doubt due, as is the opposite tendency to identify democracy with liberalism, to a historical parallelism. The young democracy strove not only for liberty, but also for economic equality, in so far as it wished to put an end to the old inequalities benefiting the old feudal upper class. Yet this striving of democracy for equality was certainly not socialist, since the old feudal privileges did not attach to capital in the modern sense, but it did at any rate bring it about that the ideas of democracy and of equality became closely linked in popular conception.

It might perhaps be said, furthermore, that a connection exists between democracy and equality to the extent that increasing equality is a prerequisite for the continued existence of democracy. Laski made himself a powerful spokesman of that view. He maintained that people who live under unequal

[1] Various authors have, however, realized that democracy and economic equality are two different things; see particulary Hans Kelsen, *Allgemeine Staatslehre* (Berlin, 1925), p. 323; James Bryce, *Modern Democracies* (London, 1921), vol. I, p. 76; and R. Bassett, *The Essentials of Parliamentary Democracy* (London: Macmillan and Co. 1935), p. 102.

(economic, social, cultural) conditions do not think alike, and that therefore the common sense of values and the will to mutual understanding, which are the prerequisites of democracy, threaten to break down if conditions become too unequal. An unequalitarian community lives always in fear of inner divisions. People in a community will have a similar interest in liberty only when, to put it roughly, they have a similar interest in its results. Liberty will not, therefore, in the long run be able to subsist without equality. Equality is the necessary condition for democracy and democracy, in turn, for liberty.

This, I believe, is roughly an expression of a right idea. But this is not an argument in favor of democracy. We cannot say that everyone who values equality has to that extent a motive for preferring democracy to autocracy. The reverse is true: if, out of love of liberty, one supports democracy, then one has a reason to desire greater equality, for without that, democracy cannot in the long run hope to survive.

The confusion of democracy and social equality may also be thought to be due to the fact that there seems to be a natural connection between these ideas in that a political system which gives the power to the common people must "naturally" also lead to an economic policy that benefits the common people at the expense of existing privilege. Equality is thought of here not as the basis of the system but as its consequence. It is possible that this is true in the long run. Economic development under democracy has at any rate up to now gone very much in that direction. But however that may be, it does not alter the fact that the political method—democracy—is one thing, and the economic policy this method leads to, another thing, and that there is nothing to prevent one from being a supporter of democracy without being a socialist, that is, a supporter of a more equal distribution of social benefits.

The tendency to make the idea of equality a fundamental idea of democracy has perhaps also, now and then, been the expression of a conscious or unconscious political inclination.

One seeks a support for the demand for equality by making it a constituent part of democracy. But quite regardless of how one appraises the demand for equality, clear thinking demands that one should keep this idea outside of democracy as a political system.

People often seek one of democracy's ideological roots in the Christian doctrine of the brotherhood of man and equality before God, and this may perhaps be taken to be a sign of an inner connection between democracy and the idea of equality. I believe that democracy has its root in Christian ideas, but I do not think that these have anything to do with social equality. The early Christians did not oppose slavery. The Christian idea of men's essential equality does not deny that one may be more intelligent, more industrious, better, more virtuous, kinder than another; nor that there might be reason for attributing importance to these differences between men. Only before God are all men equal. There, everyone counts only as one soul, equally loved by God, whose salvation rests alone with His grace. What is here expressed is not a claim for social equality, but the idea of the sacredness of man. By virtue only of his humanity, independently of individual qualities, every single individual has a claim to respect as a child of God. From here the idea finds its way to the secular humanism —homo sum—and again to the moral-political idea of the individual's autonomy and freedom.

The inquiry in this section may thus be concluded *negatively*: we cannot find any new argument in the concept of equality in support of democracy beyond that contained in the idea of liberty.

9. Democratic Mentality and its Effects Outside of Political Life: Other Forms of Institutional Democracy, and Democracy as an Attitude. Misuse of the Term "Democracy"

The attempt I have made in the preceding section at stating what seems to me to be the idea of democracy must not be taken as literally as, for instance, a chemical analysis that determines with great accuracy the elements of a compound. The democratic mentality is not something that can be measured and weighed. The reader who has not previously himself experienced the democratic ideals will hardly have understood what it is all about. The most I dare hope for is that these brief considerations which have tried to capture that democratic mentality, and, examining it from all angles, to give it definite form, may contribute to make its content more living and clear for him who has himself experienced it. The purpose of this book is not to convert autocrats to democracy, but to get those who are democrats in their "innermost selves" to understand as clearly as possible the implications of democracy.

Were I to try to straighten out the different features of democracy as revealed by our analysis, so as to make the picture's inner structure stand out more clearly, I should begin by saying that democratic mentality means *respect for the moral personality of man*. This is an attitude that has its roots in the traditions of Christianity and humanism. Christianity has given expression to this feeling in its doctrine of the infinite value of every man in the eyes of God. Kant has expressed the same in more philosophical terms in formulating his categorical imperative, which commands one always to act in such a manner as to regard humanity, within oneself as well as in every other person, as an end and never as a means only. In all humanity there lives the idea that man is sacred. In its more primitive forms that feeling expresses itself in metaphysical-religious ideas, but even emancipated from those ideas, it always remains like a taboo factor drawing a definite line of demarcation between all relativist technical-rationalist speculations over ends and means, on the one hand, and the respect for humanity, on the other.

In contrast to this is the contempt for man that is the spiritual core of Fascism. I have discussed it above when considering Hitler's critique of democracy (Chapter III, Sec. 4). Anti-humanism breaks down all barriers between man and inanimate matter. It thus leads, as a consequence, to concentration camps, gas chambers, and mass crematoria, which, to a mind that has freed itself of all taboo ideas of the sacredness of human life, are merely an expedient method for the liquidation of opponents. While that extreme line is, thank God! only rarely adopted, the lack of respect, or at least the insufficient respect for man is nevertheless characteristic of all forms of autocracy.

A special manifestation of the respect for the moral personality of man is the recognition of his autonomy, his freedom of self-determination according to his own personality, his set of values, and his ideals, as a value that should be realized to the greatest possible extent. This gives rise, among those who hold positions of power in the administration and leadership, to the wish to obtain the consent of their subordinates and not merely to coerce them. This wish reflects itself again in a number of attitudes which are partly the same one seen from different angles. There is first and foremost the idea of free political discussion as a means to mutual understanding and compromise, which expands into the idea of universal intellectual liberty. A prerequisite for this is personal security, which in its widest form leads to respect for law and order, with all their implications, as opposed to arbitrariness and brute force. This in turn amounts to the same as the preference for peace rather than the use of force.

One may outline these ideas, together with their autocratic opposites, thus:

1. Respect for man *versus* contempt for man,

whence there follows

2. Recognition of the individual's autonomy *versus* assertion of authority,

whence there follows:

3. The wish for support *versus* the wish to dominate,

which again expresses itself in the ideas of

(a) Discussion and intellectual liberty *versus* dictation and intellectual compulsion;

(b) The rule of law, particularly personal security, *versus* arbitrariness and personal insecurity, and

(c) Peace *versus* the use of force.

It is this democratic mentality that manifests itself in the political institutions of a democratic state. Yet one may also speak of democratic (or autocratic) institutions outside of political life, wherever there exists organized administration, to the extent that the above-mentioned ideas are decisive for the working of such administration. I have in mind institutions such as schools, societies, churches, joint-stock companies, political parties, trade-unions, international organizations, etc. In all of them the leadership may be more or less democratic, to the extent to which their members are given greater or lesser rights in deciding matters or in advising the leadership. The army has always been one of the most autocratic of institutions. Its keynote is discipline and blind obedience. The general is just as infallible as the pope. Even if such an institution is not absolutely inconsistent with a humane, democratic mentality, it nevertheless constitutes an element which, where the army plays a dominant role in the community, can definitely destroy or at least hinder full political democracy. The worst enemy of the nascent German democracy was the power of the officers. The idea of introducing democratic institutions into the army—such as private soldiers' deputies with bargaining power—must therefore be hailed with joy in a democratic state. Pupils' or students' councils are another result of democratic trends in organizations that otherwise are mainly autocratically administered. Purely democratic institutions are found in joint-stock companies and most associations.

There are just as many types of institutional democracy (or autocracy) as there are types of organization as defined by their object: political democracy, university democracy, corporation democracy, association democracy, military democracy, and so on. A particularly important form is industrial democracy, by which is meant the granting to workers and employees of a voice in the management and the industry and over the conditions in office and workshop.

Finally, the democratic (or autocratic) ideas may also find application in social conditions where—while there is no legal organization—there still exists an exercise of power over people, a leadership or direction. One may then speak of a democratic disposition (as distinct from institutional democracy), or human democracy. A few examples will make this clear.

In the relation between parents and children, family life and education can be based upon autocratic or democratic principles. In the former case the stress is upon authority, especially paternal authority, with the demand for absolute obedience and discipline. The child is regarded as an object to be molded, not in its own spirit but in the parents' image, and as a passive instrument for their purpose. There is no discussion, no appeal to the child's understanding; there are only orders and commands and physical and mental coercion. On the contrary, education in a democratic spirit would be based upon respect for the personality of the child and endeavor to ensure the best possible conditions for its growth. A democratic education would stimulate the child's initiative and self-reliance. The democratic educator would endeavor to explain and, through discussion, justify himself in order to win the child's consent and coöperation. Compulsion and coercion would be resorted to as little as possible. The educator, like a gardener, trims the young plant only so that it may grow stronger and bear richer fruit. His aim is to render himself superfluous as soon as possible and yield the place to an individual capable of looking after himself, freely and responsibly.

In a similar way, a great number of other social relations may be based on either of the two ideas, democracy or autocracy. This holds true of school instruction, relations between spouses, employer-employee relations, those between the clergy and the congregations; it holds true of administrations, associations and societies—wherever there is any question of leadership and guidance which might be based upon either dictation and compulsion or mutual understanding and freedom. The head of an office can turn his personnel into a group of yes-men who obey him out of fear, or he can meet them with understanding and respect as colleagues at different posts. A husband can turn into a house tyrant, or treat his spouse as a real companion and comrade. A headmaster can behave like a pope in his teachers' council, or content himself with the position of *primus inter pares*. The Roman Catholic church is markedly autocratic; the Protestant churches are relatively democratic in their relation to the congregation. In this connection it may be recalled that democratic ideas in England grew precisely out of the demand for a popular church constitution.

Wherever in these social relations there is willingness to listen to others, willingness for mutual understanding, and respect for the personality of others, there exists a democratic disposition. The good democrat is not impressed by social and conventional distinctions, by wealth and success, title and rank, any more than he despises those whom life—or the social order—has placed in humble conditions. He regards all people as his fellow men.

On the other hand, it appears to me doubtful whether the institutional forms of democracy and the corresponding ideas can be sensibly applied in the economic sphere. There is often talk of economic democracy, but it is not clear what is meant by that term. However, it seems certain that what is demanded by it is not merely a disposition of mind but an institutional order. The assumption must be, in that case, that the productive relationships in a country can be regarded as one whole, subject to a common administration, and the demand for economic democracy should mean the demand that this administration issue from the whole nation and not be reserved to a group of capitalists. But this would simply mean that the national economy should be managed by the state. There remains thus no room for any independent notion of economic democracy alongside of political democracy. The meaning of the concept is, then, only a negative one, consisting in the demand for the abolition of the present order, according to which the productive relationships are autocratically controlled by a small group, owners of capital, while certain of the conditions of production, especially the wages of labor, are laid down during negotiations or in open struggle with the workers. Economic democracy often simply means an economic system which, according to its substance, allows a more equal and equitable distribution of the fruits of production than the present one. But the use of the word "democracy" in this sense is misleading. There is then no analogy with political democracy. The latter term designates a form of government and the ideas of liberty that unfold within it. Pure problems of distribution and the idea of equality that corresponds to it lie outside of the concept of democracy. Hence it ensues that the concept of economic democracy, as it is used in everyday conversation, is a vague one which implies different elements of thought and can therefore easily lead to confusion and misunderstanding. Its two decisive elements are:

(1) The demand for state regulation of production relationships (which leaves no room for any independent idea of economic democracy alongside that of political democracy), and

(2) The demand for a more equal and fair distribution to the benefit of the broad masses (which lies outside the scope of the concept and ideas of democracy). Usage has in the meantime another firmly established designation for precisely this combination of ideas, namely, the word *socialism*. It would therefore make for greater clarity if we were to use it in place of that ambiguous and misleading term "economic democracy."

It is a corresponding fallacy to speak of cultural democracy, understanding thereby an equal access to cultural advantages such as science, literature, art, the theater, sport. Here, too, the idea amounts to a combination of a demand for state control of the production of cultural goods and a demand for equal distribution of them. The right designation for this is cultural socialism.

This misuse of the word democracy to designate economic and cultural phenomena which neither structurally nor according to their ideas are analogous to the phenomena of political democracy reaches its climax in the absurdity of the use of the term "democracy" as the designation for a form of government which according to current usage and relevant concept formation has nothing to do with democracy but is markedly autocratic and dictatorial. In the U.S.S.R. it is usual to call the dictatorship of the proletariat—which Lenin defines as the proletarian rule over the bourgeoisie limited by no law and based on violence—the most perfect form of democracy. "I admit," said Stalin, when the Soviet constitution of 1936 was inaugurated, "that the new constitution maintains the regime of the dictatorship of the proletariat." Nevertheless, he thought he could characterize the constitution as "the only completely democratic constitution in the world." Why this confusion of ideas? Are not the words "dictatorship" and "democracy" used as opposites? Indeed, simply because it is desired to exploit demagogically the good will that from old times attaches to the word democracy. Stalin does not wish to let go of that pretty word. The Nazis used quite the same tactics. They too called their dictatorship the true democracy. This is a theft of ideas and concepts, committed in order to mislead the people.

This can be cast into a short formula by saying that by political democracy is usually meant government *by* the people, while the Russians use the term as a designation for a government *for* the people—at the same time without suggesting this profound shifting in the concept. Danish and other Communists have willingly adopted these tactics and used this confusion of ideas to obscure the discussions with the Social Democrats on their position with regard to democracy. With a little good will, it should not be difficult to get clarity. Political form and economic substance are two different things and it is certain that we need a separate designation for each of them. For the political form, I do not know any other designation than the term democracy, which has always been used by preference precisely for the politico-legal method. For the economic substance, on the other hand, we have the designation socialism.

The opposite of socialism is capitalism. We thus get two sets of antitheses: democracy—autocracy, as expressing the formal distinction, and socialism–capitalism, as expressing the material one. Now if these two antitheses are combined, there arise the four following possibilities: capitalist autocracy, socialist autocracy, capitalist democracy, socialist democracy.

Of these, the first form, capitalist autocracy, was known in Germany and Italy, for instance, before the recent upheavals; socialist autocracy we know from the U.S.S.R.; capitalist democracy, the opposite combination, we know in Denmark, for instance. And finally the last form, socialist democracy, is not yet found anywhere in the world.

VI.

THE CASE AGAINST DEMOCRACY

In the preceding chapters I have described that side of democracy which appears to me to be its positive value. Now I shall look at the other side, the case against that form of government. Only when democracy is seen from both sides is there a basis for deliberate choice with full awareness of that the choice implies.

In Chapter III, Sections 3 to 5, I have discussed the main points of the criticism which, in the course of time, has been leveled against democracy. I may therefore limit myself at present to collecting and systematizing those points of view and submit their significance to a further test.

When I looked for the ideas of democracy, in the preceding chapters, I loyally warned against crediting democracy with such values as either are not always present in a democratic state or can also occur in an autocratic one. I pointed out that the question was to discover the *specific* values of democracy, that is, those which, necessarily or typically, are connected with that form of government and not with its opposite. Obviously quite the same is now required. It is very important to stick firmly to that. Too many of the complaints that are usually brought against democracy are not precisely specific for democracy, but are directed against such imperfections and shortcomings as are due to the frailty of human nature and may therefore also be found in every state, whatever its form of government. It is clear that there cannot be deduced any arguments on this basis in support of the preference for autocracy over democracy. Objections of this kind will be briefly discussed in Section 1.

Next, there is another group of counterideas, in which

there is no reason to be involved either. It is the criticism of democracy which in itself emphasizes the same essential features as were mentioned in the previous chapter, but with an opposite set of values in mind and therefore also expressed in another terminology. I have, indeed, not for a moment concealed the fact that there are people who evaluate, for instance, the will for mutual understanding that exists in a democracy in manner entirely different from mine, seeing in it merely the expression of garrulity and cowardice and praising instead heroic and ruthless determination. There is no particular interest in going further into these negative revaluations of the ideas of democracy, since they do not present new points of view to be weighed but are only expressions of another weighing of already known points of view. They are briefly discussed in Section 2.

What is most important in this chapter appears only under Section 3 where I discuss the criticism that deals with aspects of democracy that are at once specific and new.

1. THE NONSPECIFIC SHORTCOMINGS

Everyone who exercises a political function in the state—as voter, legislator, or official—is given a post in which he is expected to serve honestly, according to his best conviction of what is right and reasonable. But so far as human nature goes, there is always a risk that political power, under pressure of various kinds of desires, will be misused and applied in a way that conflicts with this expectation. In that case, the power is exercised not in order to further the common good but in order to feather individual nests or serve other narrower interests. In all such cases there exists what one might call misuse of power or corruption.

As money is the current common measure of all material values, current corruption is that which is brought about directly by the power of money tempting and threatening. King Philip of Macedonia boasted that he could conquer any town merely by first driving into it a donkey laden with gold. Since then, many have used the same method because the rich knew that it was in the long run a good investment to buy other people's honesty and political influence. Robespierre's nickname "The Incorruptible" shows that his virtue was the exception, not the rule.

Bribery, the direct purchase and sale of political influence, is the crudest and most tangible form of corruption. It may occur in relation to political power at all its levels, as a purchase of votes or as bribery of the legislative power or of officials. In the nineteenth century corruption played a great part also in the more or less democratic countries. John Stuart Mill demanded public voting about 1850 in order to do away with the flourishing votebuying. He asserted that there had never been anything done to prevent briberies because it was to the interest of both leading parties, Tories as well as Whigs, that the election should be a costly affair, so that Parliament should be accessible only to the rich. Comparatively it mattered little to them who voted, so long as they could feel certain that only people of their own class could be voted for.[1] Public opinion certainly despised him who took the bribe, but smiled at him who gave it.[2] The weapon against this abuse was an effective maintenance of penal law and the resulting gradual change of public opinion. In our own day, this form of corruption can be regarded as practically overcome in the culturally advanced democracies. In Denmark, it would not occur to anyone that he could buy a member of Parliament, a minister, or a public official, and the criminal laws relating to punishment for buying or selling of votes have thus far never been applied.

But money knows of other and more devious ways than the illegal ones. The most important of these is propaganda, the forming of public opinion by means of the control of the press and other modern means of public information. It is not unlawful to sell one's labor and one's talent to the highest

---

[1] J. S. Mill, *Essay on Representative Government* (London, 1861), p. 214.
[2] James Bryce, *Modern Democracies* (London, 1921), vol. II, p. 534.

bidder. It is a fact that the middle-class capitalist parties usually rule a press that is many times larger than what would seem to be proportional to their own party strength. The advertisers' power over the press is well known. Similarly, the paper that is strong in capital buys up and keeps new talents merely to prevent them from working in the service of opposite parties. All this brings it about that the conservative forces that are strong in capital are able to get a lead in the struggle for the minds of the people. Those forces, however, as was mentioned before, have not shown themselves able to prevent in the long run a development in a radical direction. The propaganda brings about, one might say, a secret, mental distortion. Money wields power only through persuasion. Its victim is not aware of being one, and its perpetrators are themselves presumably inclined to believe in the disinterested justice of their cause. It is easy for self-interest to disguise itself in idealistic garments, even in one's own eyes. But, as a result, suggestive propaganda, as well as corruption, leads to a perversion of political power in hoodwinking and spiritually bamboozling certain population groups into a policy that does not harmonize with their "true" interests (see Chapter V, Sec. 5).

Actual corruption also exists when political favor is bought for other than current coin. Political influence can even be misused for this purpose. An example is favoritism or patronage, when politicians exert pressure upon the administration in order to obtain public posts for friends and party colleagues. That form of corruption especially has played a big part in France. In the United states, it is well known how the party organization can be developed into a machine for mutual aid and support, in which the safeguard of private interests is intimately linked up with the exercise of public functions. A professional politician ("carpetbagger") who gradually loses every honest inner conviction and makes politics exclusively a means of livelihood also represents a degeneration that leads democracy away from its idea.

Finally, as the relatively mildest form of corruption, one might mention the inclination that sets the interests of party and party organization above the common welfare. Genuine faith in the justice of the cause will here often be entangled with personal desire for power and glory or a reckless wish to promote the interests of one's own group at the expense of all others.

The critics of democracy have often severely pointed out and deprecated the moral stagnation and the muddling of public affairs that are a result of corruption in all its different forms, party egoism, and misleading propaganda. And that criticism was fully justified. The democratic institutions are often not what they ought to be, and no one who believes in democracy and in its values has any reason to hide that fact. On the contrary, only by exposing clearly all its shady sides to the daylight is it possible to overcome them.

But the great decisive question in a balance in favor of or against democracy is whether these repulsive misgrowths are characteristic of democracy or whether the same kind of stragglers grow from any root. The latter may safely be assumed. All kinds of corruption have their roots in human nature, since it contains certain asocial tendencies. The effective way of combatting this is publicity in political life and an awakened public consciousness. These things are part and parcel of democracy. It is a historical fact that corruption a hundred or two hundred years ago, in the era of royal absolutism and at the beginning of the democratic era, was far worse than it is in our day. In the eighteenth century, Walpole could look over the British Parliament and say, "Every one of these men has his price." Robespierre won fame for his—unique—incorruptibility. As late as the nineteenth century in Britain, the system of bribery flourished. Only gradually, as democracy became more firmly established, did public criticism arise, which put an end at any rate to bribery and other crude forms of corruption. In the dictatorships, there is indeed not so much talk about corruption. Open criticism would be dangerous for the security of the state and is not tolerated. But precisely under these conditions does the rottenness grow like a fungus in the dark. It comes to the surface when the bosses occasionally undertake a mutual reckoning, or when the whole abscess bursts and discloses the striving for power, the mutual intrigues, plotting, spying upon one another, denunciations, and the party bigwigs' common self-enrichment at the expense of the common people. No, there is indeed no reason to believe that the worse aspects of human nature should find less favorable scope for development in the authoritarian states. On the contrary. "All power corrupts," a famous British historian has said, "and absolute power corrupts absolutely," and he has thus expressed a general truth which history has often confirmed. Lying and inflammatory propaganda, too, have the best scope in dictatorships. In these the population, which from childhood is brought up in uncritical submission to the system's dogmas—Blood and Soil, the Aryan Myth, or Marxism—is the defenseless victim of a systematic regimentation and planned violence for the furthering of the ends pursued by the ruling clique.

Let us therefore recognize our weaknesses and endeavor to overcome them. Democracy is no Heaven on Earth. But let us not be lured into believing that anything might be gained in that respect by giving up the publicity and free criticism which actually are the best weapons of good will in the struggle against all forms of corruption.

2. The Negative Revaluation of the Ideas of Democracy

Democracy rests upon the will to mutual understanding and assumes therefore conversation, joint discussions, public debate, and the conclusion of compromise. The supporters of democracy see a value in this. Its opponents see the matter in another light. They call debate empty talk, and compromise, lack of principle. They regard the wish for understanding as the outcome of cowardice, the lack of courage to assume responsibility, and praise instead the ruthless decision which is carried out without begging others for support. The parliamentary assemblies are called discussion clubs where the keynote is twaddle, not action. Thus two different attitudes reflect themselves in their divergent estimation of the same thing, and every individual has to form his own point of view. What for one is twaddle is for the other a sign of respect for one's fellow being's moral worth, his autonomy, as the mainstay of all social life. The theoretical critique must restrict itself to drawing attention to individual misrepresentations. People often talk, for instance, about democracy's irresponsibility. This is misleading. The characteristic of democracy is not that responsibility disappears, but that it is shared and spread over as many as possible. The ideal would be that every single citizen should feel himself coresponsible for his town's, his county's, and his country's fate. In the authoritarian state, on the other hand, the tendency is toward the placing of all responsibility in the hands of one man. In the war-crimes trials all the war criminals stood there miserably like dummies, none wishing to acknowledge any responsibility but all thrusting it from themselves onto the one who had also evaded the burden. The same mentality obtains with the average man. Politics is none of his business, it is something the Führer "arranged." It is in such a state that one may talk of irresponsibility and quite naturally so, for these items freedom and responsibility, compulsion and irresponsibility, have always belonged together.

The same revaluation is made also of the other ideas of democracy. Peace and justice, tolerance and humanity, become weakness, slackness, and slave ethics. Instead, the will to power, brutal use of violence, and the heroic struggle are praised—or else these methods are considered at any rate as unavoidable and acceptable. The ideal of liberty seems to be the only one the authoritarian ideology has not dared to tackle. The *SS.* man reached for his revolver when he heard the word culture—but it was never possible to revaluate liberty and set up conditions of slavery as ideal for the people. Instead of that, they proceeded to disparage liberty, its possibilities and its significance. They wished to make out that the liberty of which the democratic states made a display was in reality merely an appearance, a shewbread for the people, and never could be anything else; at the same time it was maintained that political freedom actually was not of decisive importance for the average man. His wish is not self-rule, but authority and leadership, not a free tongue but a full stomach. On this point, Nazis and Communists were touchingly in agreement. With true German dialectic, the Nazis further availed themselves of the trick of reinterpreting the concept of liberty to make it mean its very opposite. "True" freedom is not independence for the individual but his full subservience to the state, the people, and the Führer, who realize the individual's "true" will. Thus, they succeeded in being able to assert that the "true" freedom can only be found in the dictatorship.

3. New Points of View

(a) Since Plato, it has often been maintained that democracy is a nuisance because it is government by the incompetent. The people lack, both intellectually and morally, the necessary prerequisites for self-rule. They are ignorant, stupid, and uninterested. They are led by their instincts, not by reason, insight, and moral judgment. Popular rule must of necessity lead to incompetence, bungling, and neglect. Dilettantism and folly replace insight. Plato was of the opinion that government ought to be left to the wise and competent, the scientists, and since his time many persons—naïve and well-meaning or sly and calculating—have taken up the same argument in different variations. It has been asserted that, particularly in our own day, this consideration has weight. Government has become so complicated that it can be mastered only by experts. The more tasks the modern state draws within its orbit, the more unwieldy and complex the state machinery becomes, and errors in administration become more fateful. The complex economic context, hidden from the layman, causes economic interference to have quite different results from those envisaged at short view. Likewise those who, during a crisis, participate in a run on the banks, precisely by so doing, increase the difficulties; a state which, in order to protect its currency, introduces trade restrictions perhaps only succeeds in causing all states to become impoverished by a policy of economic isolation. Conditions today have more than ever outgrown the competence of the man in the street. He acts in part blindly. The game of foreign policy, with all its finesses, is incomprehensible to him and hardly interests him. Wilson's idea of the abolition of secret diplomacy in order to place foreign policy in the hands of the people was foredoomed to failure. The same applies in all spheres; only the well-informed expert is in a position to solve the problems in a satisfactory and fortunate way. The goal must therefore be a political system that places power in the hands of the really qualified.

As against this critique, it must in the first place be maintained that even if its assumptions are otherwise valid, it could not simply lead to a preference for every form of authoritarian government to democracy, but only the special form in which power is given to the actually qualified, the wise and competent. Unfortunately, nobody has yet been able to indicate how to determine in practice who these people are, and how to set up a system of government such that they will certainly be the ones who obtain power. It is easy to dismiss a utopia, more difficult to point out a way for its realization. In all hitherto extant authoritarian forms of government, the ruling clique has claimed to be the elite that possesses the particular qualifications which entitle it to power, but substantiation thereof has never consisted in anything but their own pretension. In the older aristocracies, noble birth was considered to provide the individual with blue blood which set him above all others. In the nineteenth-century bourgeois-capitalist society, it was the bourgeois virtues, property and culture, that were called upon for legitimation. In the modern dictatorships, the party roll is the decisive factor. At any rate, the bare facts are simply these: a certain social group has conquered power and maintains that it is the elite and therefore called upon to rule. The selection is based not upon a test that demonstrates competence, but upon an established situation of power.

At most it could be said that a dictatorship offers the best conditions for the selection of leaders and that it is therefore approximately correct to say that those who are best suited are called upon to rule. In a democracy, it is said, mediocrity itself chooses mediocrities. The commonplace person seeks in his leaders a reflection of his own pettiness and instinctively hates everyone who in any way stands out above the common herd. He only bows to him who, in the struggle for power, substantiates his natural call for leadership. In a dictatorship, therefore, natural selection sees to it that there is scope for men of real leadership, who carry the law in their own hands and rule by virtue of their inner greatness.

This theory of leader selection, which is taken from Hitler's *Mein Kampf* (see Chapter III, Sec. 4), is obviously made to fit precisely Hitler's own case, and may well also have a certain justification just in so far as that person who first seizes power and founds a dictatorship is concerned. Caesar, Napoleon, Hitler—each of them has actually proved to possess certain faculties above the average, regardless of how differently one would evaluate them. But the matter presents itself quite otherwise with regard to the whole of the remainder of the leader class in a dictatorship and the leader's successors. Here too there occurs a "selection" through "fight," that is, through cringing, ingratiation, bribery, espionage, delation, collusion, and treason, the whole of this competitive struggle for power behind the scenes according to the best gangster pattern, as the German collapse has so clearly shown. The same methods were also known in Imperial Rome and may, according to the nature of the thing, be found again in every leader dictatorship. When the leader's will is the supreme law and everyone's place in the sun depends on him, the way to power consists in winning the leader's favor by every means. But it is clear that the mental characteristics and character qualities that assure success in that struggle have nothing to do with real leadership qualities for the well-being of the people.

To this may be added, as has been pointed out by Hayek,[1] that various circumstances make it likely that every dictatorial party will find its most faithful supporters, and thus also its leaders, not among the best but rather among the worst elements of the population. The party demands from its members absolute conformity, unconditional and unqualified support for a number of dogmas and evaluations. But experience shows that with higher culture, intelligence, and human personality there generally follows a differentiation in outlook and taste that makes conformity to party absolutism and totalitarianism difficult. This results in a tendency to recruit the nucleus preferably from among coarse and single-minded fanatics who are more dominated by primitive group instincts than by trained intelligence and developed ethics, or from among the simple minded, impressionable, and characterless whom one can get to accept any ready-made creed by dinning it into their ears, or, finally, from among the cynical, unconscientious careerists who are willing for their own private gain to fall in with those who are strongest. Another circumstance that acts in the same direction is the fact that it seems easier for people to unite in a common hate, envy, and aggression against a common foe than in a positive and constructive coöperation. The common foe, whether internal (Jews, Kulaks) or external, (Encirclement, Capitalist Countries), belongs therefore among the dictatorship's prime requisites. Any organization that is to hold great masses welded together in a common iron discipline needs preferably to play upon the

---

[1] F. Hayek, *The Road to Serfdom* (London: George Routledge and Sons, 1944), p. 102–103.

instincts of hatred and aggression and is attractive mainly to natures in which those traits are dominant.

In a democracy the leader is selected through free competition for the people's confidence. Here, too, it is possible that the qualities that lead to victory are not always those which are the best qualification for leadership. Perhaps he who shouts loudest and promises most may win favor for a time, although he is merely a weathercock. All the same, there probably is no better method than open competition, which at all times puts the candidate under public criticism and popular judgment. As Lincoln said, you can fool some of the people all the time, and all the people some of the time, but you cannot fool all the people all the time. The method of open competition has the particular advantage that mistakes can be rectified, and experience has shown that in any case it is not true that the people are incapable of electing leaders who surpass the average. Roosevelt and Churchill were more than commonplace persons and were at least on a level with Mussolini, Hitler, and Stalin.

There is thus no reason to assume that "competence" has greater scope in an autocracy than in a democracy. It may be added that the criticism of incompetence in democracies rests upon a number of untenable assumptions.

In the first place, according to the principles of democracy, it is by no means the task of the common man to govern country and state. That is the task of the government. The man in the street may not conclude trade agreements, lay down the rates of exchange, or draw up laws. Many of these things are beyond his understanding, true enough. All that is required of him is that he should put his trust in others who have better understanding of those things and that he, in broad outline, shall be able to judge whether those to whom he has given his confidence are worthy of it and use it in a way of which he can approve. In order to exercise this judgment he does not require learning and science. It rests more on a sound judgment and moral honesty, and, so far as these qualities are concerned, there is nothing to indicate that they could not be found to an adequate measure among a people brought up in democratic traditions of public spirit and vigilant criticism. The conflict which, in Denmark and other occupied countries, has raged deep among the population over the problems of postwar justice may in a way be regrettable, but nevertheless, seen from another point of view, it is a sound and happy sign of the vigilant watchfulness with which a really public matter is followed and appraised by practically the whole population. There is no question here of any "incompetence," or of lack of comprehension and interest. It is good that this matter has not been left to experts, to jurists alone, but has become a question in which the entire people feels coresponsibility.

This example discloses also another error in the reasoning. The demand that government ought to be left to the wise and competent, to the experts, rests upon the assumption that the tasks of government are of a purely technical nature and may therefore be solved on a purely scientific basis so long as human knowledge is adequate. When it is a question of building a bridge of a certain capacity or a radio station with a certain range, nobody would dream of leaving those tasks to common people. Clearly those things ought to be left to special experts. In the same way, it is held, tasks of government, too, ought to be left to special experts in these domains—economists, lawyers, diplomats, sociologists. The comparison, however, is quite wrong. In order to understand this, it is necessary to remember that the only thing science can teach us is facts and their mutual, regular connections. Economics, for instance, can possibly teach us that a fall in the exchange rate will result in certain economic effects; law and sociology may teach us that a certain act of legislation may be regarded as involving certain consequences. On the other hand, science may also offer guidance when it is a question of what measures ought to be taken in order to achieve a certain desired result. The economist can possibly explain what measures would be best suited to counteract unemployment. The lawyer and the sociologist may point out what legislation would be best calculated to fight criminality in a certain area. But already here the guidance of science is limited and conditional. It will seldom be the case that there is only one way that leads to the goal. When more are available, the choice will depend on a number of opinions and judgments that are outside the domain of science.

Here we touch the crux of the matter. Science can and will, it is to be hoped, provide us with constantly increasing knowledge of how the world is ordered, how it functions, and what effects therefore one or another intervention in its mechanism will have. But all the knowledge in the world can never in any fashion directly give rise to the demand for a certain mode of conduct. Knowledge is knowledge, nor can it ever be anything else. All activity springs from a more or less conscious will or striving toward a goal. This very phenomenon of spontaneity has nothing to do with knowledge and information, and no science can teach us what our aim "ought" to be. All that theoretical insight can do is to guide us toward the goal we seek, give us the greatest possible knowledge of how we move, what will be the consequences of our actions in various respects, so that there is at any rate a possibility for our choice to be made after thorough reflection and in the light of the greatest possible insight into all the facts. Reflection and rational insight will then often rouse other impulses than the desire that is directly wakened by certain stimuli. Thus the mature, deliberate, and rational action differs from the blind and purely spontaneous one.

If now everybody were agreed to aim at a unique, common goal which could be attained only by a unique, definite way, then science would undeniably be in a position to give an unambiguous directive for the only right line of action. But none of these assumptions is true. Quite on the contrary, the fact is that people strive after a great number of different goals, and each of these may be reached by different means. Rational decision presupposes a judicious weighing of the order of precedence and relative importance of the different ends, and then of the different means, according to their smaller or greater capacity to further or impede the attainment of those ends. Since now this many-sided weighing cannot be reduced to a quantitative, objective measurement of concrete magnitudes of the same order, it is inevitable that the choice comes to depend on subjective factors and estimations as regards both the drawing up of the scale of purposes aimed at, and the means used to succeed in that direction. And since, moreover, the information science can give with regard to the relation between ends and means is often most vague and problematic, it will be understood that scientific knowledge is actually far from capable of guiding our actions unambiguously. Naturally, the greatest possible knowledge of the world in which we live is desirable if we do not wish to act heedlessly. But even assuming the best possible knowledge, there always remains a judgment and a choice with regard to where we want to go and how we wish to reach our goal. To decide this is the actual political task, which lies beyond the authority of science and the experts.

All this shows that experts are indeed of the greatest importance. Without them society would be acting blindly. But expert opinion is not the last word in the matter. The Platonic idea that the scientists are called upon to govern the state is based upon the intellectual delusion that the right deed is exclusively a question of right understanding.

Once this fallacy has been overcome, there is no longer anything paradoxical or unreasonable in the system in force in a democratic state, according to which the supreme political control rests with the people and not with the experts. Each of these two parties has its own role. The experts place their knowledge and understanding at the disposal of the people's representatives, while the latter, and in the last resort the whole people, undertake the political decision on the aims and the weighing of the means. This function, experience goes to show, is carried out best precisely by people who themselves are not specialists but who possess a sound common sense, a sense of what is stirring within the people, and the faculty of waking slumbering forces and leading the development towards new goals. Experience also shows that scientists within a people are evenly divided among the different political tendencies, which seems to suggest that their political judgment is not essentially different from that of ordinary mortals. There is hardly any doubt that if the government were left to a parliament of scientists there would be exactly the same disagreements as now among opinions representing the current political views. On the contrary, one may rather assume that the result might be even worse, if the experts were each allowed to look after those affairs of state most closely corresponding to his own domain. Experts are, so far as general judgment is concerned, often remarkably one-eyed. Their one-sided life occupation results in a corresponding one-sided scale of values. A common cottage owner who studies the expert gardener's instructions receives the impression that he ought to alter his whole way of life if he wishes to see a rose in his garden. His whole time must be spent on fertilizing, trimming, watering, grafting, clipping. The same exorbitant demands are made on him by health experts, dietitians, pedagogues, physical-training teachers, and similar specialists, and precisely the mutual incompatibility of all those demands teaches him that, when all is said and done, it is he himself who must put everything in its place by distributing his forces and interests in a suitable manner among the different ends. It is the same in political life. If the military experts were to regulate our defense system, the pedagogical experts the educational system, the churchmen the Church, the dietitians our nutrition, they would each of them overstate certain ends and quickly come into insoluble conflict. Each of them would strive to make all of us into passionate militarists, students, churchgoers, vegetarians. It is the politicians who must put things in their place by seeking a reasonable adjustment between the different interests and purposes.

The experts' task is therefore not to govern country and

state. Their place is not in the government but in the administration and on special boards and commissions. A trustworthy and expert staff of officials supplemented by specialists in different fields is a prerequisite for democracy as it is for every other form of government.

Nor, on the other hand, is it the task of the man in the street to govern the country or to form an expert opinion on all the problems of government. What is expected of the common man in a democracy is that he shall make up his mind about the political problems in their broad generality, lay down in broad outline the course to be followed, and make sure that the people's representatives exercise their mandate satisfactorily in accordance with that course. The solution of that task presupposes no exceptional intellectual faculties or profound expert knowledge. The common man's wisdom will be his sound judgment, that is, his ability tactfully and judiciously to compare and weigh a large number of great and small considerations. This ability is not innate. One may be born a poet or mathematician but one is not born with common sense. That is the result of practical experience in contact with people. It presupposes moral autonomy together with the relativism and tolerance which only maturity and practical experience bring.

The development of that ability, of course, presupposes a certain mental development and alertness in the people who are to govern themselves. I have already had on more than one occasion the opportunity to stress that fact. The decisive thing is a certain education which enables the people to judge general problems, and, in particular, an upbringing in public spirit which determines the necessary interest in public affairs. In this respect the people's participation is particularly important in popular movements and organizations, such as trade-unions, coöperative societies, producers' coöperatives, womens' organizations, educational associations, or temperance movements, as well as in local government. Common people trained and matured in work of that kind have certainly better qualifications for participating in the government of the country than many a scholar who, despite his specialized knowledge —or precisely because of it—lacks ordinary knowledge of the world and its people. It is quite untrue, as the critique alleges, that the man in the street is dull and uninterested in politics. The total vote in the enlightened democracies is often close to the maximum that can be expected when allowance is made for sickness and other impediments; in Denmark, for instance, it is about 85 per cent. As regards the level of intelligence there is not much that can be said. Experience has shown that intelligence is evenly distributed according to a sliding scale. Numbers are largest in the middle; The "normally gifted" (I. Q. 90–110) constitute 45 per cent of the population. From here, the numbers decrease evenly in both directions, giving way, respectively, to the very intelligent and the very stupid (I. Q. over 140 and I. Q. under 60). It is obvious that most people are of "average intelligence"; only a very few "highly gifted" or "pure nonentities." Every attempt at percentual grouping into different categories (see Chapter III, Sec. 3) is arbitrary and meaningless. The grouping is simply a definition of the different categories. What other measure should one have in mind, for instance, for the designation "highly gifted" than just that it is that degree of intelligence that occurs among a certain arbitrarily fixed minority of people. To use such formulations as evidence of the population's "low" level of intelligence and as argument against democracy is extraordinarily naïve.

In conclusion, the different functions that occur in a democracy, together with the claim to competence that belongs to each of them, may be thus summarized. *The people rule.* The word "rule" indicates quite well the general course-setting and -controlling role that falls to the electorate. This demands a certain education, the development of a public spirit and common sense. The politicians, that is, the people's elected representatives, govern the state, by which is meant that they take the particular decisions that are deemed suited for following the course laid down by the people. That function presupposes the same competence in an intensified form. In this the people's representatives are doubly aided by the experts. The latter's role as free experts is partly one of advising the politicians in their decisions, partly, as public servants employed in the service of the state, to carry out the directives given by Congress or Parliament and the administrative branch. In the first respect, it is theoretical scientific knowledge, in the second, it is technical ability and political loyalty, that are of chief importance.

The most striking argument against the critique of incompetence is perhaps in the last analysis the fact that the democracies exist and have existed and have solved both common and unusual tasks on the whole as well as other states have done. Bryce, who carefully studied life in the six leading democracies, came to the conclusion that they had shown themselves as capable as any of exercising the normal functions of government: to provide security from internal and external enemies, to assure honest administration of justice, to carry out an effective administration of public affairs and provide assistance to the citizens in their various activities.[1] Twice in our lifetime the democracies have waged war to a victorious conclusion against authoritarian regimes. Culturally, both large and small democratic societies are leading the way. As against these facts, all talk of democracy, the government of the "incompetent," leading to unskillfulness and misrule must become silent.

(b) In most recent times the main argument of the dictatorships against democracy has been the latter's powerlessness, its ineffectiveness or impotence. Though its leaders be ever so competent, the system itself, based upon party division, balance of power, and compromise, prevents them from being able to carry out a policy effectively and consistently according to a plan deriving from given principles. Many cooks spoil the broth. Many advisers result in endless discussions and

[1] James Bryce, *Modern Democracies* (London, 1921), vol. II, p. 577.

vacillation on all decisions. Parliaments are discussion clubs; discipline and conformity to a common purpose are rendered impossible. The idea of state retires before party interests. There is plenty of talk but no action. Everybody puts in his oar, all press for their demands and particular interests, none is capable of accomplishing anything. "For God's sake, let us put an end to that comedy, give us a leader who can put things right and get something accomplished . . ."—something like this was the leitmotiv of many who, between the two world wars, saw the only solution in strong and dictatorial government.

Now one must first of all remember that this description of democracy is by no means a picture of how it functions at its best, in the place where it has become rooted in tradition. It is actually a caricature of democracy that is resorted to, the Weimar Constitution and the other new states' rootless democracy of immature peoples. It is true enough that in those states the deep-going party divisions in connection with the unaccustomedness to coöperation threatened to bring the entire state apparatus to a standstill. As early as 1923, Germany had to resort twice to emergency powers (on October 13 and December 8) which ushered in temporary periods of dictatorship. It would clearly be unfair simply to condemn every democracy by virtue of those special experiences.

Nevertheless it has to be admitted that there is essential truth in the arguments. It cannot be denied that when a small group assumes dictatorial powers in the state there is greater scope for bold and constructive planning at long range. In a democracy it is necessary to proceed more slowly and cautiously. Party programs are quick to conceive great and fundamental plans for social organization. But to carry them out, debates and consideration of many aspects as well as difficult work are required to win over the people to new ideas. Experience has shown that even when a single party succeeds in winning a majority this still does not mean that it is able immediately to carry out its platform. The lesser effectiveness of democratic methods reveals itself also in the fact that they are temporarily suspended when, as in wartime, it is really necessary to direct all the energies of the nation in one certain direction.

It must therefore be admitted that he who values efficiency in the direction of the state has reason to that extent to prefer dictatorship to democracy. What consequences this will have for one's choice will depend partly on how highly one values efficiency; partly on the idea one has of the degree of inefficiency of democracy; and finally, of course, on a weighing of the value of efficiency in relation to the benefit of democratic liberties at the expense of which the greater efficiency can alone be obtained.

Concerning the first point, the liberals do not see any value at all in a strong and effective government. On the contrary, they see danger in every concentration of power that makes possible a far-reaching interference with accustomed liberties. There is more than enough government in the country. It is not more interference and bureaucracy that we need but, on the contrary, greater freedom for individual development and the free play of forces. The liberals will therefore always be the sincere and sworn friends of democracy. To them the argument of inefficiency means nothing at all that might endanger their democratic faith.

It is different with the socialists. Their economic ideals assume precisely an enlarging of the tasks of the state that do not allow of realization without a considerable concentration of power and effectiveness of the government. There is a choice before them. They realize that the democratic way may be long and difficult. They might, perhaps, be able to reach their goal more rapidly if they were to throw overboard democratic ideals of peace, justice, and liberty and instead achieve power by force and carry through their wishes by means of dictatorship.

It is this choice that divides the socialists into two groups: the social-democrats, who cling to democratic methods and ideals, and the communists, who traditionally are willing to give them up in favor of the greater effectiveness of dictatorship. The deciding factor in the choice is certainly primarily the extent to which the democratic ideals of peace, justice, and liberty have had a chance of realizing themselves and gaining ascendancy over minds. In Russia, the mass of the population was, at the time of the collapse of tsarism, without any of the prerequisites for real democracy; the spirit of liberty had no roots in the national tradition, and dictatorship was therefore bound to be the logical consequence, at any rate for the time being. In a country such as Denmark, things are different. Through a century of free constitutional life, through the fight for parliamentary government, through popular local government and the popular movements, the democratic idea of liberty has there become a reality to the people to such an extent that even the great majority of the socialist workers hold on to them and see their goal in a union of socialism and democracy (Social-Democracy), and not in a replacement of the present capitalist democracy by a socialist dictatorship.

The basic valuations themselves that underlie the choice cannot, as I have pointed out earlier and have thoroughly explained, either be scientifically proved or criticized; on the other hand, the conceptions of reality on which the valuations are based can be. In that respect, the communist theory is based upon an exaggerated, untenable conception of the inefficiency of the democratic system. It contends that the parliamentary way to socialism is not only longer and more difficult than direct action, but that it must at the outset be regarded as basically impossible. There is therefore no choice other than revolution and dictatorship. I have discussed more fully in Chapter III, Section 5 the content of this idea, pointed out its untenability, and stated that no doubt its practical significance is at most to justify a point of view that has already been adopted for other reasons. I daresay there is no one who has become a Communist as a result of the theoretical conviction that the democratic methods will never succeed. But once one has become a Communist because the wish to achieve quickly certain economic ends outweighs the respect for and love of democratic ideals, it is natural to accept a theory that removes all doubt and criticism by laying down dogmatically that the development toward socialism cannot take place within the framework of democracy.

VII.

THE SOCIAL CONDITIONS OF DEMOCRACY

1. INTRODUCTION

The following exposition on the last two chapters concerns only such readers as are in agreement with me that democracy is a human value, the basis of a culture that we wish to preserve and continue. From that assumption there arise a number of practical problems. How shall the fundamental principles of democracy—majority rule and civil liberties—be worked out in detail and put into effect so as to realize in the best possible manner the ideas of peace, liberty, justice, and humanity? How shall the constitutional regulations relating to the exercise of political power and to the legal status of the citizens be precisely formulated so as to create a truly democratic constitution? This technical-juridical question cannot be answered in the abstract and absolutely by constructing out of the democratic principles, once and for all, an ideal constitution as being the truly democratic one. Nobody has ever been given the task of framing a constitution without anything to go on, from *tabula rasa*, as it were. Every actual constitutional problem arises out of a quite definite situation, and is a problem of reform, the premises of which are a society with given political traditions and institutions, with a given social and economic structure. The task is always one of taking a step in a certain direction, starting out from the quite specific situation, and therefore is never the same in any two cases. It should be added that, even apart from the historical conditions that set their limit upon the freedom to reshape, the democratic principles may be realized by more than one method, conditioned by the weight put upon various considerations and ideas.

This situation brings it about that there is plenty of scope for constitutional variations, as experience also shows. Democracy does not evolve in precisely the same manner in any two countries. Each people has its characteristic institutions and traditions, each epoch its peculiar problems. The discussion of the problems of constitutional reform must therefore of necessity be bound by locality and epoch.

Before any of these constitutional problems are discussed (in Chapter VIII), this chapter will deal with some questions of more general scope. These are the questions of democracy's *social conditions*. It may be well to find out the forms for the realization of the ideas of democracy. But will the apparatus function in practice according to expectation? One has to reckon with the possibility that there are forces at work in the social fabric, in society, that will be capable of putting to shame all theoretical calculations that fail to take them into account, and to reduce the democratic institutions to illusory formalities. I have pointed out earlier that democracy is not something that can be introduced all ready-made, but that there are certain social-psychological prerequisites for its growth that are best brought about by the gradual struggle for democracy itself. In the same way, it is also conceivable that democracy has certain social-economic prerequisites without which it will be condemned to failure and decay.

In the discussion of these problems, I distinguish between a static and a dynamic point of view. The *static* point of view has as its object the compatibility of democracy with a social organization that rests on a consistent capitalist or socialist economy which is considered to be firmly established as being generally approved by the great majority of the citizens (Secs. 2 and 3). The *dynamic* has as its object the resources of democracy in a society in transition from a capitalist to a socialist economy, that is, a society where there is no longer— or not yet—general agreement on the fundamental moral and economic principles for the organization of production relationships (Sec. 4).

2. Democracy and Capitalism

It might have been taken for granted from the outset that democratic government and capitalist economy are entirely consistent. Historically, it was capitalism that paved the way for democracy. It was a bourgeois capitalism that brought about the French Revolution and the latter, in turn, democracy. Capitalism is liberalistic and, as mentioned earlier (Chapter V, Sec. 5), there is a lot to be said for the fact that the difficulties that may be connected with popular government are least under a liberal system. The less the government interferes in the economic sphere, the less also will be the tensions that may arise in connection with the exercise of political power.

Nevertheless, it is a firm part of the Communist doctrine that bourgeois democracy is merely an appearance, a deception, which is to legalize and hide the actual situation, the dictatorship of the capitalist minority over the proletariat. Into this train of thought, which has already been discussed earlier in this book (Chapter III, Sec. 5), there enter two component parts. In the first place, it is maintained that political democracy under bourgeois capitalism cannot realize itself in accordance with its own ideas. The "real" popular will does not gain expression. The most important argument in this respect is the power which the capitalist-directed propaganda and the whole of the existing system exercise over the minds of the people, so that large sections of the population are prevented from awakening to class consciousness and are persuaded to assume a conservative, counterrevolutionary attitude in conflict with their "true" interests. Capitalism can therefore quietly introduce the majority vote and allow freedom of speech. The capitalists know that so long as they control the factors of production they control also ideas, and need not fear any misuse of the political toy they have placed in the people's hands. On the contrary, the people's self-gratifying occupation with that toy will only serve to divert its attention from more serious things.

The first link of the reasoning is thus that political liberty in the sense of the people's right of self-determination is an illusion. To this is joined as the second link the conception that political liberty, both as right of self-determination and as freedom of expression, is not in itself of any decisive value. The desire for this liberty is a luxury requirement, of secondary importance for the common man. The first consideration is economic liberation, a full stomach, and not a free tongue. Therefore, since political democracy is neither of any use as a tool for a proletarian policy nor of decisive value in itself, the Communists are willing to sacrifice it in favor of a proletarian dictatorship—while at the same time they take comfort in the fact that it will only be a transition phenomenon, leading to the stateless society without coercion.

The actual content of the Communist critique may be expressed thus: Political democracy as commonly understood is a social impossibility. Democratic forms under capitalism are unable to realize their meaning and goal, satisfaction of the people's true will. If that goal is to be achieved, capitalism will have to be overcome and replaced by socialism. But that requires dictatorship and thus the dropping of democratic forms.

Similar points of view were also expressed in Nazi propaganda, which referred to the Western Democracies as plutocracies and branded them as merely formal in contrast to the true German democracy. Here, too, is the idea that in the usual democracy it is actually the rich who lord it over the poor, and that the true popular will finds its expression only in the leader-dictatorship.

The social-democratic conception in the Western and Northern democracies is distinguished from the Communist and Nazi points of view first and foremost by the fact that they do not disparage the democratic ideals. The ideas of self-government and liberty are clearly and unequivocally professed. At the same time it is recognized that it is a glaring propagandist exaggeration to maintain that capitalist propaganda renders democracy illusory. The actual facts are that capital, together with the sluggishness of the existing system, inherited traditions, and prejudices, gives the conservative forces a lead in the propaganda, but only a lead, which by no means precludes the advance and victory of radical and socialist ideas. It is true that the Conservative and Liberal parties control the press and other means of propaganda which are much more than proportional to their actual party strength, but experience still shows that the formation of public opinion is not determined by the circulation of newspapers. During the 1936 Presidential campaign in the United States, the anti-Roosevelt press in Chicago ran into one and a half million copies, while the pro-Roosevelt press disposed of a circulation of only a third of a million. All the same, Roosevelt won by an overwhelming majority. All the progress that has been accomplished in the course of time as regards the people denies the assertion that capitalism is able to hypnotize the majority into marching blindly.

As a consequence, the social-democrats do not, like the Communists, demand that political liberty should be replaced by economic liberty, socialism instead of democracy. Instead of revolution and dictatorship, they believe in a continuous development of democracy in a socialist direction. There is no reason to cast overboard political democracy and its great humane values. It is another matter that political democracy in its present form is not enough in itself, not the final goal. The latter is a union of democracy and socialism. That idea is often expressed by saying that democracy is not complete before political democracy is developed into economic freedom. The liberty that the bourgeois, capitalist democracy guarantees is of a legal nature. The citizen is protected against the arbitrariness of others. He enjoys the legal freedom of entering into agreements and making the economic arrangements he wishes, freedom to express his opinions, and personal freedom. But all this does not prevent his being subject to the compulsion arising from economic inferiority and dependence. Property and economic power mean actually the facility for ordering and commanding other people. He who owns something may prohibit others from using it or only let them use it on certain terms. He who has economic power can force others to enter into economic agreements that they would never accept voluntarily. Freedom of contract is an actual freedom only for economic equals. As a result of these facts, the security, autonomy, and development of the personality that are the positive content of the formal freedom grow only in the soil of economic independence. Real freedom for the individual is therefore not achieved before democracy has developed to a point where it also includes economic democracy. (As previously pointed out, the expression "economic democracy" is unfortunate. What is meant by it is an extension of political power to include also a regulation of the economy in the interest of the common people. As the designation of this demand for expansion and equality, the word "socialism" ought to be used.)

As far as I am concerned, I am of the opinion that the moderate social-democratic criticism of democracy under a capitalist economy is justified. Democracy is no illusion, but, on the other hand, the influence of financial power and of social prestige is such that the game is not even, and irrational factors have the effect that the people's expressed will cannot always be regarded as the genuine expression of their true and well-understood interests. This gives rise to the question: what can be done to help democracy to a sounder development according to its own idea?

First of all, all the remains of direct *corruption* must of course be fought down. The direct purchase of political influence must not be tolerated in any form. Among modern, culturally advanced nations, however, the tangible forms of corruption play so small a role that any problem of importance hardly exists.

It is a different story with the distortion of public opinion that is brought about by a venal propaganda which works on the public according to the methods of modern publicity and mass psychology. It is possible nowadays to sell political conviction just as soap or a brand of ladies' stockings are sold. The means are, if necessary, concealment, distortion of the facts, and the subtle appeal to the irrational—people's vanity, fear, envy, hatred and prejudice—together with the suggestive force of repetition.[1] By these methods public discussion is transformed from a rational debate on ends and means into a propaganda duel in which the power of money becomes more and more decisive.

Naturally, there can be no question of forbidding capital to support a political party or its public propaganda. On the other hand, it seems reasonable to me to demand that light be publicly thrown on all political subsidies, as is done at present in Sweden. The citizen who wishes to participate in political life not merely by voting and speaking personally, but also by virtue of the funds at his disposal, should be allowed

---

[1] The fundamental law of all propaganda is the assumption that people are more easily influenced by appeals to their emotions than by appeals to their reason. The best conditions for propaganda are thus present when the person to be influenced by it is in a state of emotional excitement, as, for instance, in war time, or during a crisis with great social antagonisms. The greater the need for a certain belief (e. g. in favorable reports from the front), the greater the uncritical spirit with which the propaganda reports are accepted. Experience confirms that the worse off people are, the more readily they believe evil of others. An appeal to reason and reflection is often without any effect, once the emotions are roused. "An absurd assertion can be refuted far more effectively by another absurd assertion than by a correct logical argument. A logical refutation, however perfect it may be, can have the effect of increasing the faith in the absurd assumption, merely by attracting attention to that assumption. Politicians would therefore be wise not to base themselves, before public opinion, on reason in defense of their policy, but rather in giving apparent reasons that are calculated to make an impression on the emotions of the public. The mere repetition of nonsense will often be more convincing than the best logical arguments. An almost infallible means of bringing the views of a political opponent into discredit is to accuse him of sexual immorality. If one cannot do it with any justification, one can achieve just as good an effect by doing it without justification. It is always difficult to refute defamations of that kind, and even if it were possible, such a refutation will always make a far smaller impression on the public than an unfounded accusation of sexual excesses." (This quotation, taken from a Danish author, is an account of the opinion of the Italian sociologist, Pareto).

to do so, but it must be demanded that he should give particulars of it to the public. Knowledge of what backers are financing a certain political propaganda will be enlightening in many instances as to the real tendency of that propaganda.

But in the main the efforts should be directed not so much at forbidding or in some other way preventing an irresponsible propaganda, but rather at preventing it from achieving its end. This means that the question should be of making the population propaganda-proof to the greatest possible degree, indifferent to suggestive influences that are not founded on facts and reasonable arguments. This is a big goal which is not easy to achieve. Independent judgment and critical sense are not developed from one day to the next. It is a question of a long-range task. The means consist of education and public instruction. These subjects have rightly become in recent times the focus of democratic discussion. I am convinced that in the long run the fate of democracy will depend on the schools, youth work, and public instruction. *Education for democracy* has rightly become a slogan. This, in connection with thorough economic reconstruction of society (more about that later), are the two bulwarks of psychological and material nature which are to protect the peaceful progressive development from violent upheavals of the Nazi or Communist kind.

Education is never meant to produce an abstract personality but is always adaptation of the young individual to a certain community. The problem of pedagogy must therefore be tackled sociologically. The goal of education must be determined harmony with the society for which the education takes place. Education in the U.S.S.R. therefore must be quite naturally different from that in a democratic country. The pedagogical ideas must change, subject to the change that society itself undergoes. But on that point tradition and sluggishness will often bring it about that the development gets out of step: the pedagogical ideas fall quite behind the social development. Such is precisely the situation at present in Denmark. The goal is still essentially determined by hereditary, preconstitutional, liberal-capitalist ideals. Obedience, discipline, passivity, respect for King and Church as supreme authorities, the spirit of endeavor, striving, ambition, and competitive mentality are virtues that harmonized well with the liberal absolutist society of the first half of the nineteenth century. But they no longer tally with a democratic society in an increasing socialistic development. If education is to proceed toward democracy, then its goal must be formulated in accordance with democratic functions and ideas.

Characteristically, importance must be attached not to discipline and authoritarian conformity, but to initiative and self-reliance, together with fellow feeling, a will to coöperate, and responsibility toward the community. In the relation between individual and community a middle way is thus created between the one-sided individualism of liberalism and the totalitarian trend's equally one-sided idolization of the state and the sacrament of community. This middle way is not indecision or compromise, but the only fully valid expression of the leading idea of democracy: respect for every single individual's personality and moral autonomy. The consistent liberal individualism that leaves everyone to paddle his own canoe and fight his way as best he can in the struggle against all is actually the expression not of respect for one's fellow man but of indifference and ruthlessness. At the other end of the scale, much the same holds true in totalitarian collectivism, which requires absolute regimentation and unconditional capitulation to the demands of the community. The two extremes each denote their own form of ruthlessness, on the one hand because no one cares about the fate of his fellow men, on the other hand because no one cares about their individuality and integrity. Only free democratic coöperation among equal individuals, requiring at the same time a social consciousness and fellow feeling as well as integrity of the personality, expresses a genuine respect which demands solidarity, understanding, and tolerance toward the partners in such a coöperation. This balance between collectivism and individualism is also decisive for the relation between an education for social integration and group conformity on one hand and the development of an independent personality on the other. Every society builds on certain common values, and the necessity for such a common basis of faith and ideals becomes more evident the greater the sphere of life which is drawn into the orbit of government. An elementary influence over emotional disposition is therefore necessary, the more so the further the development tends toward socialism. But on this primary basis of group conformity it is important to give scope to free development of the many-sided personality.[1]

From the point of view of intelligence, importance must be attached, in democratic education, to the independent acquiring of knowledge and to critical appraisal, instead of the authority-bound and passive acquisition of a cut-and-dried mass of knowledge which still characterizes most European education. From the point of view of subject matter, education ought, to a higher degree, to be so organized that it may help the young to understand and to find their bearings in the community in which they are to live.

The deciding thing is that these ideals leave their mark on home, kindergarten, and elementary school. It is in the earliest years of life that character is formed. Later, the job must be continued in secondary school and college, and in adult education. A certain division of labor is natural. The elementary influencing of disposition toward the "democratic creed" naturally belongs to the first stage of education, the development into a nuanced personality to its later stage.

The enlightenment of the people referred to here as a safeguard for democracy against demagogic propaganda is not to be a hotchpotch of "interesting" fragments of all universal popularized knowledge, such as is dished out in certain entertaining periodicals and appeals more to curiosity or sensationalism than to a genuine thirst for knowledge and understanding.

[1] Cf. Karl Mannheim, *Diagnosis of Our Time* (London: Kegan Paul, Trench, Trubner & Co., 1943), pp. 31–94.

It is more important to teach the man in the street comparatively thoroughly about his vocation, the facts touching most closely upon his own sphere of life, than to fill him with popular science from various domains. At least from the point of view taken here, it is not "culture" that is to be the goal of public education but the development of the ability to think and to discern, and that is best achieved by limited but real knowledge. Beyond this, a certain elementary knowledge of history, sociology, economics, and politics will naturally be important, even though it is probably illusory to believe that with such knowledge the man in the street will be able to master more involved political problems.

Last but not least, the endeavor must be made to give as many as possible a share in the higher education which alone gives access both to full acquisition of culture and to real mastery of the theoretical problems of politics. In particular, access to the higher education which also opens the door to a number of important key positions in the community ought not to be reserved to the economically privileged but should be made to depend solely on a natural aptitude for study. By this is not meant that the most suitable higher education should have in all respects the character of existing university education. The standardization of intellects and the watering down of other social groups by robbing them of their best minds, which would take place if that were done, may have drawbacks that have to be taken into account.

3. Democracy and Socialism

When the social democrats stick to traditional democracy and at the same time desire the introduction of a socialist economy, the question arises whether these two ends are compatible. Should they not be, it will mean that social democrats are striving for an unattainable goal and are forced to make a choice. Either they must stick to democracy and renounce socialism, or else stick to socialism and write off democracy. Whatever their choice, it cannot be decided in theory, of course, but must depend on which of the two opposite values will prevail in the competition. In present-day discussion, the assumed incompatibility of democracy and socialism has been used as an argument against socialism, obviously taking for granted that the idea of dictatorship is so abhorrent that the majority of people will flatly refuse such a possibility. But actually there is nothing to prevent changing the point of view so that the incompatibility is used as an argument against democracy as being unsuitable for carrying out an economic reform regarded as absolutely imperative.

The first condition for being able to form an opinion about the problem is of course to be clear about what is meant by the two terms "democracy" (or "freedom") and "socialism." The discussion suffers because both terms are often used with unclear and vague meaning. In particular, the word "freedom" is often quite indefinite and its connection with the democratic form of government quite vague. I think that in the foregoing I have contributed to the clarification of these terms. Democracy means government in parliamentary form by the majority, and democratic freedom, means the maximum of autonomy which attaches to government by consent, together with the political and personal liberties which are its prerequisites—freedom of speech and organization, together with the rule of law. On the other hand, democracy has nothing further to do with liberalism. That freedom of action, especially of economic action, will be curtailed to a certain extent under a socialist economy therefore has nothing to do with the basic question of the compatibility of democracy and socialism. The problem must be simply whether the introduction of socialism will mean the abolition of majority rule and of the specifically democratic liberties.

The word "socialism" is often used, under the influence of older Marxist ideas, as synonymous with the passage of the means of production from private to state ownership. If the word is to designate the economic ideal that is set up by modern theory in the western countries, then that definition says too much or too little. It says too much because the formal property relationship of capital cannot be regarded as the deciding factor. Only the planned control of economic life in its essentials is decisive, and with the technique of the modern state such a control may easily be achieved while at the same time the formal property right is to a certain extent left in private hands. Whether one chooses one or the other course will depend entirely on technical considerations of expediency which vary with the different spheres of economic life. It says little because state ownership or state control in itself is only a means which can be used for greatly different ends. This is often overlooked, and people believe that state ownership or control, by itself, is identical with a planned economy directed toward the equality and heightening of the standard of living of the masses. Experience has taught us differently. In Nazi Germany, the planned economy was run according to the motto "Guns instead of butter," as a means to an imperialist policy of rearmament. In Soviet Russia, rearmament for defense purposes has in the same way been given priority over production of consumer goods, and, in addition, the U.S.S.R. has largely abandoned the ideas of economic equality that characterized the early period of the Revolution. This cannot be called socialism, even if one wishes to maintain that the deviation from the ideal has happened under duress. It therefore becomes necessary to add furthermore to the definition the point that social control shall have in view increased satisfaction of requirements and economic equalization to the advantage of the majority.

Particularly in Britain and Sweden, the question has been raised and formulated whether socialization will not of necessity lead to dictatorship. This is presumably a consequence of the fact that the social democratic parties in those countries are so strong that the possibility of socialization has closed in further and has made the problem acute. During the election campaign in Britain in the Spring of 1945, it was a main point in the propaganda from the Conservative quarters that the Labour Party's victory would lead to dictatorship. In Denmark, too, this argument has been used. The position in the debate, in broad outline, is that the Social Democratic politicians do not admit the existence of any problem. They simply refer to the fact that they have a deeply ingrained love, and have a will and desire, for democracy, and that it is their intention under all circumstances to hold on to the inherited liberties. On the other hand, the assertion that socialism leads to dictatorship is made to order for Liberal and Conservative politicians who will gladly take advantage of any possibility of giving the old, slightly stale scare of socialism a new life, by playing upon the revulsion for German methods and to turn to account the boom of freedom. In their political propaganda, both parties stick to generalities and postulates. An objective investigation of the problem has been undertaken by different scientists, economists and sociologists, and among them opinion is also divided, with a tendency to correspond to the particular writer's general attitude toward socialism and liberalism.

To my mind, it cannot be denied that there are problems, difficult problems, that cannot be avoided by merely burying one's head in the sand and relying upon good will. It must be recognized that the inner logic of things in connection with the ways of human nature may bring about pressure that puts all good resolutions to shame. The Social Democrats can not therefore avoid examining the matter. They would be wise to do so, at all events. The better known and understood the difficulties are, the greater the chance of their being surmounted. Party orthodoxy alone does not do it.

One of the authors who has defended with the greatest energy the claim that socialism is synonymous with dictatorship is the British economist F. H. von Hayek, whose book *The Road to Serfdom* has rightly attracted considerable attention. His main argument is that the comprehensive plan for the organization of the entire community and all its economic resources, which socialism means, cannot conceivably be accepted in the customary democratic parliamentary forms, that is, on the basis of public debate, discussions between the parties, and majority decision. The people might indeed perhaps agree that a plan shall be laid down, and that its purpose shall be "the common weal," "welfare for all," "social advantage," or another generality. But these stock-phrases do not actually say anything. The welfare and happiness of millions cannot be measured and weighed, but depend on an infinite number of incommensurable combinations. These cannot be appraised in relation to an unique, supreme, all-comprising goal, but presuppose a whole hierarchy of ends, a comprehensive scale of values which assures each individual interest and need its own place in the system. The people and their representatives will never be able to agree on such a concrete scale of values and the plan corresponding to it. There will be exactly as many opinions as there are people. The situation will be as if a group of people agree to go on a journey together, but cannot agree where to go. The result will be that they will go on a journey that most of them do not wish to undertake. This difficulty cannot be avoided by subdividing the plan into sections and, in the usual democratic procedure, bargaining and compromising so as to achieve a just settlement. The plan is indivisible and must be considered on the long view. Its parts are organically interconnected. To adopt a plan in that way would be just as unreasonable as to lay down the strategic plan for a campaign by a democratic procedure.

The consequence is that impatience with the bungling by the democratic organs will grow. There will be a demand that the direction of the plan be "taken out of politics" and placed in the hands of experts. This can be done formally by delegating the right of decision to an autonomous organ of experts. But this delegation is so comprehensive and essential, and to such a high degree without objective directives, that if it is carried out democratic control is actually thereby given up. Democracy is now a mere appearance. A dictator will be required.[1]

Others, among them the Swedish political scientist Herbert Tingsten,[2] have furthermore contended that socialization will also endanger the political freedom of expression. Planning, it is asserted, implies an enormous concentration of power in the state apparatus. The government has to decide what shall be produced and consumed, which branches of industry shall be encouraged at the expense of what others, at what levels prices and wages shall be fixed, and how the human material shall be used in the economic process. "Can one imagine such a concentration of power in the state without a restriction of liberty, in actual fact if not legally?" The different branches of production and different social groups will fight for the control of the state so as to turn it to their own account. The group that has once obtained power will not be able to tolerate criticism and opposition, let alone strikes and boycott, which would bring into jeopardy the carrying through of the plan and their position of power. It is therefore unlikely that a socialist state could refrain from using its enormous power to carry out also an "ideological plan," that is, it would have to suspend the freedom of political expression. What would the right to publish a newspaper really signify in such a state? Even if freedom to do so were formally given, the complete regulation of production would also include the different materials that are necessary to publication, which would therefore become dependent upon a system of licenses or concessions. Since advertising would be meaningless in a planned economy, the press would depend on state subsidy. In such a state of affairs, political power, to a far higher degree than the power of capital in the present society, would

---

[1] F. Hayek, *The Road to Serfdom* (London: George Routledge & Sons, 1944), p. 42 ff.
[2] Herbert Tingsten, *Demokratiens Problem* (The Problems of Democracy) (Stockholm: P. A. Nordstedt & Sønner, 1945), p. 204 ff.

come to dominate the press, and it is inconceivable that no advantage would be taken of it to direct public opinion.

The arguments advanced to prove that economic planning is the road to serfdom sound something like the foregoing. Now, what shall we think of it?

Hayek is undoubtedly right that it is not possible by a single formula, such as "the furthering of social advantage" or something similar, to indicate the aim of planning so that its content may be inferred therefrom, but that planning presupposes a comprehensive, detailed, and concrete appraisal of all integral interests and needs, with allocation of a definite place in an order of precedence. But from this philosophic truth it by no means follows that it is to be considered impossible to arrive at the adoption of a plan by the usual democratic majority procedure. This appears simply from the fact that already under existing conditions this method is used. The state regulation that actually existed during the war, and still does exist, has perhaps not had the totalitarian character that Hayek assumes, yet it still involves in principle quite the same problem. It has been necessary to determine how production should be organized, what needs were to have priority over others, what commodities had to be imported, how raw materials were to be used, how they were to be distributed, etc. Even if these regulations are promulgated mainly through administrative bodies of experts (the Ministry of Supply and a number of special boards), it would be quite wrong to assert that democratic control was thereby abolished. Regulating bodies are responsible to the Minister concerned who, in turn, is responsible before Parliament. Public opinion, too, has shown itself to be alert and effective, concerning the import situation, for instance. The fact is that social regulation does not take place like a calculation on a philosophically founded system of values, but appears on a rough estimate as the result of the manifold evaluations, wishes, and considerations which actually live traditionally and assert themselves in a community.

It is realized that if there is a shortage of building materials, the dwelling houses must have priority over summer residences. It is also easily agreed that the import of necessary raw materials must have priority over nuts and jam. The necessitous part of the population are given a certain priority in the distribution of needed textile goods, etc. All such weighing does not allow of "proof" and cannot derive from a single principle, and yet it is possible in the customary democratic way to agree on a result, even if opinions are naturally divided, here as in other spheres, and a settlement must be sought through compromise.

There is no reason to believe that the situation should on principle present itself otherwise if planning is extended from the particular to the general. Parliament's relation to the plan may be compared with its present relation to the budget. The elaboration of a project must be left to the administrative experts in contact with a political committee. However, this does not prevent Parliament from exercising a vital influence on the organization of finances, through the uncertainty of its attitude, which influences the preparation of the bill, as well as through subsequent criticism and examination. In the same way, it must also be assumed that the political control of the economic plan will be a decisive reality, even if the elaboration of the plan in its details must be left to experts.

That it is very possible to undertake regulation in a democratic form without an objective standard of value also appears from the Civil Servants' Salary Act. In that sphere, too, it can be asserted, in full agreement with Hayek's premise, that no objective directives are possible, and that the wage system therefore presupposes a perfectly concrete code of values which assures each individual group its place in a scale. From this it should again follow, according to Hayek's argument, that each party will assert its priority, that it is quite impossible to reach a compromise and agreement, and that the wage scale therefore can only be dictatorially fixed. Experience goes to show that this is not true. Hayek's entire argument rests on abstract speculations which do not harmonize with the experience hitherto available in more limited fields.

Even if the delegation of legislative power to competent organs must presumably be quite general—Parliament can only supervise the great lines of the general plan—yet it does not signify the relinquishing of democratic control. The decisive thing in this respect is not whether objective directives may be given for the exercise of the delegated power, but that the authority may at any time be controlled and if necessary recalled, if it is used contrary to Parliament's direction and wishes. Indeed, in the last analysis the main difference between democracy and dictatorship is that in a democracy the people are in a position to dismiss the government. In this connection, furthermore, it may be added that the increasing practice of delegation of discretionary authority may be the cause of the introduction of another form of control over the administration than the judiciary control of the law courts. This will be discussed later (Chapter VIII, Sec. 4).

I therefore think that one is entitled to repudiate the assertion that the introduction of a planned economy would render unworkable the inherited democratic institutions and do away with majority rule. At the same time, the bottom is knocked out of the argument that freedom of political expression would disappear. Dictatorship—in the actual sense of denial of the parliamentary freedom of discussion (Chapter V, Sec. 5)—in the nature of things has always been connected with minority government. The ruling majority has no reason for not appealing to public opinion. I do not wish to deny entirely, however, the possibility of a majority dictatorship. It is true, indeed, that every strong concentration of power may be a temptation to use it improperly. A safeguard against this danger lies in extensive decentralization. According to the prevailing socialist view, it is not expected that a single central organ shall direct the national economy in all its details. This is simply a technical impossibility. What is intended is simply a thoroughgoing objective and territorial decentralization, a succession of higher and lower authorities, so that within certain limits there remains scope for considerable initiative and autonomy. The concrete regulation of the individual's interests in the form of issuance of licenses of various kinds will go on within these relatively autonomous subordinate organs, and there is then presumably no greater reason to fear political pressure than, for instance, in connection with the present issuance of import licenses, purchase licenses, etc.

As far as the situation of the press, is concerned, I do not take Tingsten's fears too seriously. They are based on the assumption of a totalitarian, centralized state socialism realizing itself in a system of allocations and licenses. The democratic blueprints of planned economy do not prevent the consumer's choice from working through the price mechanism. On this assumption, advertising will still have its function, even though to a lesser degree than today. At any rate, it will not be difficult to imagine some kind of subsidy to the press without pressure on opinion, for example, subsidy proportional to the actual circulation.

Over and above this more direct criticism of the arguments brought forward, some more general points of view may be mentioned which may throw a new light on the discussion.

The discussion concerns the effects of a prospective economic reorganization, the content of which can only be roughly sketched, upon the political structure of society. Since this new economic order has not as yet been realized anywhere —Russia can hardly be cited in this connection, and in any case the conditions there are so special and unfavorable to democracy that no general conclusions can be drawn—the discussion must of necessity assume a most abstract character. This is mostly based on speculations on the general trends of human nature and lacks the support of concrete experience. Under these conditions it is certainly inevitable that, to a large extent, it assumes the character of wishful thinking. In this respect, it is remarkable that there exists definite disagreement among scientists, with a clear tendency for their prognostications to be in harmony with their general inclination of sympathy or antipathy to a socialist order of society. It is mostly among the liberalistically inclined authors, those who already for other reasons or on emotional grounds are against socialization, that one meets with the allegation that planned economy leads to political dictatorship. On the other hand, there are outstanding sociologists, such as Karl Mannheim[1] and Joseph A. Schumpeter,[2] who maintain that a planned economy and political liberty are entirely compatible. In particular, Mannheim's research is quite remarkable. But also in so far as this tendency is concerned, including my own, one has of course to take into account the possibility of a certain wish-determined preconception.

Further, one must bear in mind that the actual choice is not one between accepting socialism or sticking to the good old liberal democracy. It is to be assumed that powerful forces, in particular the tendency toward large-scale production and a general psychological attitude, will in any case lead away from the laissez-faire liberalism of the good old days. The question is merely whether the planning shall be private and covert, lie in the hands of the business world's matadors, and be in the interest of their profits, or whether it shall be public and administered by the government and be in the common social interest, that is, what the great majority can approve of. The danger for liberty, then, lies not simply in socialization but in the very development toward regulation and rationalization. There is then indeed reason to believe after all that the danger is least when the control is public, and when the public is thus able to protect and maintain its hereditary liberties. It is in the people's living understanding of the value of

---

[1] Karl Mannheim, *Man and Society in an Age of Reconstruction* (New York: Harcourt, Brace and Co., 1940) p. 338 ff.

[2] J. A. Schumpeter, *Capitalism, Socialism and Democracy* (London: George Allen & Unwin, 1943), p. 235 ff.

liberty that, in the last resort, is to be found its safeguard, and that mentality will have the best chance of asserting itself when the public controls economic life.

Next I shall maintain, together with Mannheim and Schumpeter, that the organization of society in connection with economic leveling and scientific progress may be regarded as rendering unpolitical many problems which, from being political issues, will thus take the form of objective technical matters. The certain knowledge that science has acquired of the sanitary importance of vaccination, for instance, has brought it about that this question is no longer political.

It presumably will be the same, too, with different social "injections" or "operations," as their effects on society are gradually established with certainty. It may be added that many political conflicts arise out of the existing inequality, particularly the clash between capital and labor. Once these are removed, many matters will appear as technical common concerns, and there will not arise the definite clashes of interests which may lead to a struggle for power and the misuse of it at the expense of liberty and fellowship.

Finally, it must be noted that both Hayek's and Tingsten's arguments are based upon the assumption of a total, centralized state socialism. This is not the goal that Social Democrats are striving for, and to that extent they overshoot the mark. Tingsten himself admits that "there is no reason to deny the possibility of an equilibrium in which a more thorough state regulation combines with such a degree of private enterprise and free trade that the principles of political democracy in all essentials can be maintained in their traditional form." But this is indeed the essential, for all practical purposes. We can thus be agreed that democracy need not be in danger because the development continues to proceed toward socialism. Therefore, the discussion of principles is not without importance. It has opened our eyes to the dangers that may possibly exist. Later on, when we are at a further stage on our way and can better appraise the prospects ahead, the debate may be taken up anew by others who will know more than we do, and whose love of liberty will, it is to be hoped, be no less than ours.

4. Democracy's Chances in a Time of Crisis

The problems that have been discussed in the preceding section concerned the static question of the possibility of democratic ideology's functioning within a capitalist and within a socialist economy, assumed to be generally accepted by the community. We have seen that the form of democracy is compatible with the content of both, even if in both cases there may arise difficulties that in principle derive from the fact that the economic forces, whether they be directed by private capital or by the government, may threaten to render illusory the political forms, majority rule, and freedom of speech. However, there is reason to believe that it will be possible in both cases, through vigilance, to combat these difficulties.

Other problems arise when we consider a society in a period of social revolution in which powerful forces wrestle, struggling for a deep-going change of previously existing social institutions and cultural traditions. There will here arise a great ideological tension and clash of interests between the different social groups, and the question is then whether the democratic supraideology which demands the peaceful settlement of all material differences will show itself solid enough to withstand the pressure within society when passions boil over and the conflicts come to a head.

The theorists of democracy have often maintained that the democratic ideology presupposes a certain agreement on fundamental values in order to work. The condition for the individual to feel that the majority decision is just and to be willing to yield to it is that he still feels solidarity with the other members of the group despite all differences of opinion. There may be, however difficult it may be to define it more closely, a certain background of intellectual and cultural community, a certain harmony in the setting of the ultimate goal, which makes a common understanding possible. The individual must be able to identify himself with the group in order to feel that its decisions are binding and the outcome of his own autonomy. An honest person who happened to be in the company of thieves would never be able, in that company, to recognize the rights of the majority.

Under normal conditions, the community of values and the feeling of solidarity create the framework which, despite all divergences, majority and minority integrate into a whole, and give the majority decision its meaning and limitation. If the formation of parties and majorities is fairly fluid, the majority of the moment will feel a natural check on its power, because otherwise it runs the risk of losing its position as the majority. A compromise is then reached and all yield, more or less resigned to the decision arrived at. The minority, for its part, will not feel that it is an excluded group, but that it is a potential majority which tomorrow may be called upon to take over the government. This places a damper upon the opposition's criticisms as well. Government becomes teamwork between the government party and the opposition. The latter's place within the framework of the whole has been recognized most clearly in the British system, where the leader of "His Majesty's Opposition" is paid £ 2,000 a year for his criticisms.

It is a different matter, however, if a particular social group feels itself, even on the fundamental values, in definite opposition to the rest of the community. In such a case the sense of solidarity is lost. Discussion and majority principle cease to have meaning for that group; it feels that there is no way of reaching an understanding, nor is there any prospect whatever of its becoming the majority. The majority, for its part, lacks natural restraints to its desire to dominate. The relation between majority and minority loses its legal character and becomes a pure power relation. The ideas of liberty and justice have failed. The minority no longer feels ideologically bound to the whole and to the majority's decisions, whether it yields to superior force (but without loyalty and inner approval), or takes up the fight with violent means. Whether the latter happens will depend particularly on the prospects for victory in a struggle.

If therefore a divergent group is only small in relation to others, for example, a national minority, it is likely that it will yield to superior force. It does not resort to open conflict, but the state has lost for that group its character of an authoritatively binding order, and is regarded merely as physical might. In the same way, if society dissolves into many conflicting groups, none of which has any prospect of acquiring power over the others, it is likely that peace will of necessity be preserved despite the lack of ideological community. It will be different, however, if the population is divided into two mutually hostile groups of roughly the same strength. If they are, then little is required for the system to break asunder.

History knows several instances of such permanent minorities outside the framework of the community. In the sixteenth and seventeenth centuries, religious conflicts led to protracted struggles which threatened to break up the nation affected into two or more hostile camps. Here neither discussion nor compromise was possible. The minority was persecuted with fire and sword. The struggles ebbed away only when necessity gradually taught men toleration. This means that it was agreed upon to raise religious convictions themselves above the regulations of the state and to concede to the dissenters autonomy in ecclesiastical affairs.

Since the beginning of the last century, national antagonisms have played a role similar to that of the religious ones before that. Nationalism has become a new religion. National groups are persecuted and live as permanent minorities without loyalty to and feeling of solidarity with the ruling people. Here, too, the solution lies either in separation and distinct political existence—as with Ireland and Iceland—or in the granting of autonomy to the minority in national affairs.

Both these instances illustrate well the dilemma that the permanent minority creates in the democratic ideology. On the one hand there is the usual majority principle. On the other, it is felt that the full application of the majority principle in situations such as this would be a denial of democracy's own basic ideas of humanity and liberty. Why? Because the prerequisites for the majority principle, the community feeling which attaches the outvoted to the whole and makes the majority decision a common decision, are not present in these conditions. The majority decision has become tyranny and dictation, without root in the autonomy of the outvoted.

Similar problems arise if the economic and social conflicts between the different classes within a nation grow to such a tension that they in similar fashion threaten to split the nation into hostile and irreconcilable camps. The problems are even more difficult in those cases because separation and autonomy cannot, in the nature of things, be resorted to in order to resolve the conflict.

It is necessary to note that it is not the economic inequality itself as such that might imperil the community. Society has been divided at all times into a ruling and a working class, but this has by no means always given rise to social unrest. It is—in agreement with what has been said before about the significance of the ideological bond—only when the ideology which sanctions the privileges of the ruling class breaks down that the danger of a social schism arises. The explosive tensions occur therefore typically in periods of social revolution, that is, in times when a change in the technique of production relations and perhaps of military strategy brings about the dethronement of a former ruling class because it no longer performs an effective function in the life of society. Precisely because the ideologies become less and less rooted in the new social reality, they lose their sanctioning power over men's minds. The old privileges become now only odious and the objects of hateful criticism. New ideologies arise. The community breaks up. The former rulers who live on in the traditions which in bygone times reflected their effective functions feel that they are persecuted and their rights invaded. To the new men and the masses, the old privileged class, on the other hand, appears as so many parasites without any *raison d'être*, who oppose just demands. The conditions for a life-and-death struggle are present.

As an illustration of this abstract outline, one may think of the collapse of feudal society before modern capitalism. Feudal power was based on possession of land and on military service. So long as agriculture was the most important branch of production and knightly preparedness for war the most important military technique, the knights' position of power was in harmony with their functions. So long as this was the case the aristocratic-feudal ideology—of protection in exchange for allegiance and service within a rigid hierarchy of personal lord-vassal relationships, from the king as supreme overlord down to the simplest peasant—was not seriously challenged by any social class. It was not until growing capitalism and industrialization, together with the development of the science of warfare, had actually displaced the feudal lords from the effective positions of power in the community that the old ideology decayed and a new one arose that was hostile to the old regime. The contrast between the privileges of the nobility and their effective social functions now became obvious. At the court of Louis XVI the representatives of the *ancien régime* lived lives of idle luxury and splendor. The contrast between rich and poor was no greater than before. On the contrary, the position of the peasantry had improved a good deal. The decisive factor was that the old privileges had lost their meaning and in the eyes of the people had become a tribute which the working people had to slave for, to benefit a class of parasites.

There is much to indicate that we also, in our own day and age, live in the midst of such a period of social revolution, where the ideology that has hitherto legitimated the capitalist privileges is on the point of falling into decay. It is also true now that it is not the actual contrast between wealth and poverty that is the driving force. The conditions of the needy were greatly improved throughout the nineteenth century. The revolutionary impulse derives from the fact that the legitimating ideology is on the verge of losing its hold over the minds of men.

This is in turn due to a change in the effective social function of capital. So long as the capitalist ideology of free competition, initiative, enterprise, and inventiveness actually reflected an immense expansion technically, as well as economically and imperialistically, directed toward an increasing standard of living for all classes within the capitalist society, the rule of the capitalists was never seriously challenged. After the First World War, this situation changed. The capitalist mode of production has shown itself incapable of effectively utilizing the factors of production, either the natural or the human material (witness mass unemployment), and of achieving a rational distribution of the output (witness the destruction of surplus production in a world in need). The wars have shown that a great goal can be achieved only by effectively utilizing all resources under planned state leadership. Why should this not also be possible in peacetime? At the same time, the capitalists have systematically withdrawn from active management of the productive process and handed it over to another class (technocrats, bureaucrats, "the managers"). This holds true whether one thinks of the many ordinary shareholders whose only connection with production is to receive dividend tribute, or of America's "200 Families" who have withdrawn to an increasing degree to the peace of private life in order to live a life which in inconceivable luxury surpasses anything the Versailles of the Louis's could offer in its days.

This and much besides is beginning to dawn on the people. The capitalist ideology is on the point of breaking down and therefore the antagonisms are becoming more bitter. The hitherto privileged classes feel like a persecuted minority, invaded in their legitimate rights, threatened with annihilation. They are losing the feeling of loyalty toward the community, and brand the decisions of the popular majority as "class tyranny," "majority dictatorship." The have-nots, on the contrary, look with increasing irritation at the class privileges and demand that the power of the majority be used ruthlessly for their abolition. If—owing to the still extensive sway of the old ideology over the middle classes—they do not possess the necessary majority, they feel for their part that they are a permanent minority whose legitimate demand for a new order is ruthlessly suppressed by the bourgeois-capitalist majority.

It is in such a time of conflict, when the demand in the name of equity for a revolutionary change of the national economy encounters existing privileges and traditions which resent such a change as an encroachment on established rights, that democracy is in peril. Democracy is a method for peaceful social development, but the problem is whether it can master its task when the change becomes so radical as is being discussed here.

So long as the discontented constitute merely a small minority, or if the development has already gone so far that they form a considerable majority, then the danger is not so great. It culminates at the time when the two factions are about equal. Both parties will then be tempted, even if they only constitute a minority, but a strong one, to set the economic demand above considerations for the democratic right of the majority. Each side feels this inclination to show its strength, trying at the same time to support its demand with a favorable interpretation of the ideology of democracy.

In socialistic quarters[1] it is sometimes asserted that the idea of liberty has meaning and value only under the assumption of social equality. The condition of loyalty toward the state and law is ultimately that the social order permits every individual to progress in happiness and in his standard of living. A society divided into rich and poor, like two nations with

[1] E. g. Harold Laski in *Liberty in the Modern State* (London: George Allen & Unwin, 1930), and in *Revolution of our Time* (London: George Allen & Unwin, 1943).

completely different living conditions, cannot endure in the long run on a democratic basis. An expanding economy is a condition for social peace. Hitherto capitalism, through technical progress and imperialistic exploitation, has been able to grant adequate improvements in the standard of living to hold the discontent in check. But there are many indications that this time is over. The soldiers who have fought for justice and democracy will not feel like turning back to a restrictive economy, with unemployment, depressions, slums, and want, when they know that poverty is not only unjust but also unnecessary. They will demand their rights and fight for them if need be. As against a bourgeois majority, which possibly will deny their claim, it is pointed out that the democratic game in a capitalist society is not fair, and that the demand that ought to be set forth in the name of justice is in reality the expression of the great majority's true interests.

From the bourgeois side, on the other hand, there can be pointed out something which tends to indicate that threatened capitalism will not capitulate without struggle, even in the face of the majority decision. The alliance between Nazism and big industry in Germany meant in reality that capital was willing to enter into league with the lawless *condottieri* to hold down the workers. All around in other countries voices were heard saying that a Hitler could also be used there to teach discipline to the workers. Ideologically, the defense is that real democracy demands consideration for all parties, and that a scant majority decision therefore will be the expression of a ruthless majority dictatorship. Changes in the fundamental structure of society which, so to say, touch the "social contract" basis can be made only with general support.[1]

There is thus enough explosive. All the same, I believe that there is considerable hope for a peaceful development. None of the parties can be sure beforehand of winning in a struggle for power and therefore there is always a risk in embarking on

[1] So e. g. R. Bassett, in *The Essentials of Parliamentary Democracy* (London: Macmillan and Co., 1935).

this experiment. And one thing most parties can be sure of: the price of victory is the destruction of democracy for an incalculable time. Experience has taught that once dictatorship is introduced, it is very difficult to get rid of it again. Fear of that will be strong enough, presumably, so long as the desire for liberty is alive, to prevent political-power adventures and to force both parties to mutual concessions.

The only argument that violent revolution will occur in spite of everything is the old Communist thesis that it is hopeless to think that true reform can be achieved by parliamentary methods. I have already (Chapter III, Sec. 5, Chapter VII, Sec. 2) dealt with that idea and rejected it. Neither are there many more people who take this idea seriously. The argument has two parts: first, owing to capitalist propaganda, it must be considered impossible to attain a majority for a socialist reform; second, in any case it is unthinkable that the propertied will give up their position without a struggle. The first aspect is undoubtedly untenable. It may perhaps take time but in the long run the truth, if it really is truth, cannot be held down. Better than all propaganda, experience itself will expose the flaws of the capitalist system. The second aspect is the expression of a preventive point of view: let's hit first, otherwise the others will. The same argument, naturally, can quite as well be used by the other side and even this argumentation, more than anything else, is capable of conjuring up mutual distrust and creating intolerance. Instead of thus provoking a breach of the peace one ought to emphasize, on the contrary, that all previous experience in the older democracies points to the fact that the majority can expect loyalty from the minority when the majority itself has reasonable consideration for the minority and for traditional ideas. In Denmark, the development from absolute monarchy to modern democracy, with great social upheavals, has taken place without revolution and bloodshed. This line can be continued, not if a majority of 51 per cent on some fine day proclaims the socialization of all capital, but if a majority reasons wisely and considerately allows the reformation to proceed gradually so that the mentality of the conservative elements among the population can also gradually adapt itself to the development.

I believe there is good hope that the development will take place in this way.

It is becoming increasingly clear to the social democratic parties that "socialization" need not amount to the taking over of all rights of property in capital once and for all, but that the essential goal can also, and even better, be reached through a gradual extension of public control over the economic functions. On the one hand, taking over property rights is not necessary because the reality that lies in the property title may be undermined at pleasure by extending the control. On the other hand, the expropriation of private property by no means guarantees, as experience in Russia has shown, that the result will be socialism. If those who exercise state power are not subject to democratic control by the people, there is no security that state control over the production process will not be used to introduce new privileges. On the contrary, it would be strange if natural selfishness were not to cause the rulers to use their control for their own advantage. Directly contrary to the Communist thesis, it must thus be presumed that lasting socialism cannot be introduced in a revolutionary way. Revolution means dictatorship, and dictatorship will in turn, sooner or later, unavoidably lead to an exploitation of power to the advantage of the dominant ruling party, even though it persists in calling itself the exponent of the masses. Dictatorship is at best government by tutelage, and its only guarantee lies in the idealism with which the tutelage party identifies itself with the masses. According to the laws of human nature, this guarantee must break down sooner or later.

If one holds fast to the idea of progressive reform, rightly understood, there is a chance that democracy may be preserved. It is in this ideological sphere that victory will be won. *The opponent must also be overcome in his heart.* Capitalist-liberal ideology is already in an advanced state of decay. The slogans about individualism, free initiative, free enterprise, freedom of private contract, a chance for all, are, as is well known, quite hackneyed. They no longer appeal to the masses. Even the conservatives nowadays think socially to a degree inconceivable a generation ago. The capitalists themselves are on the point of losing faith in the justification of their own privileges and with it all, the will to defend them in the struggle. As the ideological process of gradual undermining continues, there is no limit to the lengths to which the gradual socialization can go, simultaneously with the maintenance of democratic institutions. And here precisely lie further guarantees that socialization will not be perverted, but will remain really and constantly an advance toward greater equality.

The concept of "majority dictatorship" is often used to justify a special defense of the interests of the propertied classes (see Chapter III, Sec. 3). The right of the majority to legislate without regard for the just interests of the minority is denied. But the question is which interests are "just" and whether it is the opinion of the majority or of the minority that ought to be decisive on that score. Those who talk of a dictatorship of the majority with a view to a majority of the left often forget that under existing conditions it is conversely a considerable part of the working population who are of the opinion that the bourgeois majority does not show sufficient consideration for their legitimate interests. The sociological reality behind the ideology is that no majority can govern democratically unless the regime is rooted in ideas of justice and righteousness, which are shared by the minority. If this community of ideas breaks down in its fundamentals, one may rightly talk of a majority dictatorship in the same way as when a national minority is oppressed. There is no longer one people, but a ruling social majority and an oppressed social minority. If such a splitting up of the nation is to be avoided, it is not enough to hold on formally to the majority's rights. It is then necessary to work constantly at the integration of the various groups' conceptions of right and justice.

The consequence of these considerations is that there is a chance that democracy may survive and lead society through a period of social conflict when the will to adhere to the values of liberty is alive and the development is allowed to proceed gradually. If, however, a small majority attempts to carry through at one stroke a thorough revolution, democracy will be lost. For either the opponents will rise in revolt—and this can only end in dictatorship of one or the other type—or else the adversaries will submit without inner consent and loyalty as an oppressed minority. In that case the unity of the nation and the democratic fellowship are also lost and replaced by dictatorship—the dictatorship of the majority.

VIII.

THE TECHNIQUE OF DEMOCRACY

1. Direct or Representative Democracy

Technically, the people's exercise of political power can be visualized as taking place in two different ways: either the people make their own political decisions directly by the "ancient plebiscite," or else they register these decisions through specialized organs particularly devised for that purpose, which act "on behalf of the people," that is, according to the people's directives and under their control. These methods may be called, respectively, direct and representative democracy.

It ought to be clear that there has never yet been any perfectly complete and pure direct democracy, nor is it likely ever to exist. Even in its primeval form it could not have been possible to make every common or particular legislative, administrative, or judicial act the object of a plebiscite. The nearest approximation to that form of democracy was the primitive Germanic society, in which legislative as well as judicial power was exercised by the assembled people at the *Thing* (Chapter II, Sec. 2). But even there most of the administrative functions were left to special organs, particularly to the king.

Under the complex social conditions of our own day it is true to an even higher degree that wide application of direct democracy is something inconceivable. The size of the population makes a direct assembly impossible, and the complexity of present-day matters of necessity demands a division of labor among specialized organs. Judicial power has been devolved into the law courts, and legislative power into what, in a narrower sense, is called popular representation.

All modern democracy is representative to that extent. All

the same, it is not without importance to be clear whether the ideal in principle, that is, apart from technical impediments, is direct or representative democracy. For the latter can be differently construed, according to whether one thinks that representation is in itself a desirable thing, or simply a technically unavoidable makeshift. In the latter case, the structure of representative democracy can be modified in different ways through institutions that originate in the ideology of direct democracy and aim to some degree at grafting its ideas and effects on to the stem of representative democracy. That which in our day goes under the name of direct democracy is in reality only such a partial impulse reflecting an ideal which hardly allows of realization in its purity, but which nevertheless in various ways can stamp and modify quite effectively the representation that is unavoidable.

Rousseau is the celebrated spokesman of *direct democracy*. Certain that the people, left alone, will always act rightly and wisely, he was also certain that the people, if they transfer the legislative power to representatives, will always be cheated and enslaved. The real source of this conviction is doubtless Rousseau's romantic primitivism. To his worship of the uncorrupted primitive man corresponds his faith in the innate instinct of the people. To this may be added, also in a romanticized light, the idyllic traditions of his home country. He speaks with ecstasy of the earth's happiest people, where one sees a group of peasants looking after the affairs of state under an oak tree, although even in Rousseau's day this idyll was essentially a legend.

This romanticism is then rationalized by Rousseau in his remarkable doctrine of how all the individual egoistic wills mystically cancel one another's negative qualities and melt together into the general will, which is always necessarily directed toward the common good. But this mystical sublimation takes place only when every individual feels himself directly and strongly linked with every other individual in society, and all individual wills stand thus in a mutual relation. If, on the other hand, the links of society snap in the people's hearts, or if partial links are formed, such as political parties, or associations based upon particular interests of some as distinct from others, then ominous particular interests will gain the upper hand and no true general will is going to arise. In the name of law, unjust decrees are then issued, the aim of which is the advancement of the various particular interests.

From these assumptions it is evident that sovereignty cannot be "represented." The sublimation is like a chemical process which takes place only when all individual wills act spontaneously in unison. The conditions for it are not present in a Parliament, where indeed only a small fraction of the nation is assembled, elected, at that, on considerations of party politics. This is the basis of Rousseau's celebrated declaration that sovereignty does not allow of representation and that the people's agents are not their representatives (by which is meant substitutes who can act as though they themselves were the people), but only proxies who cannot decide anything definitely but can only recommend matters to the people. "Every law which the people has not ratified personally is worthless, it is not law. The English believe they are free, but greatly deceive themselves. They are free only during parliamentary elections, but so soon as the members of parliament have been elected, the English people finds itself once more enslaved and counts for nothing."[1]

Thus, without Rousseau himself expressly stating it, the program for the development of democracy is clearly stated. The ideal is the direct popular decree. The people's original and spontaneous will is infallible. So far as it is necessary on practical grounds to choose "deputies," legislative assemblies, these have no authority to make decisions. They may merely draft proposals to be approved by the people. This approval may be implicit; only the people may reject the draft made by their deputies. This is the system that is called the referendum. Alongside this, the people can naturally on their own accord

[1] J. J. Rousseau, *Contrat social* (Amsterdam, 1762), vol. III, ch. 15.

and over the heads of the elected deputies pass laws, themselves. This system is known as the initiative.

According to this ideology the people require no leaders, at most they need only advisers, because they may go intellectually wrong in their judgment of what the common good consists in. The people are sufficient unto themselves, since they have an unfailing compass within themselves. Freedom consists in following that norm. The leaders will only be able to pervert the original instinct and thereby rob the people of their freedom.

It is not necessary to show that Rousseau's theory of the emergence of the general will and its innate inner correctness is pure mysticism. Only his bare, romantic belief in the people's infallibility remains.

Rousseau's belief in the natural rightness of the will of the people survived in the nineteenth century in the Utilitarians' dogmatic belief that the obvious aim of all social action is the common good, defined as the greatest possible happiness of the greatest possible number (Chapter III, Sec. 2). On the other hand, his obscure theory of the emergence of the general will is replaced among the Utilitarians by a remarkably exaggerated faith in the absolute value of open discussion as an infallible means to the right solution of all conflicts. This mystical sublimation has received a more empirical explanation in the ability of reason to overcome all resistance and through its light to bring clarity and agreement to all questions (see Chapter V, Sec. 5).

I do not know whether the supporters of direct democracy have ever allied themselves with the Utilitarians. But it would at any rate have been possible, and in that case the leading ideas of direct democracy might have been given this form:

Man is a rational being. The spontaneous popular will is always necessarily directed toward the common good and by means of a rational discussion it will also always be capable of finding the right means to that end. The people, therefore, require no leaders. They have an unerring compass in their instinct, and free, rational debate will be able to find the way toward the goal that the compass indicates. The representative organs are a technically unavoidable makeshift. Parliament has no definite, decisive competence. Its decisions are merely drafts requiring the people's approval to become law. This approval may be implicit, tacit, as long as it remains open to the people through the referendum to reject the draft. It must, further, be possible for the people to use the initiative, that is, to direct positive legislative action.

The most important practical consequence of direct democracy is the distrust of representation which finds expression in the institution of direct popular consultation (referendum and plebiscite). Something similar obtains in the case of officials. These, too, are regarded mainly as the people's deputies, without independent competence. Since, however, in this case regular ratification of their actions is impossible on practical grounds, protection against an independent and powerful bureaucracy is sought by having the officials popularly elected for short terms of office. Special qualifications are not required. If officials are not, as in Athens, selected simply by casting lots, nevertheless every citizen is regarded as suitable for carrying out the people's decisions.

It has been pointed out above (Chapter V, Sec. 5) that the idea of man's rational nature and the technique of forming public opinion, which are assumed in the ideology of direct democracy, are, according to modern psychology, a number of fatal illusions. The belief in the absolute rationality of the popular will is in conflict with the demonstration by mass psychology of the part played by emotions and irrational urges in all mass experience, which may very easily lead to snap decisions that clash with the values the people cherish in quieter moments and on the longer view. The technique of propaganda has shown how easy it is with suitable means to play on the people's emotions as on an instrument, to hypnotize them, to incite them, and then again to quiet them, according to need and desire. Against a ruthless propaganda, reason and criticism are powerless. Opinions can be produced in the propaganda ministries and instilled into a defenseless people. In the light of all these facts it is impossible to maintain one's faith in the people's instinct as an infallible guide.

The ideology of representative democracy rests on a more sober appraisal of the people's faculties and will. Direct popular decision is unreliable, not only because the people often, because of ignorance, unsteadiness, and short-sightedness, will err in judging what serves their own good, but also because the majority will often allow themselves to be swayed by ominous particular interests at the expense of reasonable consideration for the minority. The people's task is fundamentally therefore not to legislate but to elect an elite of trustworthy representatives and leaders whose task it shall be to safeguard the interests of all, wisely and with equal consideration for all, better than the people themselves can do directly, and to lead the people toward the goal that best agrees with their true interests and constant will.

These ideas found their chief spokesman in John Stuart Mill, the author of *On Representative Government*. Just as warmly as he defends the general principles of democracy (see Chapter III, Sec. 3), he is convinced that the democratic function of the people is not to govern directly but to elect representatives for that purpose from among the enlightened, capable, and tested intellectual elite. Mill sees with much fear democracy that develops into an one-sided class dictatorship. He fears the popular "instincts," and sees the best bulwark against political ignorance and majority tyranny in the inclination of the uneducated to elect educated representatives and to bow to their opinion. It may well be that the "enlightenment" Mill talks about has, furthermore, the stamp of the property owner's political conservatism (see Chapter III, Sec. 3). But this is a time-determined, fortuitous note, which does not affect the fundamental substance of the idea. Perhaps we would in our own day and age talk a little less about education and more of personality and qualities of leadership. The central point in this train of thought is that—whether owing to better insight, particular interests, character qualities, or predisposition—there actually is a decisive difference between the qualifications of different people for dealing with political problems. There is to be found a group of people who have special political qualifications, an intellectual elite of candidates for leadership. Democracy ought not to prevent their development. The aim is not to treat everybody alike. The people's primary function is, on the contrary, to give potential leaders the best chance of asserting themselves, by choosing their leaders in an open competition for the confidence of the electors.

On these assumptions it is not the people's task to legislate and rule directly, but only to direct affairs, that is, to exercise supreme authority in determining the general course of affairs, selecting the leaders, and generally exercising the ultimate control. On the other hand, the people's representative is something more than a proxy who can only act on instructions and does not possess any authority for making his own decisions. The elector must naturally elect his representative from a general acquaintance and sympathy with his leading political convictions. But it would be inconsistent with a respect for intellectual superiority and with the representative's task of leadership if the elector were to be able to exact from his representative binding declarations or to return him with binding instructions. The power must be an authority to follow the dictates of his own judgment. The idea of the representative's independent mission can also be constructively expressed by saying that he represents not only his own constituents but the entire nation. The natural limits of the representative's freedom, which remind him that he is, after all, elected to the legislative assembly as the spokesman for certain ideas and points of view, lie in his political responsibility to the electorate, —on which depend his chances of reëlection.

To sum up, the ideology of representative democracy may perhaps be expressed thus:

Man is not essentially a rational being. The great masses

are predominantly sluggish and conservative, full of prejudice and traditions, suspicious of everything new. The people require leadership. The idea of individual self-determination and responsibility is linked up with the idea of trust in leadership.

Along with the urge for independence there lies in man the urge to put his faith in the leadership of those who are wiser and more competent than himself. While direct democracy builds only upon the urge for personal independence, and dictatorship only upon the need for leadership, these two tendencies are harmoniously united in representative democracy: the leadership remains under popular control and depends on the leaders' ability to hold the people's confidence on a basis of free criticism and expression of opinion. According to this view, the representative organs are something different and more than a technical necessity. They perform an independent and desirable function; they are the expression of an elite that, better and more correctly than the people itself, directs the needs that stir within the people.

The common view of the institutions of direct popular consultation, the referendum and the plebiscite, must be altered on the basis of the assumptions of this ideology. The institution loses its dogmatic justification of "popular sovereignty" as the expression of the infallibility of the popular will. The institution cannot be recognized as a regular control over the people's representatives. On the other hand, it is not out of the question that it may under certain conditions fulfil a function in a representative democracy as well. It requires closer examination and justification (see Sec. 2).

The same holds true of the general idea of the position and function of public officials in the state. They, too, are to form an elite representing technical-administrative expert knowledge. Technical qualifications, and not their political affinities, must be the deciding factor in their appointment. Popular election is inconsistent with that. There must instead be an autonomous coöptation within a politically independent bureaucracy. Appointment must normally be for life, so that the public servant is dismissed only when incompetence or other special circumstances warrant it. These considerations are particularly important in the case of the judiciary, for which the demand of specialized ability and an absolute absence of susceptibility to outside influence are of special importance. All the same, representative democracy presupposes a certain control over officials (see Sec. 4).

Thus the ideologies of direct and of representative democracy face each other as two opposite basic views of human nature, the function in society of, respectively, the popular will and leadership. Like other ideologies they consist of a mixture of theoretical conceptions and nontheoretical values. In the first instance they are so general in their idea of human nature and the reliability of the popular will that it is hardly possible to decide where scientific truth lies. However, as far as I am concerned, I should think that experience speaks out against the belief that is expressed in the ideology of direct democracy. The decisive thing is surely values implied in the ideology. While direct democracy firmly holds to the basic democratic ideas of autonomy, self-determination, personal responsibility, representative democracy signifies a modification of these by linking them with the idea of leadership in recognition of and confidence in the greater knowledge and ability of others. Here, of course, science cannot decide the issue. Everyone must make up his own mind. I choose representative democracy.

2. Direct or Representative Democracy: Control Over the Legislative Power (Direct Popular Consultation)

Political power, "sovereignty," in a democracy derives from the people, but the political decisions themselves are mainly made by others. Nevertheless, these others are, directly or indirectly, under popular control. Democracy is an ingenious system of allocation of powers combined with measures of control. From the President or the Prime Minister down to the ordinary police constable, every single state official has been allotted his particular public duty, for the execution of which he is responsible, and authority, in which he is subject to control. Responsibility and control spread like a network throughout the entire administration of the state. They not only follow the direct line of ascent and descent with regard to superior and subordinate authorities, but may also cut right across it. In the last analysis, all these regulations aim at ensuring that all public authority harmoniously carries out and elaborates the general directives given by the people as the system's supreme authority.

Most important is the people's control over the supreme deciding power, the legislative organ. This is due in the first place to the fact that the members of the legislative assembly are elected by the people. Nor is this all. It may furthermore be claimed that the people are also in a position to make sure that their elected representatives continuously exercise the political power in a satisfactory fashion. Without such control democracy degenerates into a merely nominal one (Chapter IV, Sec. 3).

This popular control can be more or less effective. On this point hinges the decisive difference between direct and representative democracy. The control is most effective in the direct democracy (with representation as a temporary expedient). Here every decision is as a matter of principle submitted to immediate control. The referendum serves to correct the actions of the people's representatives, the initiative their omissions. In the real representative democracy, on the contrary, the control is limited to a general settlement by means of periodic elections—apart from the unorganized but nevertheless very important control that is at all times exercised by public opinion. Within its term of office, the parliament possesses an absolute power which cannot be recalled or controlled by the people. This difference in the exercise of control reflects the difference in the basic ideology, which is described in the previous section.

The institution of direct popular consultation (referendum and initiative) is thus in the first place the expression of an effective popular control over the representatives in accordance with the ideology of direct democracy.

Direct popular consultation occurs in two main forms:

(1) The *initiative*, that is, the system in which a certain portion of the people have the possibility of submitting a proposal for decision, which is thereafter made the object for a vote, either immediately or after discussion in the assembly; and

(2) The *referendum*, that is, a system according to which a resolution passed or envisaged by the representatives is made the object of direct popular consultation.

In both cases the procedure may be further qualified with regard to the object of the resolution. Thus, either the initiative or the referendum may be constitutional, legislative, administrative, financial, or related to a treaty.

According to the legal effect of the popular consultation, distinction must be made between the consultative referendum, the decisive referendum, and the semidecisive or semiconsultative referendum. The first indicates that the issue of the consultation is not legally binding on the legislative organ. Regardless of the outcome of the popular consultation, the parliament remains free to pass or reject by the customary procedure the proposal that had been made the object of the referendum. The second means that the consultation is legally binding, so that a negative outcome involves the rejection of the resolution, a positive outcome assures its adoption. The third indicates that the referendum is binding in a certain respect only; it may be that the negative outcome, but not the positive, is binding; or the referendum may be binding on the representatives of the people but not on the royal assent.

According to the conditions under which popular consultation is to be held one distinguishes between compulsory, optional, and voluntary referendums. The first means that the decisions of a certain kind, determined by their content (for example, constitutional changes), shall unconditionally be subject to referendum in order to attain validity. The second denotes that the necessity of the referendum is dependent on the stating of a certain demand for it. This demand may, in particular, emanate from a certain number of electors, from a certain proportion of representatives, or from the king. The third means that the decision whether or not the referendum shall take place rests with the legislature's own free will.

The classical countries of the referendum are Switzerland and the United States. Popular consultation in Switzerland is rooted in the ancient cantonal primitive democracy. The national traditions do not yet seem to have played any greater role. Apart from the so-called *Landgemeinde*, democratic government disappeared in the course of the eighteenth century and was replaced by aristocratic forms. The modern movement for popular consultation is connected with what is usually called the Regeneration Period, from 1830 to 1848. In those years, a number of the twenty-two cantons introduced new constitutions, which were passed through referendum, and hence that institution was extended to include general laws. However, it was not until the 1860's that the system really prevailed. This development resulted in the referendum's being also introduced into the Confederation through the revised Federal Constitution of 1874, which by an amendment in 1891 was extended to include the initiative.

Today, all constitutional changes require popular confirmation, in the Confederation as well as in the Cantons (compulsory referendum), and the people themselves may use the initiative. In matters of general legislation the referendum is compulsory in ten of the Cantons. In the remaining twelve and in the Confederation the optional referendum prevails. The initiative is recognized in all the Cantons, but not in the Confederation.

In the United States, the institution of direct popular consultation also began as the compulsory constitutional referendum. Here the idea was linked with the widespread one of a basic social contract. Hence it soon spread to cover also other subjects of special importance, in particular, financial matters. Furthermore, in practice, the use of the voluntary referendum in special cases was adopted.

A new development began about 1890 with the introduction of the optional referendum and the initiative on the Swiss model. This movement had its ground in the well-known, often-discussed situation referred to as the decay of the legislatures in the states. The most essential cause of this situation was a widespread corruption through which big business assured itself of political influence. There arose a general distrust of the legislative organs and a resulting trend toward a limitation of their originally very great power. In the first place, the position of the other state organs was strengthened, so that a distribution of powers was established. The Governor, the leader of the executive, was popularly elected; so were, to a great extent, the members of the law courts. Next, a limitation of the competence of the legislative power was attempted, partly by depriving that power of a number of important functions, partly by cutting down drastically the time of meeting, for example, to every other year only, or to every fourth year, and then only for a period of forty, fifty, or sixty days.

When Americans became acquainted with the Swiss system about 1890, the Optional Referendum became the natural keystone of this attempt to limit the power of the corrupt legislatures.

The position today may be summed up thus: Direct popular consultation does not take place in any form in the Federal Union. In constitutional questions, popular ratification (referendum) is compulsory in all the states; in fourteen of them, moreover, the people possess the initiative. In general legislative matters there is a compulsory referendum in a great number of states, limited, however, to particularly important subjects, especially of a financial nature; optional referendum is found in twenty-one of the states, and in nineteen the people have the initiative.

Apart from the fact that the compulsory constitutional referendum was introduced into Australia in 1901 and into Denmark in 1915, there began a new phase with the development of the post-1918 democracies' constitutions. In the German Reich and most of the German states, in Austria, Czechoslovakia, Estonia, Latvia, and Ireland, the referendum, or various forms of the initiative, or both were introduced. There does not seem to have been any essentially realistic political requirement or thought underlying it. The leading motive seems to have been mainly that the institution of direct popular consultation was regarded as the logical completion of democracy, and that it was therefore thought desirable to introduce it in order to give the new principle of popular sovereignty the strongest expression and the most conspicuous support. In the essentials, the Swiss model was copied without further consideration of how it would function in an essentially different political milieu. As far as is known, the institution was never called upon to play any appreciable role, and the fact that democracy soon succumbed actually or officially in most of the states mentioned precludes the drawing of practical conclusions from these experiments.

In Sweden, direct popular consultation was introduced in 1922, but only as an advisory and voluntary system at the discretion and on the orders of the legislature.

In Denmark, as has already been mentioned, the compulsory referendum on constitutional matters was introduced by the revision of the Constitution in 1915.

3. Direct or Representative Democracy: Control over the Government

Besides the parliament, the government, that is, the supreme leadership of the executive power, is the most important political authority in the state. The main question is therefore how the democratic nature of the government is ensured. There exist for that purpose three actual systems: the presidential system (United States and several other states), the council system (Switzerland), and the parliamentary system (all other democratic states).

It is obvious that a regular factual control by the people over the actions of the government—beyond the critique by public opinion—is out of the question. The control can therefore only rest in the manner in which the government is formed and dismissed. Two possibilities suggest themselves here: either the government obtains its mandate directly from the people, who elect the head of the state for a certain number of years, which is the presidential system; or else the (political) appointment is made by the representatives of the people, as in the other two systems. The main difference between these two is that according to the Swiss system, the Federal Assembly elects for a certain number of years a council, which during its term of office is politically independent of the representatives of the people; while according to the parliamentary system the government, under the leadership of a chief (the Prime Minister), is constantly dependent upon a majority of representatives.

Of those systems, judged by the effectiveness of control, the parliamentary is the most democratic. Election of an individual as an irremovable head of government is an utterly summary expression of the popular will and involves many possibilities of incalculable chances. The Swiss Federal Assembly, which counts seven members of different political shades, gives a more varied picture of the people's attitude, but the most intimate is the contact obtained in the parliamentary system, where the government at any time stands under the political control of the parliament and must resign when it no longer has the support of the prevailing majority.

It would lead too far to go into the many problems connected with the technique of forming governments, especially the development and variants of the parliamentary system.

4. Direct or Representative Democracy: Control Over Public Servants

As already mentioned, the fundamental view which attaches to the public servant's position in the state is quite different according to the ideology of direct and of representative democracy.

The first conception is characterized by fear of every form of bureaucracy corresponding to the mistrust of popular representation. It is feared that those to whom power is entrusted will become the masters of the people instead of their servants. It is stressed that the task of public officials is to carry out the sovereign will of the people, and it is assumed that this is a task that can be performed by any citizen. Therefore, no measure of competence is required for the appointment. In order further to prevent the bureaucracy from becoming a peculiar caste, a state within the state, and to assure its democratic attitude, the officials are directly appointed by the people for a short term of years. Their reëlection depends on whether during their term of office they have displayed a democratic attitude. As a natural consequence of the low standards of technical competence, public officials are generally poorly paid and not assured a pension. If the standards of technical qualifications are low, the importance attached to the political attitude is all the greater. The system culminates in the so-called spoils system, in which the officeholders are changed whenever there is a political change in government. The offices fall to the victorious party as spoils.

It is particularly in the United States that this method of filling offices has developed. But experience has not shown that it is a good method according to general opinion.[1] Popular appointment—as soon as it concerns so large a community that personal acquaintance with the candidates and their qualifications is of no importance—is no guarantee of the public

[1] James Bryce, *Modern Democracies* (London, 1921), vol. II, pp. 19–20, 147 ff., 176–177, 542.

servant's efficiency or reliability. The voter has no idea of the candidate he is voting for and therefore votes blindly according to the directives of his party. The party machine remains the absolute master of the elections, and the nominations are made from purely partisan points of view, to the injury of technical qualifications. Particularly where the bench is concerned, this leads to the most unfortunate consequences. The independence of the law counts and the integrity of their decisions are at the mercy of popular emotions.

According to the ideas of representative democracy, on the contrary, first importance is attached to the technical functions and efficiency of the public servants, not to their popular or political allegiance. The bureaucracy should be an elite which serves the people but whose task extends much further than the mechanical execution of given orders. It is a far cry from the supreme popular will to the ultimate concrete official act. The popular will is rendered concrete through a number of levels but at every level there must necessarily be considerable scope for judgment, initiative, and discretion. Every single government official must therefore, on his own initiative and responsibility, collaborate on the state's tasks. This he can do only when, by virtue of education, upbringing, and tradition, he possesses particular expert qualifications and a permanent position which enable him to devote himself to affairs of state, as a lifework.

Historically, this attitude is connected with the fact that representative democracy in Europe has developed out of the absolute monarchy. The democratic state has, as for instance in Denmark, taken over from the latter a bureaucracy of an bourgeois-aristocratic stamp, which prides itself on representing the technical "state interests," raised above party political considerations.

From this point of view the goal must be the creation of a technically well-qualified, well-trained, well-paid, and politically independent civil service. In accordance with this, a civil-service examination is required as a condition of employment for all higher offices; the power to appoint belongs formally to the king, though in reality to the bureaucracy itself; the post of public servant is normally a life occupation. The different branches of administration constitute firmly framed hierarchies in which, by virtue of seniority and efficiency, one works one's way to the top. The personnel is not replaced in case of change of government. Under changing cabinets, the civil service represents an inertia factor of expert knowledge and tradition which counteracts strong fluctuations to one or the other side in government. Like the absolute king in his time, many a popular minister has made an assault in vain on a barrier of technical considerations when conferring with the permanent secretary of his department.

The control over public servants is, on these assumptions, essentially a legal one. Apart from the administrative self-control through recourse to higher authority and from the economic control of auditing, the control lies with the law courts, partly in the form of criminal responsibility for offenses in office, partly in the form of judicial examination of the legality of the administrative acts. The political attitude of public servants, on the other hand, is regarded as a private matter which does not concern the public.

It is a question whether the whole attitude to the public servant's position in the state is not, to too great an extent, under the influence of points of view inherited from the absolute monarchy which do not harmonize with the assumptions and ideas of the democratic state, and whether the technical development, furthermore, does not make reforms in control imperative.

Politically, freedom of conscience and of expression for public servants must be the point of departure. The conditions of service must not prevent them from participating, like their fellow citizens, in the democratic-political life. Political disagreement and political criticism are, from the democratic point of view, neither attacks on the state nor enmity toward the government but, on the contrary, the very nerve of democracy. In Great Britain, the state pays the Leader of the Opposition £ 2000 a year. The demand for political uniformity of public servants in accordance with the government of the day would, furthermore, lead to the spoils system, which is ruinous to the impartiality and continuity of any system.

But a limit, and a very essential limit, there ought to be. Consideration for the security of the state and for public affairs being attended to in the spirit of democracy demand that the state shall not place its functions and thereby its own life in the hands of its enemies. Democratic society may tolerate many differences of opinion but assumes essential unity on the fundamental, the very basic, ideas of democracy. It ought not to be an unreasonable demand that democratic society choose its servants from among fellow citizens who are democrats by disposition. To deny this demand is not tolerance but suicidal thoughtlessness. The fate of the Weimar republic was sealed because, among other reasons, enemies of the republic in large numbers were allowed to fill important government posts.

That demand must lead so far that every person who is not a supporter of democracy must be regarded as unsuitable for serving the democratic society. The decisive thing in this consideration is not whether he belongs to a party pledged to overthrow the existing order with violence. It depends not on the means but on the end and the mentality. Apart from the legal and technical difficulties in making a distinction between violent and nonviolent antidemocrats, the argument in favor is that it cannot be expected that the interests of society will be democratically considered by persons who do not profess the ideas of democracy.

I shall return later to the question of the extent to which the democratic state ought to tolerate an antidemocratic propaganda. But regardless of one's attitude to this, it seems to me imperative that the state show so much will to self-assertion and respect for its own fundamental values that it does not deliver its apparatus to the enemies of the state. Even with regard to less important posts this may be of importance.

A railroad conductor or switchman, an electricity employee, a gas worker, who lacks respect for democratic law and order may be a threat to society in case of incitement to illegal strikes.

That demand can in no way come into conflict with otherwise recognized democratic principles. There is no democratic basic right for everybody to become a public servant. Freedom of expression as such is not curtailed. Only, the antidemocratically minded cannot be an official of the state while he is fighting its vital principles. To maintain that view is just as reasonable as to demand that only persons who profess the established religion may become priests in the state church; or that known antimilitarists cannot become officers in the army. Nobody would think that this would be an infringement of freedom of conscience or of speech.

To my mind, this is a matter of the greatest importance. Without a will to live no political organization can survive. The simplest expression of this will to live is that the democratic society must be governed and administered by democrats.

It is another matter that it may be difficult to put these fundamental ideas into legal rules. A rule that public officials shall be dismissed who conduct antidemocratic propaganda or act against democratic order (as by taking part in or inciting to illegal strikes), or who belong to a party of which the same can be said, will be of considerable value but is still not enough. The point is in the first place to prevent people with antidemocratic dispositions from being appointed as public servants. For this purpose, a thorough examination of applicants, supported by the opinion of reliable public-service organizations, will be necessary.

5. Direct or Representative Democracy: Unicameralism or Bicameralism?

Historically, bicameralism originated in the splitting of the English council of the kingdom into an upper and a lower house which occurred about 1340. The council originally had consisted of hereditary members—the high aristocratic vassals: the bishops, earls, and great barons—as well as of elected representatives, namely, two counts for every county and two burghers for every town and port. These latter now separated themselves into a distinct lower house. The division corresponds to the separation between the different classes or estates that is characteristic of the society of the later Middle Ages.

Following the English model, the bicameral system, with an aristocratic upper house, was introduced into France at the Restoration after the French Revolution. The Constitutional Charter granted in 1814 by Louis XVIII introduced a chamber of peers of partly life and partly hereditary members; at the beginning all were appointed by the king. The popularly elected Chamber of Deputies was elected on the basis of a highly limited franchise, dependent on the payment of high taxes.

The French Charter was in turn the model for the constitutions of that group of European states of the first half of the nineteenth century referred to as constitutional monarchies; these constitutions were established a large number of German states, by the Dutch in 1814 and 1815, the Portuguese in 1822 and 1826, the Spanish in 1834, the Belgians in 1831, and the Greeks in 1844. According to this type of constitution, the king is vested with the unity of the state, which he exercises in accordance with the provisions of the constitution. He shares the legislative power with a representative body consisting of two chambers of conservative character. The franchise for the lower house is given to only a minority of the population. The upper house is a chamber of peers filled by aristocrats, by virtue of hereditary right, royal appointment, or a very qualified franchise and eligibility.

An exception is to be noted in the Belgian constitution of 1831, which for the first time introduced a popularly elected, dissolvable, upper house. With this began a new development. The progressive democratization that took place under the influence of the revolutions of 1830 and 1848 and the social development of the latter half of the century were bound to influence also the position of the upper house. In the long run, an aristocratic upper house could not endure and maintain its position of power in a government which, to an increasing degree, was permeated by democratic principles. There were two conceivable possibilities. Either the upper chamber might in the main keep its feudal-aristocratic constitution but in exchange give up its power and become politically subordinated in relation to the popularly elected chamber, or else, if it were to continue to have any real importance, the upper house would also have to undergo a democratic rejuvenation so that it also could claim for itself the popular mandate which in democratic society is alone considered the source of political authority.

In Great Britain, the development followed the first path. The upper house has maintained its feudal-mediaeval character. Even today it is the rank of peer, that is, a member of the nobility endowed with distinct privileges (dukes, marquises, earls, viscounts, and barons) which gives a seat in the House of Lords. On the other hand, the position of this House has long been subordinate, and since 1911 it has lost all deciding influence. On general public laws it has merely a suspensive veto; on financial laws, no veto at all. The position is or has been similar in the British Dominions, which originally took the mother country as model. In Canada and New Zealand, the members of the upper house (Senate and Legislative Council) are still appointed by the governor general (the government). Accordingly, this chamber, in fact if not in law, is subordinated to the popularly elected representative chamber. In most other democracies, on the other hand, the development has followed the other path. The upper house according to the Belgian model was popularly elected, although on the basis of more qualified franchise and eligibility than that obtaining for the lower house. As the franchise to the latter was extended, resulting in equal and universal franchise, a gradual development occurred that tended to bring the two chambers nearer together. In some cases the upper chamber maintained an actually conservative character as constituted by a qualified franchise for the purpose of protection for the propertied minority against an unlimited "majority tyranny." The Danish upper house after the constitution of 1866 is an example. In the newer constitutions, after the first World War—for example, the Czechoslovakian of 1920 and the Polish of 1921—the difference in franchise was restricted only to age limits, so that the upper house was in the real sense a senate, a council of the elders. In other countries, like Belgium, Holland, France, Sweden, the difference consisted only in the indirect voting method, since the upper chamber was elected by the municipal councils which were themselves elected by universal franchise. Finally, it also occurred that the electorate was the same for both houses, while the distinction of the upper house was that it had fewer members, elected in larger constituencies for longer periods and with successive retirement at different periods (as in the states of the American Union).

This development, which brought the two chambers more and more closely together as issuing from roughly similar election procedures, was bound to raise the question: what under these conditions is the *raison d'etre* of an upper chamber that tends to become a simple duplication of the lower chamber? Already during the French Revolution, Siéyès is reported to have exclaimed: "What good will a second chamber be? If it agrees with the people's representatives then it will be superfluous; if it is in opposition to them, it will be noxious." The opinion that unicameralism must be the logical fulfilment of the democratic constitutional principles has spread more and more. In accordance with this, several of the new ultra-democratic constitutions of the years immediately following the end of World War I, for instance, those of the Baltic states, introduced pure unicameralism.

Finally, it should be mentioned that a type apart is the federative bicameralism. The "upper house" here is not of aristocratic origin and has never served for the protection of conservative interests. It is elected by and represents the federated states, in contrast to the "lower house," which is elected by and represents the citizens of the Union as one group. Federative bicameralism occurs in all federal states, particularly in Switzerland, the United States, and the Australian Commonwealth.

On the basis of this survey, the following types of legislatures in democratic states may be listed:

One chamber: France (1791 and 1793); Estonia (1920); Latvia (1922); Lithuania (1922); the Swiss Cantons; Luxemburg (1868); the Soviet Republics, Finland (1919); the Australian state of Queensland (1922); Spain (1931); and some small states. A mixture of unicameralism and bicameralism occurs in Norway (1814) and Iceland.

Two chambers, of which the upper chamber may be:

(1) *An aristocratic upper house* with hereditary or life members appointed by the Crown, as in Great Britain, and the constitutional monarchies of the first half of the nineteenth century. In a modified form it still exists in several British Dominions, in which the members of the upper house are appointed by the governor general (the government), as a rule for life. In connection with the parliamentary system of government this royal nomination, however, loses the conservative character that it originally had in constitutional monarchies. This type thus approaches the democratic. From the point of view of democracy this method may, however, appear inadequate. The political character of the chamber comes fortuitously to depend on which party is in power at the time of a member's death or resignation.

(2) *A conservative upper house*, popularly elected but elected on a qualified franchise for the protection of the propertied minority, for example, the Danish *Landsting* (1866–1915).

(3) *A democratic second chamber* based entirely or approximately on the same franchise as the first chamber. Three subtypes may be distinguished, according to whether the second chamber is based on:

(i) a higher voting age (Czechoslovakia, 1920; Poland, 1922);

(ii) indirect election through municipal councils (France, Belgium, the Netherlands, Sweden);

(iii) direct election in larger constituencies and for longer terms and with successive retirement (most of the states of the American Union).

Finally, special position is occupied by

(4) *Federal bicameralism* (Switzerland, the United States, the Australian Commonwealth, etc.). When the sovereignty of the individual states is greatly limited, so that their authority approaches usual provincial or municipal self-government, this type glides over into the one that is based on election through municipal councils. It may thus be doubtful whether one should include the senate of the South African Union in one type or the other.

As has been mentioned, the increasing similarity between the two chambers raises the question whether the upper chamber has hereafter any *raison d'être* in a consistently democratic state. When the upper chamber, too, derives its political authority from the general will of the people, it seems superfluous as a mere "echo assembly"; from left-wing quarters, too, as is well known, this conclusion has often been drawn from the principles of democracy. The upper house has been regarded as merely a historic survival and the rational fulfilment of democracy is seen in unicameralism.

This concept has in contrast found a certain confirmation in that the retention of an upper house has been most often defended on the grounds that it provides a balance of power and conservative guarantees for the propertied minority in protection against the tyranny of the coarse majority, confiscatory taxation, and other abuses. Certainly it is often pretended in general terms that the upper chamber represents quality, deliberation, and expert knowledge, and thus forms a safeguard against majority decisions that are too hasty or do not sufficiently take into consideration the rightful interests of the minority. However, in many instances it seems quite clear that it is not every minority that those who argue thus have in mind, but one particular minority, namely, the bourgeois-propertied minority, which felt itself threatened by increasing demands for social equality or even socialization. In consequence, the practical tendency has been, in one way or another, at times in camouflaged form, to give this social class a special representation or else a veto right as against the popular majority's importunate decisions.

It is quite true that the ideas of democracy assume that the majority always has reasonable regard for the minority's "rightful" interests. In accordance with this, measures that aim at impelling the majority in control at any time to bear this demand in mind cannot be regarded as undemocratic. On the other hand, it is absolutely incompatible with the democratic idea of equal political rights for all if a certain social class is given special representation or special protection in preference to others.

All the same, it would be shortsighted to reject bicameralism as undemocratic on the basis of this experience alone. It is at any rate a question whether the system cannot be developed so that, from being a survival which democratic progressive parties accept only with resignation, the upper chamber becomes an organ that serves well-understood democratic ideas.

What position is taken in this consideration depends on one's attitude to the ideology of direct or of representative democracy.

If one is a supporter of direct democracy and hence believes that the immediate, spontaneous popular will with instinctive, unerring certainty at any time decides the right thing, and regards representation as merely a technically unavoidable makeshift, it is logical also to be an opponent of the over-representation that a second chamber would involve. It is therefore a basic inconsistency, motivated by fortuitous party-determined opportunism, when conservative theorists sometimes have been at once supporters of a conservative upper house and of direct popular consultation. If one mistrusts the bare majority in the lower house, the same mistrust must also be directed against the bare majority established through the general vote. Only the hope that such a vote will turn out to be thoroughly conservative in the party-political sense may explain this inconsistency.

It is otherwise when one supports the ideas of representative democracy and believes that the "real" or "true" popular will which is to be realized is not always identical with the momentary public opinion determined by emotion and propaganda, but often is best recognized and called forth under the leadership of the people's elected representatives, a leadership elite which, to a higher degree than the man-in-the-street, possesses breadth of view, circumspection, and expert knowledge. This idea may be elaborated further, so that alongside the ordinary representative assembly which is relatively nearest to the actual currents and, as it were, first of all represents popular initiative, another organ is created which to an intensified degree possesses the representative characteristics and act to the advantage of circumspection, sober-mindedness, and continuity in government.

According to this idea, the second chamber should not favor any party or any social group, but should be a superelite, representing the most mature judgment and the best expert knowledge. This consideration has special weight in our day. The demands made on the ordinary people's representative with regard to the routine work and advancement within the party organization, the daily work in committee and in the parliament, at popular meetings and in electoral campaigns, are so overwhelming that many extremely well-qualified people, particularly of mature age, are deterred from undertaking the task. In an upper chamber elected in a suitable manner there will be a possibility of using men with qualities of political leadership who perhaps do not possess "popularity" to the same degree as those more directly in contact with the people but who still can contribute greatly to democracy as a section of the nation's best talents. One could perhaps say that, ideally, the member of the upper chamber ought to be more a "statesman" than a "politician" in the narrower sense.

The function of the upper chamber, according to this theory, should be the representation of continuity and quality which, without any partisan character, should guarantee democracy against rash or ill-considered decisions and thus ensure a stable development without the momentary fluctuations that call forth opposite reactions. There is nothing undemocratic or reactionary in this. It merely means that the state behaves like the individual who, through various checks and deliberation, compels himself not to follow every impulse but only acts after ripe reflection. As the individual "sleeps on it" before making an important decision, and mobilizes his various spiritual resources in order to consider the problem in question from as many angles as possible and make sure that the final decision derives from his whole self and not only from more peripheral layers in momentary agitation, so too, the state ought to test its decisions as soundly as possible. Bicameralism should serve this purpose, partly simply because the double discussion should create a certain thoroughness, partly and particularly because the debate in the second chamber should be calculated to place things in a new light.

In practice, different means have been used for this purpose. To ensure the continuity, longer terms of office, in conjunction with successive retirement and indissolubility, have in particular been adopted; higher voting age, because younger people are considered to be generally more easy to influence, and partial self-election by the retiring chamber have also been resorted to. Quality may be ensured either by setting up particular conditions of eligibility, or through the method whereby the candidates are nominated and elected. The first has been tried in Belgium, where the eligibility of the senators directly elected by the people is limited to the twenty-one categories enumerated in the constitution. These include, in particular, persons who hold or have held different posts, or who for a number of years have taken a leading position in economic life. Purely economic criteria also occur; thus, voters must be owners and users of real property the yield of which is at least 12,000 francs, or taxpayers whose annual tax is at least 3,000 francs. The history of the origin of this provision seems, however, to show that it is almost hopeless to try to set up such a list of categories. Either a great many groups are deliberately passed over or else the list becomes so comprehensive that it is valueless. The draft prepared by the commission met opposition on that point in the constitutional committees of both chambers; the measure was finally passed, but this seems to have been largely because it entered into comprehensive compromise negotiations between the government and the chambers.

Apart from that experiment, which hardly invites imitation, attempts have been made to ensure quality by the method in which the members are elected. Election is generally by large constituencies, where it is reckoned that local considerations come to play a smaller role. The voting age is generally higher because it is considered that the elder class of voters has greater insight and riper experience. Of greatest importance, however, are the different forms of indirect election. The indirect-voting method has as its aim that popularity and demagogic ability shall play a smaller part than technical qualifications. The voters may simply elect special electors. This procedure, however, threatens to become an unnecessarily roundabout way which does not lead beyond the usual partisan considerations. Special interest attaches to the method that is used in France, Belgium, the Netherlands, and Sweden, among others, when the election is by the municipal councils, which are themselves elected on universal suffrage. This method of election rests on the idea that the members of the municipal council possess to a particular degree training and knowledge of public affairs, not least of economic nature, and therefore must be regarded as most suitable to elect the best-qualified members to the upper chamber. Experience, particularly in France and Sweden, seems to confirm this. In both countries the second chamber holds a respected position, and it is generally felt that municipal election is one of the factors contributing most to this fact. The popularly elected representatives may also elect from among themselves the members of the second chamber (as in Norway), or the second chamber itself may elect part of its membership.

In the democratic constitutions we find combinations of the various methods discussed here for assuring the second chamber of continuity and quality, but it is not easy to establish different fixed types. The rules are not quite the same in any two states.

For deliberation about the formation of a second chamber on a democratic basis, a great many possibilities offer themselves. Political phantasy has very wide scope with regard to how it will combine the mentioned methods with others that are calculated to lead in the same direction.

6. Democracy's Self-Defense. Limitations on Freedom

In the years between the two World Wars, democracy broke down in a number of countries. Except in Spain, it happened without appreciable resistance and struggle. It was as though the strength of democracy were broken within. The democratic institutions had in reality just about ceased to function before Hitler upset the whole game.

Many people are inclined to ascribe the breakdown to the fact that democracy, in an exaggerated idealism, felt itself bound by its principles of liberty, tolerance, and humanity, even in relation to opponents who themselves did not respect those ideas but merely used them as means in a struggle against democracy and thereby against these ideas themselves. In generously placing the democratic apparatus at the disposal also of those parties whose sole aim was to destroy this apparatus, democracy dug its own grave. By clinging to the ideas of liberalism and pacifism in a world of deceit and violence, democracy prepared its own downfall.

The lesson may be derived from this that democracy, if it

is to survive, must protect itself against its inner enemies. One cannot play baseball with people who throw bombs instead of balls, nor the democratic game with opponents who are not themselves willing to observe the rules of the game. Such cheaters have to be given tit for tat. It is absurd to grant liberty to such a length that it can be applied to the end of abolishing all liberty. Democratic freedom of speech cannot consist of freedom to say anything, but only of freedom to say what is compatible with the preservation of values which democracy is to assure, among which also is freedom of speech itself.

This raises a fundamental problem: shall we by means of prohibition and force seek to safeguard that which we regard as truth and justice, or shall we give freedom to evil as well as to good indiscriminately? The problem is as a rule formulated thus: it is questioned whether or not a limitation on freedom of speech can be regarded as justified on grounds of democracy's own principles. This, to my mind, is not a good method for tackling the matter. It is not certain beforehand what the principles of democracy are, and what "rights" they produce. The question is indeed precisely how these principles are to be correctly understood and formulated so as to lead to acceptable results. In the next place, the problem is not merely whether, according to certain principles, one is "right" to limit freedom of speech, but also whether it is expedient to do so. And the judgment of this expediency ought not to be limited in advance to the point where it is based only on the special values of democracy; it must take into consideration all relevant points of view of valuation.

The correct mode of procedure must be, as usual, to account for different assumptions of values, and thereafter to discuss the problem as thoroughly and comprehensively as possible on the basis of the assumptions adopted.

An essential difference in the basis of evaluation must depend on one's general attitude to the values of democracy. I quite definitely assume that the problem is discussed only by people who are altogether supporters of democracy. Otherwise there is no problem. But among democracy's supporters it will appear differently according to whether one is unconditionally, or only conditionally, a supporter of that form of government.

By a conditional supporter of democracy I mean a person who certainly regards democracy (as I have defined it above as a form of government) and the ideas attached to it as something good, but who nevertheless considers other things, particularly economic equality or socialism, as more important and who therefore, if he is to choose between those two, will prefer economic equality to political liberty, socialism to democracy. If now such a person is of the opinion that progress toward greater economic equality can only or best be achieved by restricting freedom of speech, it is only consistent that he will support that restriction. On this assumption, the question is not whether the limitation is compatible with the principles of democracy. What these principles might lead to is put aside out of consideration for aims and values that lie outside democracy. The judgment is, one might say, external in relation to the point of view of democratic values.

Such is the case of those who, although supporters of democracy, are still in agreement with the Communists that socialism can only (or at least best) be achieved by revolution or, at any rate, by restricting democratic liberty.

The bases of valuation themselves cannot be challenged. However, it must be asserted in accordance with what was said before (Chapter VII, Sec. 4) that the actual assumption that socialism may be introduced only or best by abolishing or limiting democracy is erroneous. The situation is the reverse: without democracy (liberty), there can be no (lasting) socialism (equality).

By an unconditional supporter of democracy I understand a person who either upholds political liberty above everything else, even above economic equality, or who, at any rate, is of the opinion that the maintenance of democracy is a necessary condition for the development toward lasting socialism. On this assumption, the problem must appear different. It becomes a problem entirely within the framework of democracy itself, a question of the technique of democracy for maximum realization of its own ideas and values. It is actually the central problem in the discussion which is raised.

The question of a limitation of the freedom of speech must on these assumptions be put forward in such a way that we first are clear ourselves how the freedom of speech must be organized so as to serve its purpose in a democratic state, without considering whether it may be necessary, in order to preserve this freedom in the long run, to deviate from this ideal. Afterward, we may introduce this consideration into the investigation.

So far as the first question is concerned, there can be no doubt that freedom of speech as a democratic idea cannot mean that any verbal statement whatever should be legal. Nobody has ever asserted this. There are several kinds of verbal or written utterances that are forbidden, without this having anything to do with a limitation of the democratic freedom of speech.

(1) *Verbal or written utterances as a means whereby a certain offense is necessarily, typically, or possibly committed.* That the prohibition of utterances of this type has nothing to do with limiting freedom of speech as a democratic value will be understood at once by thinking of an example: offense against public decency by indecent remarks. The same holds true of a great many other civil offenses: inciting to hostile acts against the state through public declarations; offering assistance to the enemy through advice; disclosing the state's secret negotiations; betraying military secrets, secret negotiations, or official secrets; making false declarations or false accusations; various crimes committed for the sake of gain, particularly fraud and extortion.

Clearly, an utterance may be liable to punishment as information (because it is true or because it is untrue), as a statement of intention, and as on expression of feelings. Liability to punishment can in no way be regarded as limitation of freedom of speech as a democratic ideal.

(2) *The word as accessory to any offense whatever, regardless by what means this is directly brought about.* It is equally clear that the state punishes not only anyone who commits an offense but to a certain extent also anyone who helps in the preparation for the offense. But the preparation as well as participation will often happen through words: instigation, advice, encouragement, planning with regard to the committing of the offence.

There are very few people who will be of the opinion that the fact that it is forbidden and punishable to verbally incite another person to commit a murder should be a restriction on the freedom of speech.

As a particular and important instance may be mentioned the preparation or the participation in the preparation by word of mouth of the offense that consists in the violent overthrow of the constitution of the state. From this it follows that on the basis of the general principles of criminal law the state can forbid and punish participation in *political associations which have violent overthrow of the social order on their program* and also political propaganda for such parties. Whether it is found expedient to do so is another matter which is postponed for later discussion. The decisive factor in this question is merely to maintain that if democracy will not tolerate a party and propaganda that aim at application of violence, it means no limitation of freedom of speech as a basic democratic right. The use of force has no place in a democratic society. Consequently neither has word or action that contribute to the preparation thereof. There is nothing in democracy's own ideology which demands that one shall sit with folded hands in the face of violent attacks on individuals or on the social order. Democracy is not an expression of pacifism in the spirit of Gandhi. Nobody, not even the warmest supporter of liberty, will maintain that. It stands out clearly if we think of more advanced preparations. If a political party imported weapons, organized troops, held shooting exercises, and set up schools for instruction and training, all this with the goal of preparing the revolution, indeed nobody could be in doubt that interference with such activity and agitation is necessary self-defense. But what holds true of these obvious cases must, on principle, also hold true of the preparation by word and deed which is less advanced.

Violence and preparation for violence may (to the extent that is judged necessary) be met with violence, that is the organized power of the state. This is the more precise formulation of the idea that democracy has no obligation towards those who are not disposed to follow "the rules of the game," but has the right to give as good as it gets. (But further consequences cannot be deduced from this metaphor.) This has nothing to do with a restriction of freedom of speech as a basic democratic right. It is not a certain opinion which is attacked, but only the means that is to be used for its realization, namely, violence.

(3) *Political propaganda which is carried on by fraudulent or other dishonest means.* Just as democracy cannot tolerate violence as a means for changing social conditions, it cannot tolerate a propaganda that aims at preventing the formation of a free opinion by poisoning public discussion with all the subtle and ruthless devices of lies, slander, and incitement. Nor has this anything to do with limiting freedom of speech. No opinion or view as such is attacked, but only certain means of propagating them. I have pointed out earlier (Chapter VII, Sec. 2) that democracy's most effective weapon in combatting malignant propaganda is the elevation of education, but certainly a good deal can still be accomplished through legislation toward raising the level of public debate.

(4) I have mentioned above (Sec. 4) that the demands that ought to be made concerning the democratic attitude of public officials have nothing to do with limiting freedom of speech—just as the demand that ministers of a church must profess the Christian religion has nothing to do with limitation of the freedom of conscience.

In accordance with its function in the life of the state, democratic freedom of speech can henceforth be defined as *the freedom to propose any political opinion whatsoever and agitate for it, irrespective of its substance, but on condition that the propaganda does not make use of inadmissible means, nor aim at using violence.* Hence, there is no limitation of the freedom of speech unless the expression of certain political opinions is forbidden because of their substance.

The limitation which is advocated by many for the protection of democracy demands that propaganda which aims at suppressing freedom of speech itself, or other fundamental democratic rights, is to be prohibited. This means that the essential constitutional and legal rules which express the democratic character of the government should not be subject to free debate nor to the principle of majority decision, which loses its real meaning when free debate is suppressed. The essential principles of the constitution are thus—in order to protect democracy—canceled out of the plan of democracy. They are no longer rooted in the popular will as it forms itself freely at any time, but are laid down as indiscussible and unalterable—in the same way as the Danish King's Law in its day declared itself forever unchanging.

This demand for limitation is often justified on the grounds that it would be a logical contradiction if it were not fulfilled. It is said to be a contradiction to give freedom to such an extent that it may be used to suppress itself.

This interpretation cannot be admitted. Whether contradiction arises or not depends solely upon how the fundamental principles are formulated. It is no contradiction to maintain that one is a supporter of freedom of speech but only on the condition that this idea has support in the free will of the majority. It only expresses that one gives the formal majority principle precedence over the material principle of free speech.

Nor can there be said to be a logical contradiction in the demand for a limitation of freedom of speech in order to protect it—any more than there is a contradiction in the tobacco smoker's limitation of his own enjoyment of tobacco so as not to lose the enjoyment through excess. The question has nothing at all to do with logic, but depends exclusively on considerations of the actual expediency of one or the other mode of procedure, considered in relation to the values taken for granted.

The standpoint which underlies the demand for a limitation of liberty should then be that one must indeed thereby accept a loss that is regrettable in itself, measured in terms of the ideal of freedom of speech, but that it is worth while to agree to it since in exchange one gains a greater chance of the future survival of the freedom thus limited. The principle is: rather a lasting, although curtailed, freedom of speech than an unlimited freedom of speech in danger of foundering.

The correctness of this consideration will depend on a judgment, on the one hand, of the security that might be gained by limitation, and on the other hand, of the significance of the loss that the actual limitation itself entails. From both points of view, to my mind, weighty arguments against limitation may be brought forth.

Objection 1. The future security that may be won by a limitation of the freedom of speech is mainly illusory.

One may muzzle the people but not tie their thoughts. Public agitation may be prohibited but an underground propaganda can never be prevented. Perhaps in this way, the spread of the infection one wishes to fight may be impeded, but not even that is certain. I believe it is better to get the evil out into the open. Then it may act as a vaccination of the population by developing an antidote in the form of criticism and counterpropaganda. If the public is carefully protected so that its ear shall never hear dangerous antidemocratic talk, there is the risk that the disease may break out all at once and overcome the defenseless body. Democracy's existence ultimately rests upon the strength and life of the people's love for and faith in ideas of liberty, justice, and humanity. I do not believe that these ideas can be safeguarded by means of prohibitions. If they have not enough inner force to hold their own in conflict against other ideas, then they are not strong enough to bear the state either. When democracy in Germany and elsewhere succumbed defenselessly, it was not because it recognized its opponents' right to speak, but because, among other reasons, the ideas of democracy had never seriously taken root in those newly democratic societies.

To endeavor to perpetuate democracy by making its fundamental ideas indiscussible is to my mind an impossibility. Once the majority, or merely an important minority, has lost faith in the force of resistance of these ideas, democracy has already foundered and cannot be saved by prohibitions. It is of no avail in the long run to plug the people's ears as Ulysses did his sailors', so that they should not hear the Sirens' dangerous songs. A people can be forced to live in slavery, but not to be free. Freedom grows only out of will and faith, not out of compulsion.

I admit that the points of view I have here advanced cannot lay claim to being the expression of scientifically established truths, but can only rest upon the subjective, estimated total conception which is generally called common experience.

Objection 2. The damage to the freedom of speech that is done by limitation of it leads to far greater violation of democratic ideals than its defenders realize. It involves the obvious danger that democracy may founder, not because of exaggerated use of freedom of speech, but because of the continual limitation of it.

Once the pure argument that force may be met with force, opinions only by opinions, is abandoned, there arises the intricate question of what opinions would best profit by protection through prohibition and government compulsion. It is said that it is the fundamental ideas of democracy that are to be protected against antidemocratic propaganda.

It should be pointed out, in the first place, that there are different conceptions regarding what the essence of democracy consists of. It is in the last analysis the majority that must decide what it regards as democratic and what antidemocratic. It is likely that the conception thereof will vary so that prohibitive legislation will have an essentially different form under varying governments of different party color. In these circumstances there are serious grounds to fear that so serious and elastic a power placed in the hands of the legislature will degenerate from a protection of certain fundamental values, on which nearly all citizens can agree, into a weapon that is misused in the partisan struggle, and that before we have time to turn around, has sapped democratic liberty in the country.

But to this it may be added that, once it has been admitted that a restriction on free speech may be to the advantage of the fundamental values of democracy, one cannot escape the consequence that it may also be to the advantage of other values which are rated as high democracy or higher. Such ideas must inevitably appear when once a prohibitive legislation has been actually embarked upon. Many people certainly regard the maintenance of the capitalist system as at least as important as democracy. Why should not capitalism also be entitled to defend itself against its opponents? Exactly the same may be said of those who are supporters of socialization. Any social ideology whatever may, on the accepted assumptions, make a claim to the same right of self-defense as the democratic ideology, on condition that it has the support of the majority of the population. The result must therefore be that the majority of the moment entrenches all its essential political values with prohibition and punishment. But thereby—and this I believe everyone will realize—dictatorship is actually introduced.

The propaganda for a limitation of free speech has quietly begun at a point where the idea easily found fertile conditions. Bearing Nazism in mind, the self-defense of democracy has been suggested as something to which obviously—in this connection —practically the whole people would agree. No thought was given to the fact that this in principle signifies that the majority may demand the same protection for any other ideology to which it attaches the same weight as to democracy, and that this amounts to the introduction of dictatorship.

The result of these considerations is, to my mind, that it is vital for democracy to adhere to the clear principle: *force may be used against force*; *opinions can be combatted only with opinions*. I believe also, that in the last three of the protective measures mentioned above there actually lies most of what those who desire protection of democracy claim, namely, measures against parties that advocate the use of force, legislation against reckless propaganda, and demand for democratic dependability on the part of public servants. These, as has been pointed out, have nothing to do with limitation of freedom of speech. But neither the supporters nor the opponents of democratic defense measures have noticed this important distinction. In consequence, those in favor of defense have thoughtlessly demanded that freedom of speech itself be limited; and opponents of such defense have regarded those legitimate measures as tantamount to interference with free speech, and have therefore fought them.

It might possibly be objected against the distinction made here between views favoring the use of force and others that, even if it might be right in principle, it is impossible on grounds of legal technique. The antidemocratic parties would simply never officially pledge themselves to use force even if actually they were always prepared to resort to it. This difficulty of proof justifies altering the rule of law by virtue of an anticipation so that all antidemocratic opinions are forbidden in the absence of further evidence of violent intentions. The misgivings that I have already expressed with regard to tampering with the principle of free speech are however, for me, so serious that I am bound to consider it better in these circumstances to renounce measures against parties that intend, or are feared to intend, a forcible overthrow of society.

Even if on the basis of the principles of democracy, especially the idea of free speech, there can be no doubt about the justification of the measures mentioned above, it is naturally a question whether one would further regard them as necessary and expedient. As regards legislation for the raising of the level of public debate and the demand for the democratic dependability of public servants, I have, in accordance with the considerations I have stated earlier, no doubt that they will be beneficial and ought to be enacted as soon as possible. The situation is different with regard to measures against parties that have the use of force on their program. So long as the use of force belongs only to the theory and is postponed to a remote, indefinite future, there arise misgivings with regard to interference similar those that are mentioned above under Objection 1 against the limitation of free speech. Moves bring about countermoves, and the formation of opinion is better under control when it proceeds in the light of publicity and under criticism. It is, on the other hand, a different matter as soon as the intention of using violence assumes a more tangible character. All democrats will presumably be agreed that it is necessary to intervene in the presence of agitation for insurrection, the formation of armed corps, and other further preparations. The same ought to obtain in case of less far-reaching infringements, such as incitement to mob disturbances or to participation in illegal strikes, if the actual purpose is to cause unrest, disorganize the democratic apparatus, undermine the authority of the state, and thereby prepare the ground for a revolution. Lawlessness and mob rule ought not to be tolerated, and it is important that legislation be so arranged that not only the tools but also the actually guilty instigators, ringleaders, and backers may be made to answer. The liability of these persons should not be criminal, but political, that is, it should consist in the loss of possible political mandate. *He who does not in action respect democratic law and order shall not be admitted to the institutions of the democratic society.* This is the sound kernel in the assertion that democracy must not allow itself to be insidiously attacked from within by putting its institutions at the disposal of people whose sole aim is to sabotage the institutions of democracy and put an end to its functions.

I may thus sum up the result of the considerations put forth in this section:

Democracy ought to defend itself. As against opinions of

every kind, the only weapon should be the power of the word. Unrestricted freedom of speech ought to be a sacred principle. Prohibition and force are useless and in the last analysis turn against democracy itself. But force must be met with force. Even if a party which, according to its program, aims at violent revolution is tolerated, it is necessary to intervene effectively against all attempts to disorganize the democratic life of the community and sabotage of its institutions. Evil propaganda, too, ought to be attacked. Finally, the functions of the state ought, so far as possible, to be entrusted only to people who are not enemies of the state they are called upon to serve.

IX.

MORE THAN YOUR FREEDOM

The future of democracy is the great problem of the destiny of our time. Are the dictatorships merely casual and transitory phenomena which, like thunderstorms, purify the air and then pass off? Or are they the logical result of the social revolution of our time, the inevitable goal whither even the victorious democracies—despite their own beliefs and wishes—are moving? This no one knows, but so much is certain, that democracy in a period of social revolution such as we are now experiencing will be put to a hard test.

The portents of trouble are everywhere visible. Capitalist economy and ideology find themselves in a rapidly advancing dissolution. But when the ideological tie loosens, when the cement that binds people together into a firm social structure crumbles, the powers of violence and the dictator get their chance.

The conclusion of this drama is so momentous, not only because the end of democracy would mean a catastrophe for freedom for an interminable time, but also because the issue of the political struggle will react on the course of the social revolution.

If dictatorship triumphs, it will be all up with the dream of a socialist, that is, a classless society. How could it be otherwise? Dictatorship means that a small minority exercises unlimited control over the state apparatus and, with it, over the production apparatus, giving rise to new privileges and a new class division. A Marxist should be the first to perceive that. The development in Soviet Russia clearly illustrates what is going to happen. A new ruling class of technocrats and bureaucrats step into the place of the capitalists. The methods are different but the result is the same. Instead of exploitation by means of profits in open market operations, there is exploitation by means of wage differentiation, price fixing, and the like, the result being not socialism but what one might call technocracy.

The possibility of realizing the socialist ideals of equality and justice is therefore linked to the continuance of democracy, the people's active control of the state. This is the second great perspective of the drama.

What are now the forces that are decisive for the outcome of the mighty contest to be waged in the coming years over society's political and social fate?

Ultimately the issue depends on the power over the people's minds of the democratic ideals, which on close scrutiny are seen to be all rooted in respect for and close solidarity with the fellow human in every other individual.

But where do these ideas in turn originate and what "validity" do they possess? Are they eternal ideas, an expression of the divine in man's nature, or are they merely the product conditioned by a certain social structure and destined to perish with it? Are democracy's faithful supporters the last representatives of a dying period of civilization, fighting a hopeless battle for ideas that are doomed to disappear? Or are they the bearers of a great idea which is mankind's mark of nobility, and which can never die while the human spirit lives? Has an appeal to mankind's moral force any meaning at all, or are the ideas themselves merely an automatic by-product of the economic development?

Here we stand at the borders of a metaphysical interpretation of life, and he who wishes to remain on scientific ground would best be silent. But even without metaphysical guarantees of eternity, one can loyally perform the action the moment demands. The undisputed basis of support for this is a humanistic and Christian cultural tradition which in any case contains a spark of eternity, having through changing times and changing civilizations again and again appealed to deep aspirations in man. The language differs with a Socrates, a Jesus, a

Buddha, a Francis of Assisi, a Spinoza, a Kant—but still all have said the same: Man is sacred and inviolable.

Many are of the opinion that this thought has found at once its most sublime and its most easily understood expression in the Gospels, that every man, created in the image of God and endowed with an immortal soul, is equally loved by God with an infinite love and ought himself to love his fellow men as brothers before God. Regardless of what one thinks of the dogmas that were later erected upon the basis of the Gospels and of the manner in which the church at various times has administered the teaching of the Gospels, there is no doubt that this is one of the main pillars on which our spiritual culture rests and from which the democratic outlook can seek its inspiration in the future also.

As an institution, the church has always shown a tendency to ally itself with the world's rulers. "Throne and Altar" has often been the symbol of the forces of reaction. In countries like France and Spain, the Catholic Church has been, right to our own day, a power hostile to culture and progress, and in open conflict with the democratic republican parties as bearers of the ideals of the Revolution. On the whole it is true enough that religion as it was preached by the church, by comforting the poor and the oppressed with the hope of compensation in another life, has acted as an opiate for the people to the impediment of democratic and social progress. However, there have also been, for instance in England and Germany, reform parties of a Christian character, and in contemporary times this seems on close examination to be a sign of a change in the direction of a "Christian Realism" which emphasizes the solidarity of Christians with the entire human life, even in its political and social forms. It is perhaps particularly characteristic that the reaction against Nazism in a number of countries has shown itself in a strong advance of Christian-Popular parties.

What our time needs, more than any other, after Nazism's dissolution of all values, is a recovery of the faith in the dignity of man. I believe that the deepest source of inspiration for such a regeneration is always to be found in humanism and Christianity, which through millennia have been the foundations of our culture.

But ideals alone do not create a democracy. Democracy is a system of law, not of ethics. If ideals are effectively to shape people's social life, they must become dynamic ideas which are given substance in the form of social institutions. This means that the lofty but vague ideals must be laid down as certain standard requirements backed by the organized power of the state. That is democracy in its palpable reality as a legal institution.

It is just as important that the lofty ideals of democracy keep alive, as that they be, at all times, effectively worked out as a legal system. This is true not only on technical grounds, but also because the actual observance itself reacts favorably on the mentality. By being actually enforced as a social order, the democratic ideas gain new strength, firmness, and quality as legal concepts. The best education, as I have had on several occasions the opportunity to maintain, lies in the democratic life and the democratic institutions themselves. It is only by living in a democracy that one can fully become a good democrat.

The right technical development of democracy is thus a task of the greatest importance. If democracy is to continue in existence under changed social conditions, it must adapt itself to them. We must not lull ourselves to sleep in the mistaken belief that democracy can be taken for granted once and for all. The basic fact to be kept in mind is that the development toward a centralized, planned, state-directed economy will inevitably transfer the center of gravity of the effective "exercise of sovereignty" from the legislative to the administrative branch, to bureaus, boards, commissions, and their experts. This may be regarded as a further development away from direct democracy. As primitive democracy, in which the decisions were made directly by the people at its assemblies, was in time rendered impossible by the evolution of a larger and more complex state structure, so the economic development of our own day will in turn render impossible the unchanged continuance of our traditional parliamentary democracy in its classical form. Popular representation is not capable of mastering the complex technical tasks of state. The handing over of effective legislative power to "boards," already in full swing, will assume increasing proportions. If democracy is, nevertheless, to be preserved in its essentials, if the development is not to end in a bureaucratic absolutism, then it is necessary to develop a new technique aiming at assuring popular control over the technocrats and bureaucrats. At the same time, the greatest possible decentralization within the framework of a supreme common joint management must be accomplished. Various problems arising in this connection have been treated in Chapter VIII.

Yet democracy as a political-legal technique is not enough. If the leading ideas of mankind are not to languish they must show their power to realize the masses' obscure urge for a better-ordained social order, greater happiness, and a fuller life for the common man. It was believed at first that universal suffrage would automatically lead to all that. But after political freedom had been won, there arose a feeling of disappointment. The masses felt cheated. Many came to feel that democracy was actually powerless against the hidden influence of capital and the ideological inertia that continued to be a bulwark of capitalism. Political interest waned and revolutionary movements arose which aimed at liquidating the entire system, including democracy. This explains how great nations could at one stroke sacrifice their political liberty and throw themselves into the arms of dictatorship. Anything rather than the worm-eaten, impotent democracy! If this is not to be repeated, if democracy is to preserve its inner strength in the freedom and faith of the masses, it is necessary for it to prove its vitality in leading the masses in the economic and social sphere as well toward greater happiness and a fuller life in freedom and equality.

The fight for democracy thus goes on at once in the moral, the legal, and the economic spheres. These three are intimately interconnected. The struggle occurs every day on all fronts. It is the greatest drama of our time. We are all equally responsible for its outcome. It is not only our freedom that is at stake, but also the dream of a happier and more righteous society.

APR 2 1 1953

DATE DUE

MAY 8

FE 2
56